THE CATHOLIC UNIVERSITY (
PHILOSOPHICAL STUDI
· VOL. LXVIII

THE PHILOSOPHY OF EQUALITY

A DISSERTATION

Submitted to the Faculty of the School of Philosophy of
The Catholic University of America in Partial
Fulfillment of the Requirements for the
Degree of Doctor of Philosophy

by

SISTER M. JANE FRANCES FERGUSON, M.A.
of the
Sisters of Mercy of Georgian Court College
Lakewood, N. J.

THE CATHOLIC UNIVERSITY OF AMERICA PRESS
WASHINGTON, D. C.
1943

NIHIL OBSTAT:

FULTON J. SHEEN, D.D., PH.D., LL.D., LITT.D.

Censor Deputatus

Washingtonii, die 15 mensis Aprilis, 1942

IMPRIMATUR:

✠ GULIELMUS ALOISIUS GRIFFIN, D.D.

Episcopus Trentonensis

Trentonii, die 11 mensis Junii, 1943

Printing Statement:

Due to the very old age and scarcity of this book,
many of the pages may be hard to read due to the
blurring of the original text, possible missing pages,
missing text and other issues beyond our control.

Because this is such an important and rare work, we
believe it is best to reproduce this book regardless of
its original condition.

Thank you for your understanding.

DEDICATED

IN

GRATEFUL ACKNOWLEDGMENT

TO

MOTHER MARY JOHN, S. M., M. A., LITT. D.

PRESIDENT OF GEORGIAN COURT COLLEGE

WITHOUT WHOSE MOTHERLY SOLICITUDE

UNFAILING CONFIDENCE

AND

CONSTANT ENCOURAGEMENT

THIS WORK WOULD NOT HAVE REACHED

FULFILLMENT

TABLE OF CONTENTS

PREFACE

In the midst of a war whose fundamental issue is proclaimed to be the survival of democratic society, an examination of one of the basic concepts of that society is not only timely, it is imperative. A war that engulfs humanity has justification only if it touches humanity at its very core. Equality, being one of those essential human relations of which democracy is conceived, an attack upon the latter is not merely an attack on a method of government, it is an attack on something fundamentally human. Nevertheless, the attack was not wholly unprovoked. Something had gone wrong with democratic society. The equality it promised men did not materialize, and the freedom it boasted did not ring true. Men were unhappy, and the democratic ideals were beginning to lose their glamour. When, therefore, ideologies appeared, one of which promised men a more realistic equality and the other a more organic unity, the stage was set for world revolution. Out of this revolution men hope for a new society more conducive to human welfare.

If the democratic forces are to triumph, the democracy of Liberalism needs to be x-rayed, and the curvature of its spinal concepts straightened before men will accept again its promise of liberty, equality, and fraternity. If the classless society of Communism is to set the pattern for social living, its principles require close scrutiny before they be allowed to level the ranks of men. Finally, if peace is to have any permanent abode in man's social life, the order conducive to its emergence demands careful exposition.

For this reason the present study is concerned with the examination of a concept fundamental to three social systems. In two of them, liberal democracy and Communism, equality plays a major rôle. In the Christian social order, while not less important, equality is tempered with hierarchy. Men stand to one another as both equal and unequal. Because Liberalism and Communism predicate equality of men to the neglect of their inequality, and the organic States which have risen in protest would but reverse the order, it is necessary that the truth of the human equation be sought in that philosophy which pursues always the *via media*. From the peerless thought of St. Thomas the principles that will measure the political equality of the Liberal and the economic equality of the Communist must be drawn forth.

The present volume, therefore, falls into three major sections. Two of them will be devoted to presentation, and one to evaluation. Under presentation there will be outlined the political equality of the Liberal, the economic equality of the Communist, and the spiritual equality of the Christian.

Political equality will be approached from the standpoint of the four great modern revolutions in which the concept played an important rôle—the English Revolution of 1688 with its emphasis on the equality of men in relation to political power; the American Revolution of 1776 whose famous Declaration expressed the oft-repeated proposition: "We hold these truths to be self-evident that all men are created equal"; the French Revolution of 1789 with its famous trilogy of "Liberty, Equality, and Fraternity"; and finally the Industrial Revolution which shifted the emphasis from political to economic equality.

Economic equality will be revealed in the exposition of Communism. From the standard works of the foremost Communist leaders, Marx, Engels, Lenin and Stalin, will be gathered those egalitarian teachings which have their root in the economic interpretation of man.

Spiritual equality is a metaphysical concept. It will be examined in the writings of that superb thinker of all times, Thomas of Aquin, who best represents the Christian view; and the purpose of the examination will not be to exhume an historical curiosity, but rather to discover and expound in the thought of the immortal Doctor principles to which the modern world may well give heed.

The last section of this work will view critically the first, for our purpose is not merely to present, but to evaluate. From this criticism we hope to bring order and clarity to an ideal that has suffered much from friends and foes alike, but which yet contains a gem of truth too often hidden beneath the cloak of error.

The importance of the problem needs no defense. Equality has ever been the favorite child of democracy. But there is much confusion of tongues on the subject, and much that is written misses the mark because of a failure to understand its basic philosophy. With democracy to-day under attack it is imperative that its fundamental concepts be set forth with clarity and precision, if men are to be kept from plunging into reactions which can only add to the sum total of human suffering.

Because equality is one of such concepts, the present study hopes to dissolve some of the mist, which unfortunately blurring its contour, discloses it to the visionary reformer as the zenith of human happiness, and to the hide-bound conservative as the nadir of human slavery. Equality is neither. That it is not a panacea for human ills, nor a monster devouring liberty, we hope in the course of these pages to make clear. That it does play an important part in the structure of human society and, therefore, must have its rightful function in the new order, is the prime purpose of this work to disclose.

To her religious superiors for the opportunity afforded to pursue graduate studies, and for their ever kindly encouragement, the author expresses profound gratitude; to the Very Reverend Henry Ignatius Smith, O.P., Ph.D., Dean of the School of Philosophy, she offers grateful acknowledgment for valuable criticisms; to the Reverend William J. McDonald, Ph.D., and the Reverend Robert J. Slavin, O.P., Ph.D., are due appreciation for reading and correcting the manuscript. Finally to the Right Reverend Monsignor Fulton J. Sheen the author would express her deepest appreciation and most sincere thanks. It was he who suggested the problem, and remained throughout its development an ever fruitful source of inspiration and gracious encouragement. For his constant guidance, valuable time, and for the free access to his personal library the author will remain always indebted.

The Sisters of St. Benedict whose gracious hospitality and personal friendship added a note of joy to tedious hours understand a gratitude that words fail to convey. To all those who materially aided in this work, the Librarian of the University, and those of the Library of Congress, to Sister M. Charitina, S.M., and to Miss Eva Reiss who typed the manuscript there is due a special note of thanks.

INTRODUCTION

In the history of human thought the idea of equality bears a charmed existence. Conceded by Matthew Arnold as owing its origin as a social ideal to Meander, it has persisted in spite of vigorous onslaughts to cast its spell over prophets and reformers alike who envision in the future a glimpse of the "good life." Hailed by Thomas Jefferson as a self-evident truth, it has been denounced by William Sumner as a flagrant falsehood. Recalled by Lincoln as the proposition to which this nation was dedicated, it has been branded by Calhoun as an absurd hypothesis. Seen by De Tocqueville as synonymous with democracy, it has been equated by Dr. Butler with a democracy that is spurious. Claimed by Laski to be the necessary condition for liberty, it has been cited by Lord Acton as "the deepest cause which made the French Revolution so disastrous to liberty." Dubbed by Rufus Choate as a "glittering generality," and assailed by Emile Faguet as the "democratic tarantula," we need only turn to its devotees to find it acclaimed in equally vivid phrases. Lester Ward and Richard Tawney, George Bernard Shaw and Lewis Mumford see in it the final perfection of society; while T. V. Smith, admitting it to be false in fact, retains it as "functionally useful."

This litany of contradictions could be indefinitely lengthened, but enough has been said to show that the idea has been able to survive repeated attacks. However, ideas that are alternately interred and exhumed are never self-evident truths or flagrant falsehoods. They are a mixture of truth and error, and the confusion which surrounds a medley of affirmations and denials lies in the failure to grasp the nature of the beings which ideas represent. This failure explains the controversy that has been waged so bitterly about equality. Those who see the American Declaration of Independence or the English Bill of Rights as outmoded documents, expect from them an equality they never pretended to attain. Similarly, those who would prick the "Jeffersonian bubble" because psychologists can provide us with long lists of mental and physical inequalities are merely writing beside the point. Like-

wise, those who shake their heads over the impossibility of Utopian
societies wherein all are leveled to one rank and all enjoy an equal
share of this world's goods, need not thereby be enemies of human
progress nor callous to the depths of human woes. Equality has its
shades and its degrees. The determination of the more important
of these and their far-reaching implications is the purpose of this
study.

As a formulated doctrine, equality is usually dated as entering
the world in the eighteenth century. That it had a long history
before that date is no great task to prove. Nevertheless, with the
eighteenth century philosophers it took on what might be called
the character of a dogma, and was assigned a place in the "natural
rights philosophy" which was then current. In this connection
it was purely political in character, so that its first modern interpretation had to do with the relation of the citizen to the State.
Under this aspect it is frequently referred to as civil equality or
equality before the law.

Closely allied to political equality are religious and racial equality
and the equality of the sexes. Strictly speaking they are outside
the scope of this investigation. But in so far as discrimination
within the State, or the absence of it, is due to one's religion, race,
or sex, these types of equality are related to political equality.

The efforts to obtain political equality have been justified on the
basis of natural equality. Such equality can mean several things.
It may mean that men are equal in their physical and mental endowments, and possess at birth equal capacities for growth and
development. Their differences are the work of training and environment. It may mean that distinctions in rank, in wealth, in
political and social status, are due entirely to social arrangements,
and apart from society would not exist. This is usually the
equality that is spoken of by the social contract philosophers of
the eighteenth century. It is the equality of the "noble savage,"
the equality of men in the primitive state before they agree to bear
the yoke of civil government. It is the one usually offered as the
basic reason why men should be politically and economically equal.
It will be treated in connection with political equality. Finally,
equality may mean that men are equal in their physical essence,

that they are all equally men, and no one is more or less a man than another. Such equality will be termed in this inquiry specific, essential, substantial or spiritual equality. It will form the subject matter of the second section of the present study.

Social equality is a vague concept and any attempt to define it is apt to prove unsatisfactory. If it refers to the absence of privileged classes created by law, then it may be regarded as a phase of political equality. If it means the rise and prestige of families or groups through the accumulation of wealth and thus of power, it may be regarded as a phase of economic equality. But if social equality means nothing more than the absence of exclusive sets or groups brought together by a like preference for certain habits or ways of life, then it is difficult to see how such an equality could exist, unless men were prohibited by law, from choosing their friends from among those of similar tastes and interests. Such social formations are bound to spring up under any régime, except that of the most flagrant tyranny. We shall dismiss it, therefore, as of little consequence, and treat social equality as either political or economic depending on whether the absence of distinctions is due to the refusal of the State to create special classes, or to the possession by all the citizens of an equal share of material prosperity.

Economic equality is urged by those who see it as the next step in the realization of the equalitarian doctrine. It is the attempt to expunge all differences created by wealth by allotting to every man and woman a more equitable share in worldly goods. Its advocates would attain it through the abolition of private property, and the socialization of the means of production. It is the goal set by Socialists and Communists in their plans for the reconstruction of society.

By many, equality of opportunity is regarded as the only sane and practical form of equality. The followers of *laissez-faire* philosophy fall back upon it as the proper interpretation of the democratic formula. Basically, it operates on the principle of a "career open to talent" the right of every man to an opportunity to develop his native ability, and function in society accordingly. In so far as its denial springs from distinctions created by law or wealth it may be considered as a phase of political or economic equality.

Spiritual equality is a Christian concept. It is the equality of men before God, not in the sense that there is any mathematical parity between them, but rather that all have the same rational nature, all are equally men. Hence whatever be their individual differences, men were created for one and the same divine purpose. That purpose being spiritual in character confers on the nature destined to its attainment a certain spiritual content.

In summary, we have tried to classify the various forms of equality of which men speak, and we think we see them falling broadly under three general heads, the political, the economic and the spiritual. Political equality is the absence of all privilege created by law. Economic equality refers to the equal distribution of material goods. Spiritual equality means the equality of men in relation to their Creator. All other types we have seen as contributing to or products of these three. The present work, therefore, is dedicated to the task of investigating these three broad general types, and revealing their social implications.

PART I

Modern Concept of Equality

CHAPTER I

POLITICAL EQUALITY OR CONTRACT SOCIETY

1. THE ENGLISH REVOLUTION: EQUALITY VS. THE DIVINE RIGHT OF KINGS

A. *Historic Roots of the Problem*

The notion that all men are equal was by no means a novel doctrine introduced to the world of the seventeenth and eighteenth centuries by the political thinkers of that era. The master minds of Greece and Rome had given serious thought to the concept, and the advent of Christianity enhanced it with a meaning that the pagan world was incapable of conceiving. In the *Republic* of Plato it was thought of as an equality of opportunity;[1] with Aristotle its function was recognized in the virtue of justice, but as a leveling factor in society it was rejected in favor of a hierarchical order.[2] The Stoics taught it, and through them it influenced Roman law;[3] while Christianity, with its doctrine that all were children of a common Father, and that every human soul possessed intrinsic worth, gave it a lasting influence. And yet, equality, as we know it, is a modern doctrine, conceived and formulated by the "social contract" philosophers of the seventeenth and eighteenth centuries, and bequeathed by them to later political thinkers. Its much heralded and trumpeted appearance at this time was, however, but an emphasis, the cause of which was rooted in the Religious Revolution and the impetus to absolutism which it fostered. It was against this absolutism, as exhibited in the theory of divine right, that the

1. A. T. Williams, *The Concept of Equality in the Writings of Rousseau, Bentham, and Kant* (New York: Columbia University Press, 1907), pp. 3-4. Cf. F. Fritts, *The Concept of Equality in Relation to a Principle of Political Obligation* (Princeton: Princeton University Press, 1915), pp. 21-22.

2. Williams, *op. cit.*, pp. 5-6. Cf. Fritts, *op. cit.*, p. 23.

3. Williams, *op. cit.*, pp. 6-7. Cf. Fritts, *op. cit.*, p. 24.

1

English Revolution of 1688 was waged, and the doctrine that proved its most effective weapon was the doctrine of equality.

When the full force of the Protestant Revolt reached England, its repercussions in the political field were tremendous.[4] Tudor and Stuart kings, seeing in the theory of divine right[5] a satisfying basis for denying papal authority, were not slow to assume the absolute power in which the theory was prone to result. And when they did, they began a radical departure from the traditional English political practice.[6] With the accession of James I to the English throne the theory of divine right became a fully matured political doctrine. James gave it, not only royal benediction and explicit formulation, but exercised kingly power according to its tenets. The stage was thus set for political conflict.

The battle against Stuart absolutism was waged on three fronts: that of Parliament, which fought to regain the powers usurped by the King, was espoused by such Whig theorists as Algernon Sidney and John Locke; that of the Dissenters or Separatists, who sought to break from the Established Church too indissolubly wed to the crown to permit religious freedom, was waged by John Milton and the Puritans; while that of the Catholics, who denied that kingly power had any authority in things spiritual and gave such allegiance only to Rome, was championed by Bellarmine and Suarez. Nevertheless, all three used as their weapon the democratic formula of equality. But whereas Jesuit thinkers restated the medieval concept

4. F. J. C. Hearnshaw, *The Social and Political Ideas of Some Great Thinkers of the Renaissance and the Reformation* (London: George G. Harrap & Co., 1925). Cf. J. W. Allen, *History of Political Thought in the 16th Century* (New York: The Dial Press, 1928).

5. J. N. Figgis, *The Divine Right of Kings* (Cambridge: Cambridge University Press, 1914). Cf. C. H. McIlwain, *Political Works of James I* (Cambridge: Harvard University Press, 1918).

6. For a treatment of medieval political thought see Otto Gierki, *Political Theories of the Middle Ages* (trans. by F. W. Maitland; Cambridge: Cambridge University Press, 1922); C. H. McIlwain, *The Growth of Political Thought in the West* (New York: Macmillan Company, 1932); A. J. Carlyle, *A History of Medieval Political Theory in the West* (New York: G. P. Putnam's Sons, 1916), III; R. L. Poole, *Illustrations of the History of Medieval Thought* (London: Williams and Norgate, 1884); J. M. Littlejohn, *The Political Theory of the Schoolmen and Grotius* (New York: Columbia University, 1895).

of equality as the basis of government, Puritans and Whigs had assimilated something of another tradition consequent upon the Renaissance revival of Roman law.

The Controversy with Bellarmine and Suarez. Foremost as protagonists in the cause of liberty were two Jesuit thinkers, Bellarmine and Suarez. These offered stiff resistance to the absolutism of the Stuarts as exercised under the theory of divine right. Bellarmine was one of the most widely read controversialists of his day, and in crossing swords with him, James I not only met a devastating rival, but unwittingly served the cause of democracy by bringing Bellarmine's views into prominence.

Some years before the accession of James to the English throne, Robert Cardinal Bellarmine had written and published his best known work, *De Controversiis* (1586-1589), which, while mainly concerned with theological questions, contains one important section, the *De Laicis sive Saecularibus.* This section "treats of the natural basis and juridical origin of the State, the source of political authority, the rights and duties of rulers and of subjects, and the relations between the secular power and the ecclesiastical."[7] In this work Bellarmine states the normal medieval view, that rulers derive their authority from the consent of the people. It was against this position that James I took issue. While the details of this controversy need not detain us here, it is pertinent to note that in his exposition of the doctrine that rulers derive their power immediately from the people, Bellarmine advances as one of his arguments the fact that men being equal, there is no reason why one rather than another should dominate.

> Note, secondly, that this power resides, as in its subject, immediately in the whole state, for this power is by divine law, but divine law gives this power to no particular man, therefore divine law gives this power to the collected body. Furthermore, in the absence of positive law, there is no good reason why, *in a multitude of equals,* one rather than another should dominate. Therefore, power belongs to the collected body. Finally, human society ought to be a perfect State,

7. Robert Bellarmine, *De Laicis* (trans. by Kathleen Murphy; New York: Fordham University Press, 1928), p. 5.

therefore, it should have the power to preserve itself, hence, to punish disturbers of the peace, etc.[8]

The nature of this equality Bellarmine reveals in further passages of the *De Laicis* and in others of his works. Men are equal, not in the sense that one is not to be politically subject to another, or that all have equal powers and an equality of material possessions, but in essence; they are equal in their fundamental nature and as human beings, for they all belong equally to the same human species and are equally destined for the same end. Hence political subordination does not mean that kings or princes should rule over men, as man rules over the beast or creatures of a lower species.[9] Such rule is despotic, and befits not the essential equality of men. Political subordination, far from being against the dignity of human nature, is in full accord with the right order of society, for man is by nature social and has need of a ruler.[10] Only when rulers tyrannize over their subjects, setting themselves above others to be feared and venerated in such manner as to flatter their vanity, is man degraded, and the dignity of his nature outraged.[11] Servile subjection and political subordination are two different things. The

8. Robert Bellarmine, *De Laicis* (*Opera Omnia*, Vives ed.; Paris: 1870, III), cap. 6: "Secundo nota, potestatem immediate esse tanquem in subjecto, in tota multitudine: nam haec potestas est de jure divino. At jus divinum nulli homini particulari dedit hanc potestatem: ergo dedit multitudini. Praeterea sublato jure positivo, non est major ratio cur ex multis aequalibus unis potius, quam alius dominetur. Igitur potestas totius est multitudinis. Denique humana societas debet esse perfecta Respublica: ergo debet habere potestatem seipsam conservandi et proinde puniendi perturbatores pacis, etc."

9. *Ibid.*, cap. 7: ". . . quomodo homo dominatur bestiis, sed solum debere unum ab altero regi politice."

10. *Ibid.*, cap. 7: "Tamen politicus principatus fuisset etiam statu innocentiae; et probatur primo, quia etiam tunc homo fuisset naturaliter animal civile, et sociale, as proinde rectore opus habuisset."

11. *Ibid.*, cap. 7: "Unde ibidem subdit: 'Nam contra naturam superbire, est ab aequalibus velle timere.' Quia vero peccatores per peccatum similes fiunt bestiis, et degenerant ab ea naturae integritate, in qua creati fuerant; ideo ibidem Gregorius dicit recte post peccatum unam alteri dominari coepisse; cum terrore minando et puniendo, quod in statu innocentiae non fuisset."

former is the result of an inequality brought on by the Fall,[12] but the latter would have prevailed even though men remained in a state of innocence. For in such a state there would still have been inequality of sexes and of powers; men would have differed in stature and in intellectual and physical capacities, and the inferior would have been subject to the superior, as all right order dictates.[13]

It was against this fundamental human dignity, in which all men equally share, that the absolute monarchs of England had sinned. For, in subjecting their people to that servile obedience which the doctrines of divine right and non-resistance so stringently imposed, they not only exercised a power which was unlawful, but violated the dignity of the human person, a dignity in which king and subject shared alike, and which had its source in human freedom. Such violation is not the natural use of civil power, and Bellarmine, while recognizing the need of lawful authority, and the respectful obedience accorded it on the part of the subjects, is nevertheless adamant in his insistence that the exaltation of the ruler only makes him the servant of his people.[14]

> The individual is prior to the State, which exists only as one means to help him toward his end. All men were, therefore, essentially equal before the State; and the government, whether it consisted of a single monarch or of a dominant majority, could not utilize any man for the aggrandizement of itself or its friends.[15]

12. *Ibid.,* cap. 7: "Ad quartum dico, Augustinum loqui de servitute proprie dicta, ut ex toto illo capite patet; ubi inter alia sic ait: 'Conditio servitutis jure intelligitu imposita peccatori,' etc."

13. *Ibid.,* cap. 7: "Tamen politicus principatus fuisset etiam in statu innocentiae . . . quia in illo statu fuisset disparitas sexum, statuum, ingeniorum, sapientiae et probitatis: ergo et praefectura ac subjectio; nam in humana societate debuit esse ordo. Rectus autem ordo postulat, ut inferior a superiore regatur, foemina a viro, junior a seniore, minus sapiens a sapientiore, et minus bonus a meliore: quod autem hae diversitates tunc etiam locum habuissent, sic ostendi potest."

14. *De Laicis,* cap. 7: "Itaque revera si ulla est servitus in politico principatu, magis proprie servus dici debet qui praeest, quam qui subjectus est, ut docet Augustinus lib. XIX civitat. cap 14, et hoc ad litteram significat illud Domini, Matth. XX: Qui voluerit inter vos primus fieri, erit omnium servus. . . ."

15. H. R. McCadden, "Elusive Equality," *Thought,* VIII (1932), pp. 447-448.

6   *The Philosophy of Equality*

Bellarmine's controversy with James I found ample support in the
works of his fellow-Jesuit, Francisco Suarez. Suarez was by far
the abler philosopher, but the polemical character of Bellarmine's
works won the latter popular recognition. When, in answer to
Bellarmine's defense of the Pope's right to excommunicate heret-
ical kings and absolve their subjects from obedience,[16] James I
imposed on the Catholics of his realm the oath of allegiance, the
Pope forbade English Catholics to take the oath, on the ground
that it contained many things contrary to faith and salvation.[17] It
was then that James wrote his *Apologia for the Oath of Allegiance*,
which he addressed to "all most mightie monarchs, free princes
and states of Christendom," to "advertise to the princes of Europe
the incompatibility of the Papal claims with their own sovereign
authority."[18]

Suarez, at the request of Pope Paul V, then entered upon the
scene and produced his *Defensio Fidei Catholicae*, an "exhaustive
refutation of the English King's contention, and a defense of
Bellarmine that furnished the occasion for a much ampler theoretic
exposition of the doctrine of consent."[19] Just the year previous
he had published the *Tractatus De Legibus*, and these two works
contain the whole of his contribution to political theory. Suarez
is in complete agreement with Bellarmine that political power is
vested by God not in the ruler immediately, but in the whole
people, and the reason he advances is the same as that offered by
his fellow-Jesuit.[20] All men, before they come together in political

16. Robert Bellarmine, *De Summo Pontifice* (*Opera Omnia*, II), Lib. V,
cap. 7: "Non licet Christianis Tolerare Regem infidelem, aut haereticum, si
ille conetur pertrahere subditos ad suam haeresim, vel infidelitatem; at
judicare, an Rex pertrahat ad haeresim, necne, pertinet ad Pontificem, cui
est commissa cura religionis, ergo Pontificis est judicare, Regem esse
deponendum, vel non depondendum."
17. F. J. C. Hearnshaw, *op. cit.*, p. 122.
18. James I, *An Apologia for the Oath of Allegiance* (*Political Works of
James I*), pp. 110-167.
19. J. A. Ryan and M. F. X. Millar, *Church and State* (New York:
Macmillan & Co., 1924), p. 118.
20. Francis Suarez, *Tractatus De Legibus* (*Opera Omnia*, Vives ed.;
Paris: 1856), Lib. III, cap. 2: "Ratio prioris partis evidens est, quae in
principio est tacta, quia ex natura rei omnes homines nascuntur liberi, et
ideo nullus habet jurisdictionem politicam in alium, sicut nec dominum:
neque est ulla ratio cur hoc tribuatur ex natura rei his respectu illorum
potius quam e converso."

society, are free and equal, and there is no reason from nature why one should impose his will upon another.[21] This is simply the medieval teaching that was handed down from Augustine, who taught that the divine origin of political authority was necessitated by the fact that all men being created equal, the right of man to command men cannot come except from outside humanity.[22] Augustine is here referring to the ultimate divine origin of civil authority, but it is significant to note that he bases it on the natural equality of men before the "pact of society."

This notion of equality which Bellarmine and Suarez inherited from the Augustinian tradition, did not imply a dead leveling of society. Society was still hierarchial; it was still based on the principle of gradation. But men, as men, were not to be subject in their persons to another, nor were they to be used as means to the attainment of another's end. Rather, political society was to be the means whereby each man attained his own individual end, and governmental authority was the necessary instrument for the preservation of that society. Hence the ruler, receiving his power from the people, becomes their master only that he may better become their servant. In his capacity as ruler he is above them; in his nature as a man he is equal to them; but in so far as he ministers unto them, he is beneath those whom he serves.

Such doctrine was necessarily anathema to the divine right theorists, and James I accorded it the honor of being burned, when he sentenced the *Defensio Fidei Catholicae* to be the fuel of a public bonfire in London, a few months after it had been printed.[23] But the burning of political tracts need not necessarily erase the

21. Suarez, *Defensio Fidei Catholicae* (*Opera Omnia*, XXIV, p. 209): "Exemplum est de libertate hominis, quae servituti opponitur, est enim de jure naturali, quia ex vi solius naturalis juris homo nascitur liber, nec potest sine legitimo aliquo titulo in servitutem redigi; jus autem naturae non praecipit omnem hominem semper manere liberum, seu (quod perinde est) non simpliciter prohibit hominem in servitutem redigi, sed solum ut id non fiat vel sine libero illius consensu, vel sine justo titulo et potestate."

22. St. Augustine, *De Civitate Dei*, xix, 15 (Dod trans., Edinburgh: T. & T. Clark, 1888). Cf. Gustave Combes, *La Doctrine Politique de Saint Augustine* (Paris: 1927), p. 81.

23. A. Rahilly, "The Sources of English and American Democracy," *Studies*, VIII (1919), p. 201.

ideas they propagate, and while James bequeathed to succeeding
Stuart kings his theory of State, he did not thereby obliterate the
democratic ideas of his opponents.

The Rôle of Milton. The notions of popular sovereignty based
on the concept of equality which Bellarmine and Suarez advanced
soon began to make, in Puritans and Whigs, strange bedfellows.
The chief spokesman of the Puritans was John Milton, who in his
Tenure of Kings and Magistrates (1649), and again in the
Defensio Pro Populo Anglicano (1651), voiced anew the doctrine
of popular sovereignty based on the natural freedom and equality
of all men.[24] But the equality of Milton is of a different stamp
from that of Suarez and Bellarmine, deriving, not from Augustine
and the normal medieval view,[25] but related more to a political
tradition whose modern version was ushered in with the Renaissance revival of Roman law. Its equality was one of origin rather
than of destiny, of condition rather than essence, and its conception
of society more that of an aggregate rather than an organism.[26]

The Theory of Hobbes. During the period of the Protectorate,
the theory of royal absolutism suffered no dearth of political
philosophers to bolster up its claim. Most noteworthy among
these was Thomas Hobbes, who as royal tutor of Charles II, was
naturally absorbed by the controversy going on between the Stuarts
and the champions of political liberty. During the Puritan Revolution and the subsequent overthrow of the Stuart regime, Hobbes
fled with the defeated Royalists to France. While in exile he
published *The Leviathan*, or the *Matter, Form and Power of a
Commonwealth, Ecclesiastical and Civil* (1651). In this work,
Hobbes, to the embarrassment of his royal patrons, and to the
confusion of democratic theorists, combines the theory of absolute
monarchy with the theory of popular contract. Kings reign, no
longer by divine right, but through the consent of their subjects,

24. W. A. Dunning, *History of Political Theory* (From Luther to Montesquieu; New York: Macmillan Company, 1910), pp. 242-244.
    25. George Bull, "The Two Traditions in Political Philosophy," *Thought*,
VII, pp. 404-417.
    26. McCadden, op. cit., pp. 444-458.

who to escape the nightmare of brutish warfare in the pre-social state, abjectly give over to one of their members all their rights and liberties forever in return for peace and security. Absolute rule men contracted for, and to absolute rule they must forever submit. With his doctrine of consent, Hobbes stepped from the Royalist camp, but his conclusion barred his entrance within the democratic lines. In his political theory he stands alone, the hybrid of two opposing theories. Yet his influence is far-reaching.

The doctrine of consent was not new, but the theory of social contract was.[27] Likewise the pre-political state was not an innovation, but Hobbes' description of it was distinctly novel. To the men of the Middle Ages the *pactum societatis* was not a formal contract made by free and equal solitaries in a pre-political state where man played the wolf to his fellows, but an agreement expressed or tacit, whereby men, social by nature and recognizing their need to obey a ruler, freely consent to submit themselves to one of their own choice.[28]

To the mind of Hobbes, on the other hand, pre-political man is by nature antisocial, so engrossed in the pursuit of his own selfish ends that he must necessarily be at war with his fellowmen. Consequently, war and struggle are the natural activities of men, the escape from which could only be had when men so covenanted one with another, that each gave up his natural freedom, and equal rights to the goods of the earth, and resigned them to one selected member, in order that by complete obedience to this newly created authority, the "Leviathan," men might obtain the peace and security lacking in the primitive state of nature. In this new State, since "each gives up all his rights the conditions are the same for all and an equality is again reached combined with peace and order."[29]

But the equality which men acquire in the "Leviathan" is the complete antithesis of the equality they possessed in the "state of nature." In that primitive condition, equality meant merely the absence of those inequalities which are due to institutions and conventions. All possessed equal natural rights but since right is

27. Dunning, *op. cit.*, p. 302.
28. St. Augustine, *Confessions*, iii, 8 & 15. Cf. Combes, *op. cit.*, p. 79.
29. Williams, *op. cit.*, pp. 9-10.

indistinguishable from might,[30] the only salvation for man is to surrender all his rights to a civil power, which he contracts with his fellows to set up. From then on all are equally slaves, possessing only such freedom as arbitrary power may see fit to give. Thus from one extreme, man has gone to the other, and the equality lost, as well as the equality gained, has in no way added to the dignity of man's estate.

The equality which Hobbes provides is a far cry from the equality of Bellarmine and Suarez, as well as the medievalists and the Christian Fathers, and his theory of social contract is even more so. The transfer of divinely given authority from the community as a whole to the selected ruler, becomes for Hobbes the contract of individual with individual to so pool their respective rights and powers, that there is formed one great powerful authority, the "Leviathan" which is but the sum of the powers of all the subjects.

> I Authorize, and give up my Right of Governing my selfe, to this Man or to this Assembly of men, on this condition, that thou give up thy Right to him and Authorize all his Actions in like manner. This done, the Multitude so united in one Person, is called a Commonwealth. . . . This is the Generation of the great Leviathan or rather that Mortall God, to whom wee owe under the Immortall God, our peace and defense.[31]

Though Hobbes sought to justify the unlimited power of the Stuarts, the Royalists, who would have none of his brand of absolutism, had to look to other quarters for speculative support. "They preferred to lose their cause in the strength of Charles and Filmer than to gain it with the aid of the artillery forged in the factory of the Devil."[32]

The Views of Filmer.   Robert Filmer, whose posthumous work, *Patriarcha,* was published in 1680, became the Royalist philosopher

30. David Ritchie, *Natural Rights* (New York: Macmillan Company, 1924), p. 83.
31. Thomas Hobbes, *Leviathan* (London: 1651), p. 131.
32. C. E. Vaughan, *Studies in the History of Political Philosophy* (Manchester: University Press, 1925), I, p. 23.

par excellence. Recognized by divine right theorists as the proper exponent of their views, he was deemed by the Whigs as the opponent most worthy of attack. Filmer had been private theologian to James I, and his closeness to that source of royal absolutism, won him the benediction of Anglican divines and Cavalier retainers. Of his orthodoxy there was no question. Filmer sought a basis of royal power that would meet the rationalist thinkers of the seventeenth century on their own ground, but which at the same time would satisfy the theological bent of divine right supporters. He found it in his patriarchical theory of sovereignty. To the contract theorists of the Hobbesian stamp, the natural equality and freedom of men made civil society but a conventional institution. Although it was to the "men of nature" they went for their source of authority, the political institution they erected was but nature shorn of its primitive freedom. Filmer would show civil society to be natural, and he would do it by an attack on the natural equality of men and any government formed through the "clumsy paraphernalia of social contract."[33] In his *Observations Concerning the Originall of Government,* he answers the contract theorists. In his *Patriarchia* he refutes the political doctrine of Bellarmine and Suarez.

Filmer clearly perceived that all arguments in favor of popular sovereignty rested upon the doctrine of the natural equality of men. The successful refutation of that equality would therefore mean the death knell of such sovereignty. The natural subjection of children to their fathers, and of these fathers in turn to the eldest parent was Filmer's answer to the natural equality of men. By the possession of the first fathers of absolute power over their children, and the inheritance of such power by the rightful heir, Filmer justifies the absolute power of kings. Rule by divine right may be traced to God's grant of power to the first fathers of the race, and since children may never lawfully rebel against their parents, neither may subjects ever lawfully rebel against their king.

The Influence of Sidney and Locke. Whig philosophers saw in Filmer material worthy of their steel, and Algernon Sidney and

33. Dunning, *op. cit.,* pp. 254-261.

John Locke drew their swords in defense of the Whig claims.
Sidney lost his head in the battle of words, for Charles II executed
him in the latter part of his reign.[34]   But Locke lived to see
James II banished forever from the English throne, and then published his *Two Treatises on Government* to justify the "glorious
revolution" that put an end to Stuart absolutism.

The first Treatise is given over entirely to the refutation of
Filmer, while the second sets forth Locke's constructive theory on
the nature and origin of government.   Like Hobbes he takes as
his point of departure individual man in the state of nature.   The
function of the State he seeks in its origin, and since he is looking
for grounds upon which to base limitations to political power, he
thinks the natural condition of men before there was a State will
provide the answer.   Hence he premises a state of nature in which
men enjoy perfect freedom and equality.   This is the historical
primitive state that existed before the organization of men into the
body politic.   Here men were so free and so equal that no one
could assume authority or jurisdiction over the rest.

> To understand political power aright, and derive it from its
> original, we must consider what estate all men are naturally
> in, and that is, a state of perfect freedom. . . .   A state also
> of equality, wherein all the power and jurisdiction is recip-
> rocal, no one having more than another, there being nothing
> more evident than that creatures of the same species and rank,
> promiscuously born to all the same advantages of Nature, and
> the use of the same faculties, should also be equal one amongst
> another, without subordination or subjection. . . .   This
> equality of men by Nature, the judicious Hooker looks upon
> as so evident in itself, and beyond all question, that he makes
> it the foundation of that obligation to mutual love amongst
> men on which he builds the duties they owe one another,[35]

34. Sidney's *Discourses on Government* were an attack on the Court party
and a refutation of Filmer's *Patriarcha.*   He agreed with Bellarmine and
Suarez that civil authority comes to the ruler only through the consent
of the people.   Such was the "common notion written in the heart of every
man."   Algernon Sidney, *Discourses on Government* (New York: Deare
and Andrews, 1805) I, pp. 313-355.

35. John Locke, *Of Civil Government* (Everyman's Library ed.; New
York: E. P. Dutton & Co., 1936), pp. 118-119.

At this point Locke parts company with Hobbes, who, as we have seen, conceived the state of nature to be one of war, *homo homini lupus.* Locke found it otherwise. The men who lived before civil organization regimented mankind, patterned their lives in accordance with the law of nature. Thus tranquillity and not war characterized pre-political man.

> The state of nature has a law to govern it, which obliges everyone, and reason, which is that law, teaches all mankind who will but consult it, that being all equal and independent, no one ought to harm another in his life, health, liberty or possessions. . . .[36]

In this state men were endowed with certain natural rights, as for example, those to life, liberty and property. And all were equally so endowed. Should one violate the rights of another each was empowered to execute the natural law and punish the transgressor.

> . . . the execution of the law of Nature is in that state put into every man's hands, whereby everyone has a right to punish the transgressor of that law to such a degree as may hinder its violation.[37]

It was this individual execution of the law of nature, that made the state of nature inconvenient for peaceful living, and necessitated the formation of the civil State.[38] This State came into being when each individual contracted with every other individual to give up his natural right to execute the law of nature, and vest such power in the community as a whole. The sum of the rights donated constituted the complete authority possessed by the community. Since men did not give up all their natural rights, but only those which authorized each to punish offenders of the natural law, the community was vested with this power and no other that it determine what constitutes a breach of nature's law, and inflict

36. *Ibid.,* p. 119.
37. *Ibid.,* p. 120.
38. *Ibid.,* Bk. II, ch. 9, *passim.*

just punishment on the malefactor.[39]   Thus peace was ensured, and man left free to pursue unhampered the acquisition of whatever might help him to enjoy temporal happiness.[40]   Such is Locke's concept of government: (1) a *state of nature*, wherein all are equal, and each in consequence of which is empowered to enforce the mandates of the law of nature; (2) a *social compact* by which each relinquishes this right to the body politic, and consents to follow the will of the majority; (3) an *authority* limited to only such power as will execute the natural law in the preservation of property; (4) a *termination of that authority and the establishment of a new government* when the bounds set have been exceeded for what is necessary for the preservation of the general welfare. Since the Stuart kings exceeded the power vested in them by the community, and disregarded the laws which the English people had enacted, their authority was forfeit, and a new government in the persons of William and Mary was necessary to replace it. Such was Locke's justification for the "glorious revolution" a justification that won him the title "Father of Modern Liberty." And that there might be no further doubt in the minds of the present or succeeding monarchs as to the extent of their powers, the Bill of Rights was framed, a contract between the king and Parliament, designating the rights and powers of each.

B. *Philosophic Roots of the Problem*

In summing up the events leading to the dethronement of royal absolutism in England, it may be stated that the theoretical grounds of that historic struggle can be reduced to the controversy regarding the source of political power. Against the claims of the English monarchs that their power to rule was a direct grant from God, and therefore subject to no human limitation, the democratic forces countered that kingly power is always dependent on human consent, and advanced as the basis of their argument the doctrine of human equality. Such equality recognizes the right of no man to assume political jurisdiction over his equals unless fully con-

---

39. *Ibid.*, Bk. II, ch. 9, sec. 129-131.
40. *Ibid.*, Bk. II, ch. 11, sec. 135, p. 94.

sented to by those same equals on whom his rule is to be imposed.
But though human equality is offered as the basic reason why civil
power must in some way have a popular source, the democratic
forces split on the character of that equality, and as a consequence
on the exact location of the *ultimate* source of political power.

The Two Democratic Traditions. The reason for this split
centers in the two opposed democratic theories already mentioned,
Christian and pagan. The former was begotten of a principle of
equality that recognized no essential differences among men. It
therefore predicated that among equals no one had the right to
assume power over the rest, and hence the right of man to rule
men must be divinely conferred. This was the teaching of St.
Augustine[41] and it remained the normal medieval view, adopted
and elaborated by St. Thomas who refused to conceive that even
in the state of innocence there was no need for authority.[42] It was
this tradition that was espoused by Bellarmine and Suarez, who
brought their medieval heritage to a fuller development when they
applied it to the situation in England. These two Jesuit thinkers
were insistent in their claims that out of deference to human
equality God centers civil power immediately in the multitude. But
since the multitude cannot exercise this power, they agree to select
one of their own members, who shall wield it in their name. Having transferred to this one the power to rule, they consent to obey
the authority thus erected, in whatever does not run counter to
human nature and its end. It is thus that kingly power is subject
to popular consent, and limited by the purpose which in the divine
plan of the Creator, the equal natures of men are destined to
achieve. In such view human equality becomes not only the basis
of popular sovereignty, but the reason why civil power must ultimately be divine.

The Pagan Tradition. The second tradition in democracy we
have designated secular or pagan, because it views man apart from
any obligation to his Creator. It sees him only in reference to his

41. St. Augustine, *De Civitate Dei,* xix, 15.
42. St. Thomas Aquinas, *Summa Theol.,* I, Q. 96, art. 4.

origin and temporal happiness, never in relation to his final goal.[43]
This tradition emanates from a notion of equality vastly different
from that of the Christian. Though both speak of the natural
equality of men, to the one, nature refers to essence; to the other,
it signifies the *primitive,* that state in which men found themselves
before conventional institutions and customs conditioned human
relations. In this "natural" state men were equally free, because
as yet all were unhampered by the restraining influence of civil
law. Whatever may have been the nature of the causes impelling
men to put on the shackles of political subjection (and theorists
are not one in their explanation of why man became political),
this much is certain—political power arose out of some sort of
understanding among free and equal men that certain of their
powers must be relinquished and conferred on some central authority. The extent of this authority, therefore, depends on the nature
of the contract made. It is thus that the "natural" equality
of men demands the popular origin of government, and the control
of civil power has its seat in the people's will. To this school of
thought Locke, Milton and the Puritans subscribed, while Hooker[44]
and Sidney were not untouched by its influence. Hobbes, as has
been pointed out, accepted its premises, but the nature of his social
contract brought wholly different conclusions.

The function of equality in the shaping of modern democratic
systems is thus evident. The constitutional monarchy set up in
England after the Revolution of 1688 set the pattern for modern
experiments in democratic governments. The effect of the English
example was world-wide, and wherever the theory of government
by the people took hold, the notion of equality lay at its very
foundation. But since the content of that equality signifies something wholly different to the two schools of democratic thought, the
modern democracies set up differ in proportion as their fundamental principles differ. The Christian notion of equality and the
function that it plays in social life will be the subject of investigation in a later section of this study. The equality that is of im-

43. Bull, *op. cit.,* pp. 404-417.
44. George Bull, "What Did Locke Borrow from Hooker?" *Thought,*
VII, pp. 122-135.

mediate concern is essentially related to a democratic trend that fathered the modern liberal democracy. Its influence entered the English struggle, and determined largely the character of political equality that marks so many of the democracies of our day.

The lineaments of this tradition need detain us but little. It is sufficient merely to note that they may be traced to the influence of Stoic philosophy on Roman law, wherein the concept of law as will issued from a notion of political authority which sprang from the equal grants of power on the part of free and equal solitaries in a state of nature. This view of law as the embodiment of will was uppermost in the whole of the Roman jurisprudence, and culminated through the *lex regia,* whereby the people made over to the emperor their whole power and authority in the absolutism of the Caesars. It was thus that rights became legal rights, and freedom but the power to do what the State permits.

With the triumph of Christianity within the Empire, these pagan law concepts lost their influence and to a great extent lay dormant. Christianity taught that civil authority had limitations other than individual or imperial will, limitations whch sprang from a natural law which had in common with the Roman jurists and the Stoics hardly more than a name. Being the manifestation in human nature of the eternal law of God, it was intimately bound up with the equality springing from that nature. St. Augustine, particularly, broke away from the naturalism of the earlier Romans, and his teaching on equality put a limitation on civil power that was unknown to the Roman jurists.

It was not until the Renaissance that the full force of the Stoic-Roman tradition was again felt in European jurisprudence. With the revival of Roman law this philosophy of law as will began to seep into European political thought. In France, particularly, the pagan political views took firm root, engendering a tradition in French politics that has endured to the present day. France was the first among the nations of Europe to achieve national independence and solidity, and it did so on the basis of a philosophy that could easily usher in a regime of absolute power. When the French kings sought to establish their supremacy, and weaken the power of the feudal barons they were offered in support of their claims a notion that was nothing more than the revival of the *lex regia* of pagan Rome, to which was added the further pagan principle of the prince as *legibus solutus*, not only above the law but its very incarnation.[45]

But if pagan absolutism had worked its way into French political thought it was opposed by another current of pagan politics. In the *Vindiciae Contra Tyrannos*, that much heralded pamphlet of French democracy, the people became the medium for the transfer of power, and the magistrate but the representative of the popular will. The importance of the *Vindiciae* and its influence on later political thought has been summarized by Laski as follows:

> . . . the theory of state upon which the *Vindiciae* rests determined the character of political speculation from the end of the sixteenth century until the advent of Rousseau. So long as the aim of political philosophy was to outline the area of abstract right determined *a priori* as a field subtracted from the rights of individuals, the Monarchomatic tradition exhausted the requirements of a liberal outlook. Prynne and Rutherford both drew their nourishment from this source; and the ideas of the Levelers rest upon a kindred foundation. Through Locke, it is at the base of the thoughts of Price and Priestley. . . . And Locke himself derived the substance of his ideas from the French thinkers of the Counter-Reformation.[46]

The notion of political society as the creation of the popular will received further impetus from the writings of Grotius,[47] Pufendorf[48] and Burlamaqui. These men are credited with having popularized the contract theory of government, which later political writers assumed as an established fact. This theory as already pointed out, rests on a concept of human equality that views men as equal because in the absence of political organization no man

45. Carlyle, *op. cit.*, VI, Pt. III, ch. 5; Pt. IV, ch. 3.

46. *A Defense of Liberty Against Tyrants* (ed. by Harold Laski; London: G. Bell & Sons, 1924), p. 54.

47. Littlejohn, *op. cit.*, intro., pp. v-ix.

48. Samuel Pufendorf, *De Jure Naturae et Gentium* (trans. C. H. and W. A. Oldfather; Oxford: Clarendon Press, 1934).

is subject to the will of another. Each is autonomous in the sense that no man or group of men has as yet received power to subject others to his rule.

C. *The English Controversy and the Two Democratic Traditions*

Though England, prior to 1688, still clung to its medieval heritage, there were not wanting political theorists who had become indoctrinated with the continental strain just outlined. Hobbes, Locke, Milton and the Levelers, are alike in their concept of men as free and equal before the formation of civil society. To them, as to the continental thinkers, society was a pactitious affair, through which men transfer all their rights to the ruler, as in the case of Hobbes who thus justifies the unlimited power of the monarch, or only such as is needful to keep peace and tranquillity, as in the case of Milton, Locke and the Levelers. But this is merely the pagan notion of equality, which concedes men to be equal in origin and condition, in so far as nature has bestowed on each equal natural rights or powers, by which they are equipped for self-preservation and development.

The concept of equality upon which the Schoolmen based their theory of government, was something quite different from this. Government was not the creation of individual grants of power, but the natural development of man's social nature. Its establishment meant not the loss of any individual rights, but their guarantee and protection. While there was an equality of rights rooted in specific natures, these rights had less to do with origin than with destiny. They gave to man no authority over another; and what no individual possessed, no aggregate of individuals could claim. Authority was something divine, and man bowed not to the will of his fellowman, but to the law that expressed the divine plan of his Creator.

2. The American Revolution: All Men Are Created Equal.

When the American Colonies severed their political affiliations with Great Britain, the principles upon which they resisted British rule were stated in that now famous second paragraph of the Declaration:

> We hold these truths to be self-evident that all men are created *equal*, that they are endowed by their Creator with certain inalienable rights, that among these are life, liberty and the pursuit of happiness. That to secure these rights governments are instituted among men, deriving their just powers from the consent of the governed.

These principles are essentially the same as those upon which the English Revolution of 1688 claimed justification, namely, that government is valid only when it rests on the consent of the governed. Although the "glorious revolution" put an end to the tyranny of the King, it substituted, as far as the Colonies were concerned, the tyranny of Parliament. Since the Colonies claimed they were not represented in that body, they insisted that they could not be governed by it without their consent. Hence they refused to recognize its jurisdiction.[49] When George III upheld the action of Parliament and disregarded the protests made to the Crown by the American subjects, there was nothing left for them to do but to assert their right to throw off the yoke of a government that had become destructive of the ends for which it had been erected.

Now the statement that governments are valid only when they function with the consent of the governed, rests upon the conviction traditional in western civilization that men are by nature equal, and are possessed of certain rights that governments must not only respect, but preserve. But if men are equal in nature there is no basis upon which one may set himself politically over another unless with the consent of those on whom his rule is to be

49. C. H. McIlwain, *The American Revolution* (New York: The Macmillan Co., 1923), ch. 4.

imposed.[50] Furthermore, the doctrine of inalienable rights, that is, the possession of powers which man may never delegate, prevents established governments from becoming absolute in rule. When absolutism is assumed, government becomes but a thing of force, which man is justified in overcoming; for a rule imposed on men, not for their common welfare, but to satisfy the intention of the ruler, is without any rational foundation.

Such were the views of the American leaders on which they based their armed resistance when Great Britain resorted to force. The ideas were not new. They had had a long history in European politics, but as has been outlined in the preceding pages, they were given an interpretation during the period from the Renaissance to the eighteenth century, which was quite different from their significance to the men of medieval society. From which tradition do the American notions spring? From the pagan ideas revived by the Renaissance and reinforced by Protestant thinking, or are they of Scholastic lineage? On the anwer to this question depends the dissolving of the present confusion as to whether the second paragraph of the Declaration expresses but "glittering generalities" and "out-moded theories," or the more stable basis of unchanging truths. The answer is imperative, for one view makes government an artificial contrivance, the other the urgency of nature. The prevalence of one theory or the other has on social life effects of far-reaching but vitally different character.

That there is a close parallel between Scholastic political philosophy, and the basic principles of the American theory of government, has been admirably shown in several studies,[51] where the Virginia Bill of Rights, the Massachusetts Declaration of Rights, and the Declaration of Independence, on the one hand, and the writings of St. Thomas and Cardinal Bellarmine on the other, have been compared section by section. A perusal of these studies

50. *The Works of James Wilson* (ed. by James DeWitt Andrews; Chicago: Callahan & Co., 1896), II, pp. 507-508.
51. E. F. Murphy, *St. Thomas' Political Doctrine and Democracy* (Washington: Catholic University Press, 1921), ch. 7. Cf. J. C. Rager, *Democracy and Bellarmine* (Washington: Catholic University Press, 1926), pp. 137-139. S. J. McNamara, *American Democracy and Catholic Doctrine* (New York: International Catholic Truth Society, n.d.), pp. 113-114.

leaves one in little doubt of the agreement between the political
principles of the great Scholastics and the historic documents
which contain our principles of government. Space permits the
citation of but a few of these parallels, which shall be limited to
the respective positions on equality.

> *Vir. Decl. R.:*   That all men are by nature equally free and
> independent, and have certain inherent rights, of which, when
> they enter into a State of society, they cannot, by any compact
> deprive or divest their posterity; namely, the enjoyment of
> life and liberty, with the means of acquiring and possessing
> property, pursuing and obtaining happiness and safety.[52]
> *St. Thom., 2 Sent.,* d. 6, q. 1, a. 4, ad. 5:   Men are not
> superior to each other according to the order of nature.[53]
> *St. Thom., 2 Sent.,* d. 44, q. 1, a. 3:   Nature made all men
> equal in liberty.[54]
> *Summa Theol.* 2a, 2ae. q. 104, a. 5:   In two respects, the
> subject is not bound to obey his superior in all things: first,
> in the case of a command on the part of a greater power;
> secondly, if the latter orders something in which the former
> is not subject to him.   Hence in such affairs as appertain to
> the inner volitional life, man is not beholden to man, but to
> God alone.   His obedience is due in regard to his external,
> bodily activity; yet in those acts which belong to the nature
> of the body, God alone is his superior; for all men are equal
> by nature.[55]
> *Decl. of Ind.:*   All men are created equal[56]
> *Bellarmine:*   In a commonwealth all men are born naturally
> free and equal.   *De Clericis,* ch. 7.
> There is no reason why amongst equals one should rule rather
> than another.   *De Laicis,* ch. 6, note 2.[57]

Do these passages portray merely a verbal likeness, but under-
neath represent the two antithetic traditions in democratic theory?
Or, are the Americans and the Scholastics one in their view of
man's equality?   That the American Fathers interpreted equality

52. E. F. Murphy, *op. cit.,* p. 179.
53. *Ibid.,* p. 180.
54. *Ibid.,* p. 180.
55. *Ibid.,* p. 180.
56. *Ibid.,* p. 207.
57. Rager, *op. cit.,* p. 138.

in the same sense as the Scholastics is evidenced by their writings and by the concept of sovereignty they held. In the Scholastic notion of equality, no man has a right to impose his will on another, for in those things that pertain to his end or purpose as a man, "he is not beholden to man, but to God alone."[58]   But in a community composed of equals, since no valid reason can be advanced why one rather than another should dominate, power belongs to the collected body; but as the collected body of itself cannot exercise this power, the community must delegate it to some individual or group of individuals. Such is the doctrine of St. Thomas for whom the end of the State is determined by the end of man:

> To order anything to the common good belongs either to the whole people or to some one who is vicegerent of the whole people, and therefore the making of a law belongs either to the whole people or to a public personage who has care of the whole people, since in all other matters the directing of anything to the end concerns him to whom the end belongs.[59]

Bellarmine, writing on this same point, is in agreement with St. Thomas. Explaining the popular origin of government, he says:

> (Secular) power resides as in its subject in the whole state, for this power is by Divine law. But Divine law gives this power to no particular man, therefore Divine law gives the power to the collected body. For there is no good reason why, in a multitude of equals, one rather than another should dominate. . . . By the same natural right, this power is delegated by the multitude to one or several, for the state cannot

58. *Summa Theol.*, II, II, q. 104, art. 5: "Et ideo in his quae pertinent ad interiorem motum voluntatis, homo non tenetur homini obedire, sed solum Deo."

59. *Summa Theol.*, I, II, q. 90, art. 3: "Ordinare autem aliquid in bonum commune est vel totius multitudinis, vel alicuius gerentes vicem totius multitudinis. Et ideo condere legem vel pertinet ad totam multitudinem, vel pertinet ad personam publicam quae totius multitudinis curam habet. Quia et in omnibus aliis ordinare in finem est eius cujus est proprius ille finis."

of itself exercise this power, therefore it is bound to delegate it to one or to several, and this authority of rulers considered in general is both by natural law and by Divine law.[60]

Now if these passages mean anything, they mean that government based on the consent of the governed is the necessary consequence of the essential equality of men. From equality understood in this sense, it follows that men being equal in nature, they must necessarily tend to the same end, an end outside the determination of the State. Having a duty to pursue that end, they have an inherent right to the means necessary to attain it. It is in consequence of this, that men have inalienable rights, which are antecedent to all positive law, and which the State is bound not only to respect but preserve. How clearly this was understood by the Founders of our country is demonstrated by their persistent demand that men have certain inalienable rights, to secure which governments are instituted among men. And because men are equal these governments must derive their just powers from the consent of the governed. This doctrine of inalienable rights lies at the very basis of our government, and is the foundation upon which rests the supremacy of law and the divisions of sovereignty.

That the Founding Fathers had a clear perception of these principles, may be gleaned from an examination of their writings, and that they wove these principles into the very fabric of our Constitution, the decisions of the Supreme Court definitely confirm. No one fought more vigorously for the incorporation of these ideas into our Constitution than did James Wilson, one of the most dominant figures in the Conventions that determined our course as a nation. Recognized by Washington as the ablest lawyer in the Convention, he was appointed to the Supreme Court on Washington's advent to the Presidency.[61] This great American jurist has left us in no doubt as to his position on the doctrine of equality, and in that position he is true to the Scholastic tradition.

In civil society previous to the institution of civil government, all men are equal, of one blood all nations are made; from one

60. *De Laicis*, cap. 7.
61. Ives, "St. Thomas and the Constitution," *Thought*, V (1930), pp. 567-586.

source the whole human race has sprung. . . . With regard to all there is equality in rights and obligations; . . . the natural rights and duties of man belong equally to all. Each forms a part of that great system, whose greatest interest and happiness are intended by the laws of God and nature. . . . As in civil society, previous to all civil government, all men are equal, so in the same state all men are free. In such a state no one can claim in preference to another superior right. In the same state no one can claim over another superior authority.[62]

This same conception of equality was held by another political leader of the American Revolution. Hamilton, in asserting the existence of the natural law, and the equal subjection of all to this law, concludes:

Hence, in a state of nature, no man had any *moral* power to deprive another of his life, limbs, property, or liberty; nor the least authority to command, or exact, obedience from him, except that which arose from the ties of consanguinity.

Hence, also the origin of all civil government, justly established, must be a voluntary compact between the rulers and the ruled; and must be liable to such limitations, as are necessary for the security of the *absolute rights* of the latter; for what original title can any man, or set of men, have to govern others, except their own consent?[63]

It is significant that Jefferson, who is conceded to be the most radical of the Founding Fathers, did not go beyond this notion of equality in drawing up the Declaration of Independence. While there is question of his interpretation of natural right, and while he may have been influenced by the pagan view, this influence has not entered into either the Declaration, or the Virginia Bill of Rights, of the preamble of which he is the author. He was absent during the drawing up of the Constitution;[64] therefore, he could have had no active part in the expression of its principles.

62. *The Works of James Wilson, I,* pp. 273-275.
63. *Works of Alexander Hamilton* (ed. by C. C. Francis; New York: 1851), II, pp. 43-45.
64. E. Channing, *Students' History of the United States* (New York: The Macmillan Co., 1926), p. 199.

The doctrine of equality on which rests the American theory of the supremacy of law as against mere arbitrary will is strikingly brought out in the case of Yick Wo, a Chinese, who unable to become an American citizen was denied the right to carry on his laundry business. Justice Matthews in delivering his opinion on the case expressed himself as follows:

> The law is the declaration and limitation of power. It is indeed, quite true, that there must always be lodged somewhere, and in some person or body, the authority of final decision. . . . But the fundamental rights to life, liberty and the pursuit of happiness, considered as individual possessions, are secured by those maxims of constitutional law which are the monuments showing the victorious progress of the race in securing to men, the blessings of civilization under the reign of just and equal laws. So that in the famous language of the Massachusetts Bill of Rights, the government of the commonwealth "may be a government of laws and not of men." For the very idea that one man may be compelled to hold his life or the means of living, or any material right essential to the enjoyment of life at the mere will of another seems to be intolerable in any country where freedom prevails, as being of the essence of slavery itself.[65]

No clearer statement could be made of the Scholastic concept of equality than that contained in these words of Justice Matthews. In all that pertains to man as man, in all that pertains to the well-being of his personality, man is never subject to another man, "he is beholden only to God." It is the same idea that was expressed by Bellarmine.

> Men are born equal not in wisdom or grace or qualifications, but they are equal in their fundamental nature and as human beings. From this equality we correctly conclude that no man has a right to dominate or tyrannize his fellowmen. Man dominates over beasts, he rules the fishes of the sea, the birds of the air, and the other animals by despotic rule, but his fellowmen, he merely governs or directs politically.[66]

65. J. C. Bancroft Davis, *United States Reports* (New York: Banks Law Publishing Company, 1920), CXVIII, p. 370.
66. *De Laicis*, cap. 7.

When the Declaration of Independence proclaims that all men
are created equal, it is not reducing all to the dead level of blind
material nature, nor is it speaking of the equal freedom of all to
express and enforce their wills. Such is the Stoic concept that
Locke adopted, a concept that would give to all men equal power
to do whatever each chooses. This is curtailed only by the yoke
of civil government, which is always equal to the sum of delegated
powers. Such a theory places no restraint on government, which
may always do whatever the majority decides. Those who decry
our Declaration of Independence and sneer at its "glittering generalities" know of no other meaning for its doctrine of equality
than that of the Stoic leveling to an identity of powers. It is this
notion that lies behind the statement of Arthur Twining Hadley, a
former President of Yale, when he says in reference to the
Declaration:

> Few of us at present would be ready to subscribe to quite so
> broad a statement as this. We know that the right to liberty
> is not inalienable, but may be forfeited by misconduct. We
> know that the supposed equality of all mankind is something
> that has never been actually realized in human history. In
> fact, the signers of the Declaration of Independence them-
> selves can hardly have meant what they said to be taken
> literally. Most of them were aristocrats, many of them were
> slave-holders; some of them defended human slavery on
> principle. They were simply stating the theory of democratic
> government as it was understood in their time, and as it has
> been expounded by the great prophet of modern democracy,
> Rousseau.[67]

Dr. Hadley gravely errs. That Rousseau, in whom pagan
democracy reached its full bloom, inspired the Declaration, is a
statement lacking foundation in fact. Yet it illustrates the blind
spot in the thinking of so many modern writers on American
political theory, a blind spot that extends from pagan Rome to the
Renaissance and the Reformation, and leaves a void of some thousand years of political thinking. But fortunately for America, the

67. Arthur Twining Hadley, *The Conflict Between Liberty and Equality*
(New York: Houghton Mifflin Co., 1925), pp. 1-2.

Founding Fathers did not suffer from the same disease, and
whether they knew it or not, the political thought of those same
thousand years worked its way into the very warp and woof of the
political structure of our nation. No wonder a recent student of
democracy could reach the following conclusion:

> Two centuries before Columbus discovered America geo-
> graphically, it would seem that Aquinas has located it politi-
> cally. In his politics our country is in embryo. He differs
> from the founders of our republic and their achievement, only
> as the summer from the spring-time, or the full-blown blossom
> from the humble seed. To admit the merit and democracy of
> the United States, is to concede the same presaging Thomistic
> thought. In the right-bills of our sovereign states, in the
> document of our Declaration of Independence, in the *rationale*
> of our Constitution, his finger appears. An invisible guest,
> he was present at the founding of our nation; as he is also
> present through its preservation. So long as she is true to
> justice and reason, the spirits in which she was conceived, our
> country cannot die. But justice and reason express the
> political apostolate of Aquinas, and are the very substance of
> his message. And in justice, the people must find their due:
> which is democracy. In reason, they must accept duty as well
> as claim right; which is the salvation of democracy.[68]

3. THE FRENCH REVOLUTION: LIBERTY, EQUALITY, FRATERNITY

As in England and America, it was the loss of liberty in France
that made the cry for equality so poignant. In medieval society a
hierarchial order had developed as the result of a mutual interchange of services. Lord and vassal, serf and villein recognized
certain seigneurial privileges on the one hand, and certain tenurial
obligations on the other. The feudal barons thus became a "class
par excellence, exempt from the toils of daily life precisely in order
that they might turn all their activities to the service of the commonweal."[69] With the passage of France from a group of feudal

---

68. E. F. Murphy, *op. cit.,* pp. 211-213.
69. Guido de Ruggiero, *History of European Liberalism* (London: Oxford University Press, 1927), pp. 8-9.

patrimonies to a consolidated nation such services became defunct, leaving a hierarchical structure devoid of meaning. Tithes and dues, which in the feudal scheme of things had a purpose became with the consolidation of the nation under the monarchy an unwarranted and empty tribute to an absentee lord, whose services to his people had long since ceased. Yet it was in view of these defunct services that the same lords, were they spiritual or temporal, claimed immunity from a just share in the national debt, leaving the lower classes to carry the burden alone.

But if a hierarchical order had lost its meaning in French life the disappearance of ancient liberties was partly responsible. As the monarchy gradually superimposed itself on a feudal society there was a corresponding decline in those institutions of freedom which had grown up in medieval France. Though both English and French Kings climbed to power through the humiliation of feudal barons the Tudor-created aristocracy of England never bowed as humbly to royal favor as did the Bourbon courtier. It was the knowledge of this fact that led de Tocqueville to say that while in France the aristocracy had lost their powers but kept their privileges, in England they had lost their privileges and kept their powers.[70] That is why the power of the Estates General, the great national assembly of France, never rose to the heights of the English Parliament. Instead of controlling the prerogatives of the Crown and protecting the rights of the people, as did the British assembly, it merely "laid their complaints at the foot of the throne, with no assurance that they would be listened to."[71]

When royal extravagance left the national treasury empty neither prince nor prelate was asked to economize. The Third Estate alone was expected to furnish the bulk of the nation's needs as well as the demands of a dissolute Court. With dues to the nobles and tithes to the clergy, and an array of taxes to the central government, in return for which they received scant consideration from prelate, prince, or king, the French peasantry were reduced to a pauperism, which the gaiety and splendor of Versailles and the

70. Alexis De Tocqueville, *L'Ancien Régime* (Paris: 1887), p. 147.

71. Sir Thomas Erskine May, *Democracy in Europe* (London: Longmans, Green & Co., 1877), II, p. 23.

galling immunities of the privileged, served but to fan the flames of discontent. Yet not violence, but constitutional methods, were the means sought by the French people to remedy the gross inequalities that were rotting the substance of a nation. If any leveling tendencies were present to wipe out social distinctions, they came not from the humble tillers of the soil, who made up the majority of French people, but from the rich bourgeois, writhing under the scorn of a titled noble who boasted an ancient lineage but an empty purse.[72] It was this bourgeois that became the spokesman for the Third Estate, the same bourgeois who bought his way into public office,[73] and too often reaped a fortune from the taxes farmed from the poor.[74] Egged on by a pernicious philosophy that was alone needed to complete the picture of the influence that wrought havoc in French society, it was his lips that framed the Revolutionary slogan, "Liberty, Equality and Fraternity," a formula vague enough to cover as much or as little as the framers intended, and inflammatory enough to kindle the passions of a suffering people.

A. *Revolutionary Philosophy*

Whether the philosophy of a century that called itself "enlightened" was the direct cause of the Revolution, or whether the economic conditions of the country brought on that historic struggle, may be left to others to decide. One thing, however, is beyond question. Had the French *Philosophes* thought otherwise than they did, the current of French politics might have entered wholly different channels. The Revolution was inevitable; that it took the turn it did, is due in no small measure to the political thought that preceded it. The actors on the philosophic stage and the drama they portrayed will bear reviewing, if the political concepts that permeated the Revolution, are to be properly understood. Many factors entered into the training of the *Philosophes*,

72. Kingsley Martin, *French Liberal Thought in the Eighteenth Century* (Boston: Little, Brown & Co., 1929), pp. 70-75.
73. Carlton J. H. Hayes, *Political and Social History of Modern Europe* (New York: The Macmillan Company, 1924), I, pp. 453.
74. Martin, *op. cit.*, p. 73.

and the shaping of the philosophy for which they stood. The mathematical formalism of Cartesian philosophy, the scientific discoveries of Newton, the anthropological data of the explorers, and the classical tradition in literature, all combined to produce the eighteenth century French Rationalism of Voltaire and Montesquieu, Helvetius and Holbach, Diderot and the Encyclopedists, with Rousseau as the consequent reaction. The nature of this Rationalism is aptly set forth in the words of Laski:

> It is essentially an attempt to apply the principles of Cartesianism to human affairs. Take as postulates the inescapable evidence of stout common sense, and reason logically from them to the conclusions they imply. That common sense, all the philosophers believed, will give everywhere the same results; what it is to the sage of Ferney it will be in Pekin or the woods of America. It is a kind of a psychological geometry built upon the belief that human nature is everywhere the the same.[75]

Reason could thus discover the laws of nature as Newton had discovered the law of gravitation. Observe, compare, deduce, and you can discover all there is to be known. Nature is everywhere the same, and her laws are invariable. The instrument for plumbing her depth is human reason. Apply this to all natural phenomena, mountains, minerals, monkeys or men, and you have the key that unlocks the secrets of the universe. Miracles, revelations, prophecies are the superstitions of the "unenlightened." There is no supernatural; there is only the natural, and God is its First Cause. He not only made the universe, but He made it go, and then promptly forgot all about it. All we have to do is to find the principles upon which it works, and we have reached the pinnacle of knowledge. Religion there is, and morality, but of a purely natural kind. Heaven has been brought down to earth, and the supernatural fictions have been translated into scientific facts.

Thus preached Voltaire, and Diderot, and Holbach, and a flippant French society applauded the new gospel. Nature and nature's laws were the magic words on the lips of the learned, and

75. F. J. C. Hearnshaw, *Social and Political Ideas of Some Great Thinkers of the Age of Reason* (London: George G. Harrap & Co., 1930), p. 15.

the lives of the primitives in the forests of America and the jungles of the tropics became the standard or norm for measuring human nature. The rational was the aboriginal, and the natural was what was left when the canons of civilization were stripped off. Take the method of Cartesian philosophy, the findings of Newtonian physics, and the data of the explorers, and wrap them up in the abstract phrasing of the classic spirit, and you have the Rationalism of the Age of Reason.

Voltaire and Montesquieu brought the spirit from England, where both had visited, and become enamoured of English freedom. The former in his *Letters on the English*,[76] succeeded in making many thousands of readers see England as he had done, as a land of freedom and opportunity, where common sense reigned; the latter, seeing France through the eyes of a Persian, satirized existing institutions, political, religious and social, with just the right amount of wisdom and wit to suit the tastes of the day.[77]

Voltaire. It was Voltaire, more than anyone else, who popularized English thought and political institutions in France, while his virulent diatribes against Catholicism and Christianity spread abroad a "Voltairism," that was synonymous with impiety. If we look into his political conceptions little of positive value is to be found. His was the work of destruction, and his resounding blows at the ancient regime, with its institutions of privilege and its suppression of human rights, cleared away the obstacles which damned the rapidly rising flood. "He was the pioneer, the trail-blazer, whose task it was to level rather than construct; dynamite and the axe are his weapons, and his path is not beautiful to the eye."[78]

Such political philosophy as was his is perhaps best expressed in his *Essay on Customs*,[79] where, beginning with the natural, that is, the primitive, he argues to an order of society founded on the natural law, natural religion and natural rights. Over against this is the *empire of custom,* the actual world, built up on the

76. *Lettres anglaises.*
77. W. A. Dunning, *A History of Political Theories* (From Luther to Montesquieu; New York: The Macmillan Co., 1919), p. 391.
78. Hearnshaw, *op. cit.,* p. 139.
79. *Essai sur les moeurs.*

accumulation of innumerable traditions. The task of the political thinker is to bring this latter into harmony with the natural order which reason has discovered. Hence he attacks the existing laws, the established religion, and the maimed rights of the absolutist regime of the age. Man in his natural setting is the base from which to attack the existing institutions that would rob him of his birthright.[80] While Voltaire does not hold up the primitive as the perfect state of existence, he does view it as lacking the injustices of civilization. Man in the natural state has a propensity for society; he is not the solitary being of Hobbes, or the later Rousseau. Strip man of the evils of civilization, and then build a society on rational principles, and you reach the perfect state.

Voltaire, however, is no egalitarian. Admitting an equality at the primitive level, he blames inequality on nature's paucity, coupled with the fact that she gave man a lust for power, wealth, and pleasure.[81] While he does not explicitly say it, the implication is clear; political power belongs to the strong, and the mass of mankind can expect no participation in its exercise.[82] He was bitter in his denunciation of privilege, and insistent in his demands for

80. Hearnshaw, *op. cit.*, p. 140.

81. Voltaire, "Egalité," *Dictionnaire Philosophique* (Paris, 1816), VI, pp. 232-235: "Il est clair que les hommes, jouissant des facultés attachées à leur nature, sont égaux; ils le sont quand ils s'acquittent des fonctions animales, et quand ils exercent leur entendement. . . . Si cette terre était ce qu'elle semble devoir être, si l'homme y trouvait partout une subsistance facile et assurée et un climat convenable à sa nature, il est clair qu'il eût été impossible à un homme d'en asservir un autre. . . . Tous les hommes seraient donc nécessairement égaux s'ils étaient sans besoins; la misère attachée à notre espèce subordonne un homme à un autre homme: ce n'est pas l'inégalité qui est un malheur réel, c'est la dépendance. . . .

Une famille nombreuse a cultivé un bon terroir; deux petites familles voisines ont des champs ingrats et rebelles; il faut que les deux pauvres familles servent la famille opulente ou qu'elles l'égorgent: cela va sans difficulté. Une des deux familles indigentes va offrir ses bras à la riche pour avoir du pain: l'autre va l'attaquer et est battue. La famille servante est l'origine des domestiques et des manœuvres; la famille battue est l'origine des esclaves. . . .

Il est impossible dans notre malheureux globe que les hommes vivant en société ne soient pas divisés en deux classes; l'une des riches qui commandent, l'autre des pauvres qui servent, et ces deux se subdivisent en mille, et ces mille ont encore des nuances différentes."

82. Hearnshaw, *op. cit.*, pp. 152-153.

toleration and freedom of expression, yet one feels that when Voltaire suffered from the pride of the nobles or the power of the Church for his impious attacks, he cried out for equality with those above him; when he looked below, he saw himself superior to the mass of men for whom he had no love.

Montesquieu. If the part played by Voltaire in paving the way for the Revolution was the demolition of the *ancien régime,* rather than any constructive plans for popular government, the part played by Montesquieu, while no less destructive and no less faint in its espousal of democracy, had at least the virtue of a positive contribution to the theory of political science. In his *Persian Letters,*[83] Montesquieu attacked, among other things, the injustices of French civil life; in his *Spirit of the Laws,*[84] he makes a definite contribution to political science.

Montesquieu, like Voltaire, was a Rationalist, perhaps the most learned of his day. Like Voltaire, he too had visited England, and canonized the English constitution as the sacred citadel of liberty. Influenced by the Rationalist spirit, he sees government to consist of the adjustment of universal principles of the natural law to special conditions. In the pre-political state, the laws of nature rule directly.[85] As men advance in political society, the laws they formulate must harmonize with those of nature, and be in accordance with the climatic conditions of the country, and the character of the people.[86] Only when laws do this is government natural. Hence there is no one best form of government, the type adopted being dependent on the place and the people.

Where participation in government is the privilege of the whole, as in a democracy, the animating temper must be devotion to the community, and a spirit of equality. Where all have an equal share in government, class distinctions breed hatred and discontent. The laws of a democratic state should, therefore, encourage

83. *Lettres persanes,* 1721.

84. *L'Esprit des Lois,* 1746.

85. Montesquieu, Baron de, *The Spirit of the Laws* (trans. by T. Nugent; New York; Colonial Press, 1900), I, pp. 3-5.

86. *Ibid.,* I, p. 6.

equality in every way, and be framed to prevent the acquisition of great wealth, which leads to power and destroys equality.[87] But Montesquieu had no particular love for democracy, and though he conceded it a place in the scheme of governments, and recognized equality as its principle, there was no wish for its establishment in France. Nevertheless, his writings gave encouragement to the nobles and the *Parlements* to seek a return of their suppressed powers and his spirit hovered over the Conventions that directed the course of the Revolution. Yet his theory contains important defects. His concept of natural law showed the influence of classic antiquity, of which he was no mean student. It was likewise influenced by Newtonian physics. The natural law is the law of nature as it operates in man. But since man's characteristic faculty is reason, the natural is the rational. This is nothing more than the Stoic concept of reason as the law permeating nature, and Montesquieu in his studies in Roman history could hardly have escaped its influence. Democracy he can only interpret in terms of the classic forms, and equality has reference only to condition, which is the Stoic version.

Rousseau. While Voltaire won the ear of the literary world, and Montesquieu was hailed by the judicial, Rousseau played upon the heartstrings of the mass of the common people.[88] Though he lacked the logic of Voltaire and the learning of Montesquieu, he could write with a passion strong enough to arouse the emotions of the inarticulate multitude, and express the sentiments lying dormant in the breasts of an oppressed people. And he did it with a literary style that has never lost its appeal.[89] If his doctrines preached an individualism that could end only in social anarchy, they likewise preached a collectivism that can be justly styled a Marxian forerunner. Thus he is responsible for the two main concepts which the French Revolution has bequeathed to modern democracy—the notion that one is free to do anything not forbidden by law, and the equally prevalent notion that law is but the

87. Montesquieu, *Spirit of the Laws,* I, pp. 41-45.
88. Hearnshaw, *op. cit.,* pp. 170-171.
89. *Ibid.*

expression of human will. The one is the current notion of liberty, the other is the current notion of authority.

It is his concept of equality that lies at the basis of Rousseau's political theory; and the nature of that equality, the story of its destruction, and of its final acquisition, is the theme of his whole political output. Entering the political arena through the well-worn gateway of the "state of nature," he paints in the *Discourse on the Origin of Inequality among Men*, the picture of man in nature's Eden. Here is a sinless creature whose natural goodness shines forth in two virtues, the primary sentiments of self-interest and pity. By the first he is extremely selfish; by the second extremely sensitive to the sufferings of others.[90]   In this state,

> the noble savage, that ideal creature of the eighteenth century imagination, lives his simple, sinless, happy, and careless existence. He is an essentially solitary being; he wears no clothes and feels no need of them; he has no property and does not want any; he finds his scanty necessities amply supplied by the lavish bounty of nature. He is devoid of knowledge of both good and evil; he is free from most of the diseases of civilization, and he has no consciousness of the approach of death. There are no restrictions on his perfect liberty; his equality with his fellows is complete.[91]

The equality of Rousseau's primitive, however, differs from that enjoyed by the primitive of the Rationalists. With the latter, men are equal by virtue of the common possession of reason; with the former, the basis of equality is had in feeling. It is at this level that the common or universal element is found, on the basis of which all men are equal. The intellect tends to divide men into classes, but at the level of ordinary feelings mankind is one, and social distinctions cannot exist.[92]

> Men are naturally neither kings, nor great, neither courtiers, nor rich; all are born naked and poor, all are subject to the miseries of life, to its chagrin, its needs, and its sorrows of all kinds; finally, all are condemned to death. This is what is

90. Dunning, *op. cit.*, p. 12.
91. Hearnshaw, *op. cit.*, p. 187.
92. Alfred Tuttle Williams, *op. cit.*, p. 22.

true of men. . . . Begin then by studying human nature, that which is most inseparable from it, that which constitutes the best part of humanity.[93]

In time, however, reason developed and man began to fashion tools, coöperate with his fellowmen, build permanent homes, live in groups, and finally to acquire property. This was the original sin, and from it inequalities arose, engendering jealousies and strife. To preserve peace, the enactment of laws was found necessary, and the invention of all the devices of government. Man's primitive freedom was wholly lost, and in its place was substituted the tyranny of the rich over the poor.

> The first man, who having enclosed a piece of land, bethought himself to say, *this is mine*, and found people simple enough to believe him, was the true founder of civil society. What crimes, what wars, what murders, what miseries and horrors might not have been spared the human race by that one, who, pulling up the stakes, or filling up the ditch, had cried to his fellowmen, "Beware of listening to the imposter; you are lost if you forget that the fruits belong to all, and that the earth belongs to no one person."[94]

But evidently no such saviour of humanity at that moment appeared, and man entered upon a condition of sin and misery. In this condition he was doomed for centuries to live, falling ever deeper into bondage, seeing his species divided into rich and poor,

93. J. J. Rousseau, *Émile* (Paris: n.d.), p. 240: "Les hommes ne sont naturellement ni rois, ni grands, ni courtisans, ni riches; tous sont nés nus et pauvres, tous sujets aux misères de la vie, aux chagrins, aux besoins, aux douleurs de toute espèce; enfin tous sont condamnés à la mort. Voilà ce qui est vraiment des hommes. . . . Commencez donc par étudier de la nature humaine, ce qui en est le plus inséparable, ce qui constitue le mieux l'humanité."
94. "Discours sur l'inégalité," *Political Writings of J. J. Rousseau* (ed. by C. E. Vaughan; Cambridge: Cambridge University Press, 1915), p. 169: "Le premier qui ayant un terrain s'avisa de dire, *C'est à moi*, et trouva des gens assez simples pour le croire, fut le vrai fondateur de la société civile. Que de crimes, de guerres, de meurtres, qui de misères et d'horreurs n'eût point épargnés au genre humain celui qui, arrachant les pieux ou comblant la fosse, eut crié à ses semblables: 'Gardez-vous d'écouter cet imposteur; vous êtes perdus si vous oubliez que les fruits sont à tous, et que la terre n'est à personne.'"

noble and peasant. The depths of this degradation was reached in the France of Rousseau. Human misery and human inequalities had attained the tragic proportions which eighteenth century France, with its principle of privilege and unreasonable social distinctions, too plainly showed. On all sides were vast inequalities, social and political: ragged peasants and brocaded nobles, rich bourgeoisie and starving proletariat, the tax-exempt upper classes and the masses bearing the brunt of the national debt. Such was the depth to which humanity had sunk since that fateful day when the first sinner, enclosing a piece of ground, bethought himself to say, *this is mine*. Was there any hope of redemption? Could men ever return to that garden of primitive felicity? No longer were there forests where men could roam freely, untrammeled by the shackles of civilization. The world was too small for the teeming millions to return to "nature." The New Jerusalem was to be found, not in the forest, but in accommodating mankind to the necessity of civil society. Property was a fact that demanded acceptance, and science had come to stay. Redemption could be had, only by recovering liberty without abolishing law, and restoring equality without surrendering property. Fallen man was not hopeless. There was a way to wash away his sins, and win him a new freedom and a new equality more glorious than the first. That way was through the social contract, by which men renounce their unequal freedoms, and constitute themselves a common will in which all equally participate. All are subject to that common will in an equal degree, and all are equally free, since, in obeying the whole of which one is a part, one is only obeying himself.[95] This is the essence of freedom.

The common will thus becomes the redeemer of mankind, for each individual, giving up his natural rights to the community as a whole, creates a body politic with a life and will of its own, distinct from its members. This is the *general will*, the *State*, and each individual, possessing an equal and inalienable part of its sovereignty, gains back the rights he has given up.

95. H. J. Laski, "Portrait of Jean Jacques Rousseau," in *Dangers of Obedience and Other Essays* (New York: Harper Bros., 1930), p. 190.

Finally, each man, in giving himself to all, gives himself to nobody; and as there is no associate over whom one does not acquire the same right as he cedes to others over himself, one gains the equivalent of all that he has lost, and a greater force for the conservation of what he has.

If then we remove from the compact what is not of its essence, we shall find that it reduces itself to the following terms. "Each of us puts in common his person and all his power under the supreme direction of the general will, and we receive in a body each member as an indivisible part of the whole."[96]

Rousseau's doctrine of the *general will,* and the consequent notions of freedom and equality, caught the popular fancy. Sovereignty had descended from the King to the people. All are equally rulers, and all are equally ruled. Freedom and equality are inextricably bound together. He is free who obeys only himself, and all are equal since no one is subject to another. Only in the doctrine of the *general will* could such freedom and equality be gained. France, having caught a glimpse of its meaning and implications, could be satisfied with nothing less.

B. *The New France*

Rousseau's theory had a profound influence on the rise of the new France. Both the Constitution of 1791, and the *Declaration of the Rights of Man* are evidence of his influence. The latter declares:

Men are born, and always continue, free and equal in respect of their rights. . . . The end of all political associations is the preservation of the natural and imprescriptible rights of

96. "Social Contract," *Political Writings of J. J. Rousseau,* II, Bk. I, ch. 6, p. 33: "Enfin, chacun, se donnant à tous, ne se donne à personne; et comme il n'y a pas un associé sur lequel on n'acquière le même droit qu'on lui cède sur soi, on gagne l'équivalent de tout ce qu'on perd, et plus de force pour conserver ce qu'on a.

Si donc on écarte du pacte ce qui n'est pas de son essence, on trouve qu'il se réduit aux termes suivants: 'Chacun de nous met en commun sa personne et toute sa puissance sous la suprême direction de la volonté générale; et nous recevons en corps chaque membre comme partie indivisible du tout.'"

> man . . . the nation is essentially the source of sovereignty.
> . . . Political liberty consists in the power of doing whatever
> does not injure another. The exercise of the natural rights
> of every man has no other limits than those which are neces-
> sary to secure to every *other* man the free exercise of the same
> rights; and these limits are determinable only by law. . . .
> Law is the expression of the general will of the community.
> And all Citizens have a right to concur either personally or
> by their representatives, in its formation.[97]

Thus is political equality established and the privileges and class
stratifications of the *ancien régime* outlawed. The nature of this
equality was dictated by the character of the inequalities which
obtained in pre-Revolutionary France.

> Since the most conspicuous of them were juristic, not eco-
> nomic, it was, in the first place, legal privilege, not inequality
> of wealth, which was the object of the attack. A distinction
> was drawn between the *egalité de droit* and the *egalité de fait*,
> between formal or legal equality and practical or economic
> equality. The primary aim of the reformers was the achieve-
> ment of the first, since, once the first was established, the
> second, insofar as it was desirable, would, it was thought,
> establish itself. It was to abolish legal impediments to eco-
> nomic enterprise, and to the employment by the individual of
> the wealth which his enterprise yielded. It was, in short, to
> create a democracy of property owners who should also be
> producers.[98]

It is this legal equality on which the *Declaration of Rights* most
earnestly insists. Since this document declares that all men have
equal rights, all should have a like share in government, and all an
equal right to public office.[99] Now to understand this principle of
equality as enunciated by the *Declaration*, it is necessary to determine on what basis that document justified such equality, and on
what grounds it abolished the class structure of society which had
hitherto prevailed in France. Abuses in France were many and

97. David Ritchie, *Natural Rights* (New York: The Macmillan Co.,
1924), appendix, pp. 290-294.
98. R. H. Tawney, *Equality* (New York: Harcourt, Brace, 1931), p. 110.
99. Lord J. E. D. Acton, *Lectures on the French Revolution* (London:
The Macmillan Co., 1910), p. 106.

manifest, but the abuse of a privilege is not a sufficient reason for its abolition. There must be sought a fundamental principle on which to base the abolition of inequality, and the leveling of society. Political thinkers sought that principle in nature, by which they meant, not specific nature which constitutes the essence of man, but that primitive condition in which men found themselves before they took on the garb of social life and regulated their lives according to the canons of civilization. The way the first men lived was to be the norm for directing civilized life.

C. *The Character of French Equality*

When the prophets of "enlightenment" spoke of the natural equality of men, and the equality of natural rights, they meant the equality of men in the raw, the equal liberty that each possessed because as yet there was no civil power to restrain some and permit others the freedom of unrestraint. Hence equal natural rights meant the equal freedom of every primitive unrestricted by the positive law to use his power in whatever way he chose. Hence when one primitive in the state of nature said to another, "I have the *right* to do this," he meant, "I am just as *free* as you are to use my *power* to do this. I am just as free to pluck this apple from this tree as you are to pluck the same apple from the same tree." Such freedom is the freedom from all law except the physical law of nature. And as it was the operation of the latter law which determined who finally got the apple, men saw the need of another law to avoid constant warfare and bring harmony into the realm of human intercourse, as well as equality into the material possessions of men.

This new law arose from the individual wills of men entering into a social contract. Since no one of the contracting parties was as yet subordinate to another, no one would agree that such law should limit one more than another. It must bear on all alike, since all form it, and all agree to it. In other words, *reason* dictates to man that he order his acts to conform in some way to the order and uniformity of nature, so that there will be on the human level the same smooth functioning of natural law as exists on the sub-human level. This is an expression on the part of man of that universal law of *reason* that permeates nature. It is *reason,* the force behind nature, bringing order to the human sphere in much the same way as it brought it into the sub-human.

Now this is definitely the Stoic concept of equality, which lies at the basis of the pagan tradition in democracy. Whether that tradition is right or wrong does not concern us here. What is of concern is to determine whether the French concept of equality falls within such tradition, or whether it forms part of the Christian tradition which so greatly shaped the rôle of equality in the English and American Revolutions. That the French concept of equality is of the Stoic variety, is clear from a comparison of the Stoic notion with the principles of the *Philosophes* who so greatly influenced French political theory throughout the revolutionary era. When we reflect that French Rationalism was bound up with Renaissance Humanism, which politically felt the touch of Stoicism,[100] we can understand how the *Philosophes* came to adopt such views. And when we further reflect that the French lawyers who played so prominent a part in the Revolution, were imbued with the French tradition in Roman law,[101] we find it hard to conclude that the equality spoken of in the French *Declaration* was anything other than this same Stoic strain.

Such a concept demands that when human laws come into existence they must respect that natural freedom enjoyed by man before the formation of a civil society, and provide that every man be restrained in the exercise of his natural rights only to the extent that such exercise in no way harms the same right in another. In other words, human law is to put that amount of restraint on men, and only that amount, which will equalize differences in natural powers, and thus equalize men in the possession of material goods.

How much this concept determined the course of French politics, the *Declaration* clearly manifests.

> The exercise of the natural rights of every man has no other limits than those which are necessary to secure to every other man the free exercise of the same rights.[102]

100. M. F. X. Millar, "Stoicism in Modern Thought," *Thought*, III (1928), p. 457.
101. M. F. X. Millar, "Does the Majority Rule?" *America*, XXXII (1925), p. 585.
102. Ritchie, *op. cit.*, appendix, p. 291.

D. *Summary of the French Struggle*

The relation equality bears to the French Revolution may now be summarized as follows. The basic cause of that historic upheaval was the conflict between an artificial society arranged on the basis of political privilege, and the theory of society as a contractual institution erected by men who enjoyed equal freedom in a state of primitive nature. With the destruction of the *ancien régime*, men formed a new society based on the original social contract, which contract provided that the equal contracting parties give over such rights or powers as are necessary for general welfare. The combined wills of the individual contracting parties determine what constitutes the general welfare, and therefore which rights are to be ceded. This *general will* acts through representatives, who from time to time propose measures to it to determine if such measures conform to the *general will*. The majority decides the answer. Now since the *general will* is the sum of the individual equal wills, and law is the expression of that will, all may participate equally in civil affairs, and receive at the hands of civil authority equal treatment in return. The condition of power men possessed in the primitive state of nature is thus preserved within the limits of the general welfare, and the equal freedom of primitive men to exercise their powers, becomes the equal freedom of civilized men to a like exercise curtailed only to the extent necessary for social peace. When this is achieved, the equal freedom of every man to exercise his rights will result in an equalization of material conditions.

E. *Influence of French Egalitarianism*

French egalitarian principles were not confined within the boundaries of the French nation. With the overthrow of autocracy in France, the democratic trilogy of "Liberty, Equality, Fraternity" became the symbol of the philosophy of Liberalism which quickly spread over Europe, setting up parliamentary government in countries where the feudal structure was breaking down. Nor did England[103] and America escape the impact of the Stoic-Liberal

103. Helen R. McCadden, "Elusive Equality," *Thought*, VIII (1933), pp. 444-458.

view. Though autocracy in these latter countries was unseated mainly on the basis of political principles rooted in the Christian tradition, many of the later political thinkers not only lost sight of their own political heritage, but in espousing the Stoic-Liberal amalgam, sought to wed their own political foundations to an alien tradition.

In England, Burke, particularly, fought bitterly to stem the inroads of the newer trend. His *Reflections on the French Revolution*, his *Appeal from the New to the Old Whigs*, his *Impeachment of Warren Hastings*, and his *Tract on the Popery Laws*, all eloquently attest his vigorous disapproval of a political philosophy imported from the continent, and rapidly taking root in English political thought. It was this philosophy that gave substance to the notion prevalent in England that Parliament was supreme, and the voice of a parliamentary majority was the last word in law.[104] It was also the philosophy from which Bentham drew his inspiration, and which today nourishes the political and social views of such current theorists as Laski and Hobson.

In America, Carl Becker[105] and T. V. Smith[106] understand it as the source of American political ideals, and the latter, particularly, interprets the Declaration's enunciation of human equality to be one with that of Hobbes, Locke, and Rousseau.

As the Stoic-Liberal view of human equality gained hold on the modern mind, the Augustinian-medieval concept given prominence by Bellarmine and Suarez, receded into the mists of a dim past. Liberalism rode triumphantly in the political arenas of France, England and America, and its concept of equality taught men that the doctrine of equal rights, and the equal freedom of every man in the sphere of politics would soon bear fruit in a like equality in the realm of economics. The extent to which political equality realized by the three great revolutions fructified in an economic equality is the story of economic Liberalism.

---

104. George Bull, "The Two Traditions in Political Philosophy," *Thought*, VII (1932), pp. 404-417.

105. Carl Becker, "After Thoughts on Constitution," *Yale Review* (1938).

106. T. V. Smith, *The American Philosophy of Equality* (Chicago: University of Chicago Press, 1927).

4. The Industrial Revolution: Equality of Opportunity

Through three revolutions modern man sought for equality with his fellows. This quest for political equality carried with it the hope that economic equality would soon follow. Once men were free to pursue on an equal footing whatever economic calling they chose, disparities of wealth were expected to vanish quickly. Yet once men were politically free and equal, even though they were equipped with methods of production and transportation that might effectively banish abject poverty from the earth, they fell again into violently opposed classes. One of these, small in number, controls not only the goods of the earth but the means of production itself; the other, representing the mass of mankind, knows only misery and dire want. Thus the Industrial Revolution, flourishing among men politically free, brought on a condition which these words of Pius XI aptly describe:

> Towards the close of the nineteenth century the new economic methods and the new developments of industry had sprung into being in almost all civilized nations, and had made such headway that human society appeared more and more divided into two classes. The first, small in numbers, enjoyed practically all the comforts so plentifully supplied by modern invention; the second class, comprising the immense multitude of working men, was made up of those, who oppressed by dire poverty, struggled in vain to escape from the straits which encompassed them.[107]

Two explanations are offered for this anomaly, the explanation of Marx, and the explanation of economic Liberalism. They are not unlike. Indeed, there is a close affinity between the two, for both find their immediate ancestry in the natural law philosophy of the eighteenth century. The former will be dealt with in a later chapter, the latter will engage our attention here.

---

107. Pope Pius XI, *Quadragesimo Anno.*

A. *Economic Philosophy*

Economic Liberalism is the application of the philosophy of Individualism to economic life. Just as political Liberalism sprang into being as the result of the individualistic interpretation of man's relation to the State, so economic Liberalism is an attempt to explain man's relation to the laws of economy. We have witnessed the play of Individualism in the political order as Locke and the natural law philosophers elaborated their atomic concept of the State. Thus arose political Liberalism, a theory which would limit the exercise of civil authority to a mere restraining of men from violating the property rights of their fellows. It is in this, that economic Liberalism takes its rise. Just as civil society operates according to certain natural laws, beyond which its authority may not extend, so economics has its natural laws, which the State is impotent to change. Should it try to do so, it disrupts economic life, and throws out of balance the whole national economy.

The chief exponents of this view were the Physiocrats of France, the Classical Economists of England, those apostles of the "dismal science," Malthus and Ricardo, and the Utilitarians of whom Jeremy Bentham and John Stuart Mill are the outstanding spokesmen. In the teachings of these men the seeds of economic Liberalism took firm root, and the practical man of affairs, finding its doctrine well suited to his acquisitive desires, resisted vigorously all legislative attempts to curtail the bargains he chose to drive. Liberalism had taught that man's property was his own, and his absolute right to its possession made any attempt on the part of the State to direct its use an unjust infringement of his natural liberty. Free competition in business was also man's natural inheritance, and the equal bargaining power it provided made contracts inviolable. On the strength of this philosophy, the privilege and status of the *ancien régime,* and the monopolies protected by government were swept away. In their place was substituted a society in which men were possessed of the same legal rights and enjoyed equality before the law. All occupations and professions were thrown open to talent and men were free to buy and sell, trade and invest as best suited their opportunities for gain. In such a society inequalities based on legal privilege were made impossible. If other inequalities were still present they were the sign of personal capacity which nature itself had distributed unevenly.[108]

> The inequalities of the old regime had been intolerable because they had been arbitrary, the result not of difference of personal capacity, but of social and political favoritism. The inequalities of industrial society were to be esteemed, for they were the expression of individual achievement or failure to achieve. They were twice blessed. They deserved moral approval, for they corresponded to merit. They were economically beneficial, for they offered a system of prizes and penalties. So it was possible to hate the inequalities most characteristic of the eighteenth century and to applaud those most characteristic of the nineteenth. The distinction between them was that the former had their origin in social institution, the latter in personal character. The fact of equality of legal rights could be cited as a reason why any other kind of equality was unnecessary and dangerous.[109]

So argued the captains of industry when they were reminded that the abolition of legal privilege was a small boon to the millions who were economically oppressed. So they argued likewise, when it was pointed out that "the wider diffusion of economic opportunities" consequent upon the "abolition of capricious favors" did not produce a society free from class domination, but merely substituted distinctions of wealth for distinctions of birth. Nevertheless,

> A society marked by sharp disparities of wealth and power might properly . . . be described as classless, since it was open to each man to become wealthy and powerful.[110]

But though the blessings of *laissez-faire*, and the career open to talents, might produce sheer romance, when an occasional ditch-digger abandons his shovel and assumes the authority of a railway czar, it is small consolation to those on the fringe of starvation to know that an economic regime that affords one of their members

108. John Dewey, *Liberalism and Social Action* (New York: G. P. Putnam's Sons, 1935), p. 37.
109. R. H. Tawney, *Equality* (New York: Harcourt, Brace & Co., 1931), p. 122.
110. *Ibid.*, p. 123.

the palace of a prince, bestows on the others the opportunity to experience only insecurity and want.[111]   And it is small consolation to be told that economic inequalities are the necessary result of legal equality and economic liberty.

Free competition and equal bargaining power become so many empty fictions when the small producer is snuffed out by the great corporation, and when the lone laborer must accept the terms of the employer or suffer further unemployment should he doubt his equality to the firm to which he offers his services. Jerome Davis sums up the situation pithily when he says:

> Every individual is supposed to have the free right to make contracts. Each person can contract to sell property or to sell his services. This assumes, of course, that the individual is really free to sell his labor. Oftentimes this freedom is a mockery, as when some fifteen million people are unemployed. Again, how much freedom to sell one's labor does the individual have in actuality if he belongs to a union in a coalmining county and is blacklisted by the operators? To the extent that natural resources are owned and controlled by the few, the many are no longer free to sell their services except on terms of that privileged few. Freedom of contract thus becomes freedom to offer labor at the terms of the owners or freedom to starve or exist on such charity as can be secured if one refuses.[112]

If the bourgeois Liberal boasted that he put an end to legal privilege and status of birth, substituting in their place freedom and equal opportunity for all, he little realized that industrial capitalism was rearing in their stead privilege of wealth and economic status.[113]   Hereditary privilege might claim its exemptions on the basis that it took the trouble to be born; economic privilege offers as its claim to distinction mere quantity of possessions. But hereditary privilege was the outgrowth of function, and even though that function was no longer exercised, tradition was there to give honor

---

111. Fulton J. Sheen, *Liberty, Equality, and Fraternity* (New York: Macmillan Company, 1938).

112. Jerome Davis, *Capitalism and Its Culture* (New York: Farrar and Rinehart, 1935), p. 36.

113. H. J. Laski, *The Rise of Liberalism* (New York: Harper & Bros., 1936), p. 268.

to its claim. Privilege of wealth, on the other hand, too often grew out of a shrewd ability to drive a sharper bargain than a mere honest competitor. Nor was the new economic privilege less loathe to assume authority and power. No sooner had it destroyed the autocracy of political power than it set up an autocracy of its own. Free competition, so necessary to the early Liberal, gave way to economic dictatorship, once the new aristocracy rose to power. The fact of this economic dominance did not miss the keen eye of Pius XI, when he wrote:

> . . . it is patent that in our days not alone is wealth accumulated, but immense power and despotic economic domination are concentrated in the hands of a few, and that those few are frequently not the owners but only the trustees and directors of invested funds, who administer them at their good pleasure.
>
> This power becomes irresistible when exercised by those who, because they hold and control money, are able to govern credit and determine its allotment, for that reason supplying, so to speak the life blood of the economic body, and grasping as it were, in their hands the very soul of production, so that no one dare breathe against their will.
>
> This accumulation of power, the characteristic note of modern economic order, is a natural result of limitless free competition, which permits the survival of those only who are the strongest, which often means those who fight most relentlessly, who pay least heed to the dictates of conscience.[114]

Just as Liberalism supplanted the landed proprietor with a new *noblesse* who quickly usurped power, so it supplanted the feudal peasant and medieval craftsman with the farm laborer and factory hand, thereby creating the proletariat, or the class of propertyless wage-earners. It merely, therefore, substituted one class system for another, a substitution fraught with more antagonism than the system it supplanted,[115] because the distance between the two classes is no longer the distance between humble and noble birth, but rather the distance between great material possessions on the one hand, and a great want of them on the other. It is the distance between the cotton-king and the share-cropper, the plutocrat and

114. Pope Pius XI, *Quadragesimo Anno.*
115. Laski, *The Rise of Liberalism,* pp. 268-269.

the pauper, and it is not made easier by the "tendency of Liberalism to regard the poor as men who have failed through their own fault."[116]

Deep across the new industrial society, therefore, has cut two inequalities, the inequality of power, and the inequality of circumstance. By the one, the new peerage of business rules dictatorially, not only in economics, but in politics as well. By the other, mankind is divided by a deep gulf between the affluence of the few and the bare subsistence of the many. Thus did Liberalism, which revolted against the autocracy and class stratification of the old regime, end by inaugurating a new autocracy and a new class stratification which controlled the very means of existence and entrenched itself behind state power. In this new division of society into classes, the few who are very rich enjoy the vast wealth produced by the labor of the many who are very poor.

B. *Equality of Opportunity*

If such be the state of things that have come to pass as a consequence of the new revolution in industry, may we not pause to reflect upon this question? What equality, if any, could have been born of the Industrial Revolution? And what of its traditional heritage? Certainly that equality was neither political nor economic. If any egalitarian principle was fathered by the new industrial techniques, that principle purported to be the principle of equal opportunity. Not only did the equality of men before the law guarantee to every man the equal freedom to engage in whatever economic enterprise he chose, but it guaranteed that no one man or group of men be given preference in the pursuit of an economic goal; and it further guaranteed the immunity of commerce and industry from the restraint of political power so long as the equal rights of men suffered no infringement at the hands of unjust deeds.

In the theory of economic Liberalism men bargained one with another as free and equal individuals and they competed in the economic arena with no impediment but the impediment of indi-

116. *Ibid.*, p. 297.

vidual capacity. In the *career open to talent*, individual acumen and personal skill won the day. The spoils of victory went to him whose superior ability outstripped the mental endowments of a less gifted rival. As this was nature's law operating in the field of economic endeavor any restraint upon its free operation by the interference of political power, merely meant introducing once more the artificial for the natural, and as a consequence throwing the natural operation of economic forces out of balance. If men saw the fruits of their labor as the rewards of individual ability and effort they could not complain that their unequal conditions in life were the result of unfair advantage. They were experiencing the equality of nature to this extent, that there was no restraint on the exercise of their economic powers other than the restraint of physical nature. If the operation of unrestrained economic forces resulted in inequalities of wealth, it was nature's way. If in their commercial and industrial pursuits men bargained as equals, if they competed as free and equal individuals in the marts of the world, if they contracted one with another on the basis of equal freedom from the hampering restrictions of legal codes, the fact that they did not end equally only showed that individual merit alone graded men economically.

Such was the theory that explained the impasse to which humanity was reduced when the new industrial techniques got under way, an impasse resulting from the application of liberal philosophy to economic life. Had Liberalism failed? Was its espousal of human equality but the espousal of an illusion? Certainly, men left to themselves had demonstrated their inequality, an inequality so appalling that human theorists had need to take stock of their philosophical speculations. And take stock they did. Liberalism had had its day. Applying its concept of equality, an equality resulting from the absence of legal restrictions, it showed that men equally free to engage in whatever economic activities they chose (providing such activity did not violate the exercise of the same natural right in another) were merely experiencing the inequalities imposed by nature. Since nature's laws were inexorable men had no choice but to submit to the blind material forces of which they were the helpless victims. But there were others to whom the Liberal's answer was not final. There was another chapter in human history that was yet to be written, a chapter that began where the Liberal ended, and gave man a glimpse of a newer life, a glimpse that should make life in this vale of tears a little more endurable. But before pursuing the ray of hope held out in Marxian theory, it might be well to study the debacle of Liberalism in the country that gave birth to Communism.

CHAPTER II

ECONOMIC EQUALITY: CLASSLESS SOCIETY

1. TRANSITION TO COMMUNISM: BOURGEOIS EQUALITY

The political revolutions of the seventeenth and eighteenth centuries, whatever their immediate incentive, were undoubtedly attempts to set up a liberal State as a reaction against the absolutism that sought to stem the disintegrating forces incident to the decay of medieval society. The reaction was justified, for absolutism, imposed, as it was, on a feudal structure of society ill-suited to autocratic rule, only rendered such organization meaningless. But once royal power was curtailed and the feudal structure destroyed, the equality and freedom resulting were of a dubious character.

The political revolutions did not realize the glorious dream of liberty, equality and fraternity, nor did *laissez-faire* economics provide equal opportunity for all to obtain material security and reasonable comforts.[1] Rather did the new freedom play into the hands of the rapacious few, and before the nineteenth century had gone very far the inspiring ideals of the eighteenth were converted into instruments of economic and political power, more enthralling than the authority they had so lately displaced. As expressed by one modern writer the

> leveling of social classes which the eighteenth century liberals
> expected to be the result of liberty and democracy had not
> come off. Instead there had arisen a new upper class and a
> new tyranny. The submerged classes were just as submerged
> and just as numerous as before, and were held in bondage
> by sacred individual rights which ironically belonged to them
> in common with all humanity, but which only their masters
> could exercise and enjoy.[2]

1. Chester C. Maxey, *Political Philosophies* (New York: The Macmillan Co., 1938), p. 490.
2. *Ibid.*, p. 565.

53

The failure of Liberalism in England, France, and America to effect the liberty and equality it promised soon brought its inspiring ideals into ill repute. Branded as shibboleths of speculative philosophy, or ridiculed as the myth and folklore of Capitalism, natural law and natural rights descended into the limbo of exploded theories. Nevertheless, the dream of equality did not fade. Though the attempts to establish it in England, France, and America present indeed a sorry tale, the doctrine of equality found new champions in Germany, where the bourgeois liberal movement vainly strove to unseat one of the remaining strongholds of autocracy.

A. *Kantian Equality*

It was Kant, who in the words of Marx, developed the "German theory of the French Revolution."[3] Influenced by the dominant ideas of eighteenth century political thought, especially those of Rousseau, he sought to cast them into the categories of his critical philosophy. Men are free and equal, and the State is the result of contract. This contract, however, is not an historical event, but a rational principle that directs social relations.[4] It is, however, in his doctrine of the freedom of the will and the absolute worth of the human person, that Kant comes closest to the principles of political Liberalism. Realizing that social life made unlimited freedom impossible, Kant sought in the realm of transcendental ideas the perfect freedom that was the cherished ideal of the liberal spirits. Here man reigned supreme, and no one but himself could determine his choice. He was free to choose the rational or the irrational, and no one could bid him nay. Reason alone, was autonomous and only that was forbidden which reason could not elevate to a general law. The *categorical imperative* was each man's individual reason bidding him to exercise his freedom only by choosing such acts as would be capable of universal performance. "Act as if the maxim of thy action were to become by thy will a

3. Cited in Sidney Hook, *From Hegel to Marx* (London: Victor Gollancz, 1936), p. 142.
4. Dr. Harold Höffding, *A History of Modern Philosophy* (trans. by B. E. Meyer; London: The Macmillan Co., 1900), II, p. 90.

universal law."[5] But only on the supposition that all men are equal in their capabilities, could such a law of right be formulated. For if an act is moral only when it is capable of universalization, unless every man is capable of making the same judgment, no universal law could be formulated, and what one recognized as a general rule of conduct, would conflict with the generalization of another.[6]

Kant thus made men free and equal, not on the basis of any fictitious state of primitive society, but on the basis of a self-imposed law which each was equally capable of raising to a general rule of society. No longer need man submit to a supernatural ethic, and the laws of society need be no more than the collection of those universal maxims that each perceives to be his own rational mode of action. It was Kant's version of Rousseau's *general will*,[7] translated into the transcendental categories of his system.

B. *Hegelian Hierarchy*

Hegel sought to vindicate the liberal view, not indeed on the basis of natural right and social contract, nor even on the doctrine that the individual will was autonomous. Rather he sought in history the perfect realization of freedom. Bourgeois Liberalism had divorced thought from reality. Its principles did not coincide with the facts. In Hegel there was to be no such divorce. The real and the rational were to be identified in a system of thought in which an absolute union of nature and mind could be realized, and in which the ideal could be viewed as embodied in the actual. The center of Hegelian philosophy was a new logic, wherein was elaborated a new intellectual method, the dialectic, by which the synthesis of the ideal and the real was to be accomplished. Fundamentally, the dialectic is a process by which development takes place through a union of opposites. As a property of thought, it

5. *Ibid.,* II, p. 86.

6. A. T. Williams, *The Concept of Equality in Rousseau, Bentham, and Kant* (New York: Columbia University Press, 1907), pp. 40-45.

7. W. A. Dunning, *Political Theories from Rousseau to Spencer* (New York: The Macmillan Co., 1926), pp. 130-136.

causes concepts to generate their opposites, through the process of negation. The newly generated thought, manifesting as it does, the error or limitation inherent in the original concept, is, nevertheless, richer in content than the first. But being itself negated, a third concept comes into being, a union of the two preceding opposites, and containing within itself all the perfections of both. Through this triadic movement of *thesis, antithesis* and *synthesis*, thought is developed, and truth is attained.[8]

Hegel used the dialectic as a key to all history, showing that historical processes are carried on by the opposition of inherent forces. All nature and all thought are made up of contrary forces, through whose opposition a new reality more adequate than either emerges. Here was the formula for all history. In its light, historical progression consists of a series of social forms whose inner contradictions are the moving forces that cause one historical period to be supplanted by another in which freedom is more perfectly realized. When, therefore, liberal philosophers view man as possessing perfect freedom in the full exercise of all his natural rights in the state of nature, they err. Men are by nature free only in the sense that they have an undeveloped power to become such.[9] In reality they are slaves to passion. Society does indeed place on them a limitation, but it is not a limitation of their freedom, as much as a limitation of their brute emotions and rude instincts.[10] Hence the freedom of man in the state of nature to give unrestrained expression to his passions, is only a partial freedom. The anarchy that ensues necessitates the opposite of that freedom, the constraint of civil society, in which a higher freedom emerges, the freedom of the citizen. But civil society, an aggregate of families, is only an imperfect social organization. It is the State that is the perfect embodiment of the idea, and, therefore, the perfect realization of freedom.[11]

Not only did Hegel's philosophy combat the Individualism and Liberalism of the French Revolution, but it aimed to show the

8. Höffding, *op. cit.*, II, p. 180.
9. G. W. F. Hegel, *The Philosophy of History* (trans. by J. Sibree; London: 1900), p. 40.
10. *Ibid.*, p. 41.
11. *Ibid.*, p. 41.

German people that in the spirit of Individualism so characteristic of their political dealings, and illustrated in the independence of the petty principalities that made up the German nation, was to be found the real bar to freedom. Real freedom, real independence, as well as real greatness, may only be had in a strong national State, for "the national State, when combined with Protestant Christianity, is unique in producing the highest kind of freedom."[12]

The necessary triadic movement of history culminating in the all powerful State in which the individual, wholly submerged, attains the most perfect freedom, is Hegel's answer to the Liberal's dream. Not bloody revolution, but progressive development of the idea attaining self-consciousness in the human mind, is the force by which men become free.[13] As for equality, there is no place for it in the Hegelian State, unless one may speak of the equality of submission. The State is not a collection of atomic individuals, but a hierarchy of ascending organization in which individuals "only as members of estates, of classes, of guilds and associations, and of local communities, acquire moral dignity, the right to participate in the life of the State."[14] Natural right, far from being the individual's claim against the government or his fellowmen issuing from a social contract, becomes the dignity conferred by his place in the social organization, and the expression of duties arising therefrom.

C. *Karl Marx*

Karl Marx, as a Young Hegelian was dissatisfied with his master's philosophy and the impossibility of finding in it any practical remedy for the political and social degradation of the German masses. The Idealism of Hegel had not produced the union of the real and the ideal it had promised. What was needed was not a philosophy spun out of the abstract realms of thought, but a revolutionary philosophy, born not of the mind, but of the economic womb of society whence all human problems spring.

12. G. H. Sabine, *A History of Political Theory* (New York: Henry Holt & Co., 1937), p. 639.
13. Hook, *op. cit.*, p. 78.
14. Sabine, *op. cit.*, p. 643.

Neither in religion nor in politics is to be found the source of social
ills, and the attempts of bourgeois Liberalism to bring about
political freedom and equality have only exchanged one set of
masters for another. Philosophies that set up an ideal man in an
ideal society, are merely dealing with metaphysical abstractions.
Reality is basically material; and the history of man, as well as
the real understanding of his nature, is to be found in the history
of material production. Out of this arise social processes, and out
of it, likewise, emerge human needs and purposes. The dialectic is
not the self-development of the concept, as Hegel taught. The real
dialectic is the class struggle which is constituted by the mode of
material production. This is the force behind all history, and all
human thinking as well.[15] Consequently, when bourgeois Liberalism prates about liberty and equality, as though these were innate
primitive endowments of individuals divorced from society, it is
small wonder that its attempts to realize such abstract ideas disrupt the whole of society, breaking up into a multiplicity of atoms
the social totality demanded by economic processes. Political
equality is a chimera, because it is alienated from economic life.
The social classes have their origin, not in political favoritism and
legal privilege, but in the methods of economic production. To
understand history, one must understand the cycle of economic
methods in which class struggle, the moving force of history, is
rooted.

In the dialectics of class struggle, and in the materialism of
economic production is hidden the secret of real equality. Until
this is attained, all else is spurious, for man is primarily not a
political animal, but an economic one. Such, in general, is the
formula of Marx, and his answer to the futile attempts of Liberalism to construct a society of equals. An examination of his theory
will reveal the nature of the economic equality which he sees as
the panacea for human society and the crowning glory of human
freedom. Bourgeois equality has failed. Proletarian equality must
take its place, for out of the womb of capitalist production a new
class has emerged, in whom the society of equals will at last be
realized.

15. T. A. Jackson, *Dialectics* (London: Lawrence & Wishart, 1936),
pp. 290-383.

2. The Proletarian Revolution: Classless Equality

The failure of political equality to provide the masses with economic security offered Marx a point of departure from which to launch a political and social program that would not only destroy the last vestiges of autocracy, but would even wipe out the liberal State as well. Marxism was, in fact, more a reaction against Liberalism, than an attack on any prevailing form of absolutism. Indeed, according to Marx's philosophy, the bourgeois liberal State was a necessary phase of political and social evolution, and the bourgeois revolutions were indispensable conditions for the emergence of the proletarian class, whose revolution would usher in the culminating point of human freedom.[16] It is paradoxical that Marxism, the official philosophy of Communism, though claiming to be a repudiation of bourgeois liberal principles is in fact Liberalism carried to its ultimate development.[17] Liberalism would curtail authority to the mere enforcement of the natural laws of human society. Marxism would abolish authority altogether in favor of the social conscience of men whose perfect conformity to the natural laws of society renders external coercion unnecessary.[18]

It was the failure of Liberalism to extend the fruits of its principles beyond the boundaries of the bourgeoisie that caused Marx and his followers to scornfully reject the freedom and equality that were its proud boast. The freedom promised by the "bourgeois" revolutions became in the mind of the Communists the freedom of the capitalists to plunder and exploit, and the freedom of the workers to sell their labor for bare subsistence. Equality, which in the liberal view of things, meant an equality of rights, and the equal status of all before the law, became contemptuously regarded by the advocates of Marxism as a remnant of petty bourgeois

16. G. H. Sabine, *A History of Political Theory* (New York: Henry Holt & Co., 1937), p. 689.

17. A. J. Penty, *Tradition and Modernism in Politics* (London: Sheed & Ward, 1937), p. 7.

18. Frederick Engels, "Socialism, Utopian and Scientific," in *Karl Marx, Selected Works* (New York: International Publishers, 1936).

prejudices, an empty slogan which permitted the commodity owners and the capitalists to oppress the toiling masses.[19]

> In the bourgeois republic, even though it is the freest and most democratic one, "freedom" and "equality" cannot be and never have been but the expression of the equality and freedom of the commodity owners, of the equality and freedom of capital. Marx, a thousand times in all his works . . . explained this and laughed at abstract explanations of "freedom" and "equality," at the vulgarizers like Bentham who did not see this and concealed the material roots of this abstraction.
> "Freedom" and "Equality" in the bourgeois system . . . and in the bourgeois democracy will remain formal, meaning in fact *wage slavery* for the workers (who are formally free, formally enjoy equal rights) and *supreme power* for capital.[20]

This attitude of contempt toward "bourgeois equality" occasioned by its so-called class character, was accompanied by a new demand for equality, a proletarian demand, which was not only a "reaction against the crying social inequalities, against the contrast of the rich and the poor" but "a reaction against the bourgeois demand for equality."[21]

> The proletarians took the bourgeoisie at their word: equality must not be merely apparent, must not apply merely to the sphere of the state, but must be real, must be extended to the social and economic sphere. And especially since the time when the French bourgeoisie, from the Great Revolution on, brought bourgeois equality to the fore-front, the French proletariat has answered it blow for blow with the demand for social and economic equality, and equality has become the battle-cry particularly of the French proletariat.[22]

19. S. H. M. Chang, *The Marxian Theory of the State* (Philadelphia: University of Pennsylvania Press, 1931), p. 85.

20. V. I. Lenin, *On Deceiving the People with Slogans about Liberty and Equality* (London: Martin Laurence, 1919), p. 120.

21. Engels, *Anti-Dühring*, p. 120.

22. *Ibid.*, p. 120.

Nevertheless the bourgeois demand for equality was a necessary condition for the rise of the proletarian demand, for in the materialistic conception of history, which is the essence of Marxian philosophy, equality is explained as follows:

> The idea of equality . . . both in its bourgeois and in its proletarian form, is itself a historical product, the creation of which required definite historical conditions which in turn themselves presuppose a long previous historical development.[23]

In order, therefore, to understand the significance of this new demand for equality, this proletarian demand, which is Marx's contribution to the equalitarian doctrines, we must view it in connection with his theory of history, a theory which holds that all social institutions, and all social movements are the necessary products of the economic modes of production.

A. *The Economic Interpretation of History*

In the philosophy of Marx there were two influences of prime importance, the dialectics of Hegel, and the materialism of Feuerbach. But there was one other who helped weave these two elements into an integral whole. Pierre Proudhon was the first to point out to Marx the dialectical development of human society.[24] In the class struggle, in the ever-recurring combat of the upper and lower classes of society, was to be found the real conflict of opposites, from which new social levels emerged. The elements of Marxian philosophy were thus assembled. In the methods of material production and in the dialectics of class struggle Marx found the key to all history, and elaborated his famous theory of historical materialism. A study of this theory will reveal the communistic doctrine of equality which was Marx's answer to the bourgeois equality which he condemned as a spurious and pseudo equality.

23. *Ibid.*, p. 121.
24. C. J. McFadden, *The Metaphysical Foundations of Dialectical Materialism* (Washington: Catholic University Press, 1938), pp. 27-28.

Its Chronological Development. The theory of historical materialism, or as it is frequently called, the economic interpretation of history, was not wholly original with Marx or his faithful collaborator, Friedrich Engels. Frequent allusions to it had been made in the writings of several of the early socialist thinkers in England, France, and Germany, but these precursors of Marx, be they Saint-Simon, Fourier, Louis Blanc, Proudhon, Lorenz von Stein, or others, made at best sporadic attempts to point out the relation between economic practices and the political, legal and social conditions, with which they co-exist. It was left to Marx, not only to formulate such relations as a theory, but to emphasize the importance of that theory by making it an essential constituent of his system.[25]

He first gave utterance to the theory in the *Deutsch-Franzosische Jahrbuch* (1844), and gradually developed it in succeeding works until he published his *Contribution to the Critique of Political Economy* (1859), which contains the most systematic statement of his view that the driving force of history is to be found in the production and exchange of the material necessities of life.[26] In his excoriating attack on Bruno Bauer which he entitled *The Holy Family,* or the *Criticism of Critical Criticism,*[27] Marx gives one of his early intimations of the economic basis of history. Bauer's social philosophy leaned too heavily on German Idealism to suit Marx. While the former believed that social evils arose out of the material conditions of life, he held they persisted only because of the ignorance of the rulers and the ruled. It was futile to attempt to reform mechanisms of social life, until a revolution was brought about in the ideas and attitudes of the people. Ideological reform must precede an economic one. Men must first be brought to the level of critical self-consciousness before they could see that evil institutions were but the reflex of evil thinking. But for the masses this is impossible. Concerned as they are with the concrete and the material, they cannot follow the loftier reaches

25. E. R. A. Seligman, *The Economic Interpretation of History* (New York: Columbia University Press, 1934), pp. 50-56.
26. F. J. C. Hearnshaw, *A Survey of Socialism* (London: The Macmillan Co., 1929), p. 235.
27. *Die Heilige Familie, Kritik der kritischen Kritik* (1844).

of the spirit. Hence, only in the philosopher-critic is social salvation to be found. To Marx all this was rank heresy, and his
answer to Bauer and his school was *The Holy Family,* a devastating attack on speculative Idealism, but containing the germs of his
materialistic conception of history.[28] Referring to Bauer and his
associates, Marx herein writes :

> Do these gentlemen think that they can understand the first
> word of history as long as they exclude the relations of man
> to nature, natural science and industry? Do they believe that
> they can actually comprehend any epoch without grasping the
> industry of the period, the immediate methods of production
> in actual life? . . . Just as they separate history from natural
> science and industry, so they find the birthplace of history not
> in the gross material on earth, but in the misty cloud forma-
> tion of heaven.[29]

But theories emanating from the "misty clouds of heaven" held
for Marx no reality, and German Idealism received more than
one flagellation at the stroke of his virulent pen. In *German
Ideology,*[30] a joint work with Engels, he again contrasts the
idealistic with the materialistic conception of history.

> In direct contrast to German philosophy, which descends from
> heaven to earth, here the ascent is made from earth to heaven.
> That is to say, we do not start from what men say, imagine,
> conceive, nor from men as described, thought of, imagined and
> conceived, in order thence and thereby to reach corporeal
> men ; we start from real, active men and from their life-
> processes also show the development of the ideological reflexes
> and echoes of this life-process. Even the phantasmagoria in
> men's brains are necessary supplements of their material life-
> process, empirically demonstrable and bound up with material
> premises. Morals, religion, metaphysics and all other ideology
> and the corresponding forms of consciousness thus no longer
> maintain the appearance of independence. They have no

28. Sidney Hook, *From Hegel to Marx* (London : Victor Gollancz, 1936),
pp. 98-125.

29. Karl Marx, "Die Heilige Familie," *Gesamtausgabe* (Berlin : 1932),
Abt. I, Bd. 3, p. 327.

30. *Die deutsche Ideologie* (1845).

history, they have no development; but men, developing their material production and their intercourse, change, along with this their real existence, also their thinking and the products of their thought. It is not consciousness that determines life, but life that determines consciousness.[31]

It is, however in the *Misery of Philosophy*, a polemic written in 1847 against Proudhon, that Marx gives the first clear formulation of the new philosophy.

The social relations are intimately attached to the productive forces. In acquiring new productive forces men change their mode of production, their manner of gaining a living, they change all their social relations. *The windmill gives you society with the feudal lord; the steam-mill, society with the industrial capitalist.* The same men who establish social relations conformably with their material productivity, produce also the principles, ideas, the categories, conformably with their social relations.

Thus these ideas, these categories, are not more eternal than the relations which they express. They are *historical and transitory products.*[32]

All these utterances served to clarify in Marx's own mind the theory he was elaborating. Its classic expression, however, was reached in the *Communist Manifesto*, a pamphlet written in collaboration with Engels in 1848. Here the whole of human history is summed up in the language of historical materialism. In his preface to the English edition Engels states the fundamental proposition forming the nucleus of the Manifesto:

That proposition is: That in every historical epoch, the prevailing mode of economic production and exchange, and the social organization necessarily following from it, form the basis upon which is built up, and from which alone can be explained the political and intellectual history of that epoch. . . .[33]

31. Marx & Engels, "Die deutsche Ideologie," *Gesamtausgabe*, Abt. I, Bd. 5, pp. 15-16.
32. Karl Marx, *The Poverty of Philosophy* (London: Martin Laurence, 1936), pp. 92-93.
33. Marx & Engels, *The Communist Manifesto* (New York: League for Industrial Democracy, 1933), p. 56.

Numerous passages in the works of Marx and Engels repeat this same theme. To cite them all here would be needless repetition. Hence it will suffice to end this chronological expression of the theory by quoting from the later works of these two founders of the system those selections which give their more mature view. In the preface to his *Critique of Political Economy* which appeared in 1859, Marx gives a lucid summary of his historical theory.

> In the social production of their means of existence men enter into definite necessary relationships which correspond to a definite stage of development of their material productive forces. The aggregate of these productive relationships constitutes the economic structure of society, the real basis on which a juridical and political superstructure arises, and to which definite forms of social consciousness correspond. The mode of production of the material means of existence conditions the whole process of social, political and intellectual life. . . . At a certain stage of their development the material productive forces of society come into contradiction with the existing productive relationships, or, what is but a legal expression of these, with the property relationships within which they had moved before. From forms of development of the productive forces these relationships are transformed into their fetters. Then an epoch of social revolution opens. With the change in the economic foundation the whole vast superstructure is more or less rapidly transformed.[34]

In a later work of Engels, *Socialism: Utopian and Scientific,* written shortly before Marx's death, there again appears with unmistakable clearness the essence of the theory which lies at the heart of the whole Marxian system.

> The materialist conception of history starts from the principle that production, and with production the exchange of its products, is the basis of every social order; and that in every society which has appeared in history the distribution of the products, and with it the division of society into classes or estates, is determined by what is produced and how it is produced, and how the product is exchanged. According to this

34. Karl Marx, "A Contribution to the Critique of Political Economy," pref. in *Handbook of Marxism* (ed. by Emile Burns; London: Victor Gollancz, 1935), pp. 371-372.

conception, the ultimate source of all social changes and political revolutions are to be sought, not in the minds of men, in their increasing insight into actual truth and justice, but in changes in the mode of production and exchange; they are to be sought not in *philosophy* but in the *economics* of the epoch concerned.[35]

The Economic Basis of Social Relations. From the foregoing citations one concludes that the materialistic conception of history would make economics the basis of all social relations. The reason for this is simple. Marx would reduce all human activity to the basic drive in human nature, the drive to exist. In this primal instinct Marx sees all other actions of men, all their aspirations and desires, all their intercourse with their fellows, ultimately rooted. Men are differentiated from animals by no other characteristic than the production of their means of subsistence.[36] Since the will to exist is the paramount law of human nature, then the effort to obtain the material requisites needful to sustain life, must condition all other efforts. Consequently when men enter into manifold social relationships, when they build various social institutions, political, religious, economic, they do so with one aim in view—to facilitate the acquisition of life's necessities. If, therefore, one wishes to understand the social institutions prevailing in any epoch, the ideologies that arise, one must not make the mistake of believing that the latter determine the former. Rather both are determined by the productive forces operating within the age, and evolve as the necessary protective agencies of the manner in which the men of the period produce and exchange the material necessities of life. Change the mode of production and distribution of material goods, and the vast superstructure erected to preserve it will crumble, and a new superstructure will of necessity arise to guard and preserve the new productive forces that have come into being. Such is the material and economic foundation of all history. It is, however, a foundation that is static. There is needed a dynamic element to account for the progress in history, and Marx provides such an element in the dialectics of class struggle.

35. Engels, *Socialism, Utopian and Scientific,*" *op. cit.,* p. 165.
36. Marx & Engels, "Die deutsche Ideologie," *op. cit.,* Abt. I, Bd. 5, p. 15.

The Class Struggle: The Dialectics of Materialism. The class struggle, as an integral part of historical materialism, is but the application of the dialectic formula to history. Combined with the materialism of economic production it is simply Marx's philosophy of dialectical materialism as he sees it working itself out in human history. Just as Hegel saw the advance of truth through the conflict of two opposing ideas, so Marx sees the advance of history through the conflict of two opposing classes. The *Communist Manifesto,* whose opening sentence reads, "The history of all hitherto existing society is the history of class struggle,"[37] is a detailed description of how human society evolves through this conflict of opposing classes. Engels in his preface to the *Manifesto* declares:

> . . . the whole history of mankind . . . has been a history of class struggles, contests between exploiting and exploited, ruling and oppressed classes.[38]

These classes take their nature and origin from the mode of material production and exchange in which the men of any age find themselves engaged. Indeed the very concept of class is intimately bound up with the manner in which men wrest from nature the very necessities of life.

> What constitutes a "class" in the Marxian sense? Basically it is a specific relation to the mode of social production for the time being in operation. It is a social expression of that which, in base, is the social division of labour.[39]

It is in the division of labour that the Marxian class take its origin. In primitive communistic society, when the means of production were collectively owned, and men produced individually the goods they consumed, classes were non-existent.

> As men first emerged from the animal world . . . in the narrower sense of the term . . . so they made their entry into

37. Marx & Engels, *The Communist Manifesto,* p. 59.
38. *Ibid.,* pref. to 1888 ed., p. 56.
39. T. A. Jackson, *Dialectics* (London: Lawrence & Wishart, 1936), p. 458.

history; still half animal, brutal, still helpless in the face of
the forces of Nature, still ignorant of their own: and consequently as poor as the animals and hardly more productive
than these.   There prevailed a certain equality in the conditions of existence, and for the heads of families also a kind of
equality of social position—at least an absence of social
classes—which continued among the natural agricultural communities of civilized people of a later period.[40]

But as human society increased in numbers, and mankind split
into separate tribes and communities, men became more and more
adept in securing their means of livelihood.   Soon production
exceeded the bare needs of individual maintenance, and men
learned to exchange their surplus products.

The increase of production in all branches—stock-raising,
agriculture, domestic handicraft—enabled human labor power
to produce more than was necessary for its maintenance.   It
increased at the same time the amount of daily work that fell
to the lot of every member of a gens, a household, or a single
family.   The addition of more labor power became desirable.
It was furnished by war; the captured enemies were transformed into slaves.   Under the given historical conditions, the
first great division of social labor, by increasing the productivity of labor, adding to the wealth, and enlarging the field
productivity, necessarily carried slavery in its wake.   Out of
the first great division of social labor arose the first great
division of society into two classes: masters and servants, exploiters and exploited.[41]

Thus entered into history the two classes whose contradictory
character would supply the opposing forces by which human
progress was to be effected.   The one, owning the means of production, becomes the exploiting class, the class that appropriates
the surplus products and controls the social institutions of its
epoch; the other, possessing nothing but its labor power, becomes
the exploited class, the class which, while producing the goods by
which the whole of society is sustained, shares in none of its

40. Engels, *Anti-Dühring*, pp. 200-201.
41. Frederick Engels, *The Origin of the Family, Private Property and
the State* (Chicago: Charles H. Kerr, 1902), p. 195.

products, with the exception of the barest minimum necessary to recoup the bodily strength needed for its labors. In the early stages of a certain era of production, when the mode of production is as yet in its formative period, these classes are wholly unconscious of their class character. They are merely physical entities, differentiated one from the other solely by the way in which they find themselves placed as regards the possession of the means of production. They are as yet without knowledge of their common interests, or the fact that the affluence of one rests upon the surplus products it has extorted from the labor of the other. But when the productive forces peculiar to the epoch are more fully grown, when they reach the period of ripe maturity, they disclose

> to the clear view the ghastly mechanism by which the social order works to the detriment of one class and to the aggrandizement of the other. The ripened material conditions throw a flood of light before the abused class, disclosing the source of its sufferings, and indicating the inevitable methods to be employed for its emancipation.[42]

With this awakened class consciousness, the group which heretofore was merely an aggregate, playing a like rôle in the process of production, now emerges as a class in the proper sense of the term, possessed of a knowledge of its historical mission, and the part it is to play in producing the new society in which it will have secured its own emancipation, by the overthrow of the ruling class which maintained the old order and was the cause of its subjugation and misery. These stages in class development Bukharin describes as follows:

> Class psychology and class ideology, the consciousness of the class not only as to its momentary interest, but also as to permanent and universal interests, are a result of the position of the class in production, which by no means signifies that this position of the class will *at once* produce in it a consciousness of its general and basic interests. On the contrary, it may be said that this is rarely the case. For, in the first place,

42. M. M. Bober, *Karl Marx's Interpretation of History* (Cambridge: Harvard University Press, 1927), p. 101.

the process of production itself, in actual life, goes through a
number of stages of evolution, and the contradictions in the
economic structure do not become apparent until a later period
of evolution; in the second place, a class does not descend full-
grown from heaven, but grows in a crude elemental manner
from a number of other social groups; in the third place, a
certain time usually passes before a class becomes conscious
of itself through experience in battle of its special and peculiar
interests, aspirations, social "ideals" and desires, which
emphatically distinguish it from all other classes in the given
society. . . . The result is that a class discharging a definite
function in the process of production may already exist as an
aggregate of persons before it exists as a self-conscious class;
we have a class, but no class consciousness. It exists as a
factor in production, as a specific aggregate of production
relations; it does not yet exist as a social, independent *force*
that knows what it wants, that feels a mission, that is *conscious* of its peculiar position, of the hostility of its interests to
those of the other classes. As designations for these different
stages in the process of class evolution, Marx makes use of
two expressions: he calls class *"an sich"* (in itself), a class
not yet conscious of itself as such; he calls class *"fur sich"*
(for itself), a class already conscious of its social rule.[43]

Class antagonism is now fully developed. The oppressed class
completely recognizes the nature and source of its sufferings and
degradation, as well as the means it must take to free itself from
bondage and usher in a new social order in which it will not only
realize its own liberation, but become the dominant and ruling class
in the bargain. Perceiving the incongruity between the new productive forces, now in full bloom, and the existing social order, and
realizing their dependence on these forces, whose operation is
inhibited by the structure of the old regime, the oppressed class
finally breaks into open revolt.

At a certain stage of their development the material productive forces of society come into contradiction with the existing
productive relationships, or, what is but a legal expression for
these, with the property relationships within which they had

43. Nikolai Bukharin, *Historical Materialism* (New York: International
Publishers, 1925), pp. 292-293.

moved before. From forms of development of the productive forces these relationships are transformed into their fetters. Then an epoch of social revolution opens. With the change in the economic foundation the whole vast superstructure is more or less rapidly transformed.[44]

New and higher productive relationships now come into being. The former exploited class assumes control of the means of production, and erects the social institutions protective of its new interests. But no sooner does it rise to a position of dominance than a new class emerges on whom it fastens the fetters of economic bondage from which it has been so lately released, and the struggle between the exploited and the exploiting begins anew. To sum up this doctrine of historical materialism in its broad outlines, we have seen how

> . . . the mode of production determines the relations of property which are in their real form the relations of production, and these relations of property at once create classes, owners and non-owners, exploited and exploiting, and further create class antagonisms and struggles. "No antagonisms, no progress. That is the law which civilization has followed down to our day." Thus the materialist conception of history resolves itself into a class struggle conception of history. Only socialism, or communism, will end this historic era, or rather this "prehistoric" era, of class struggles by abolition of private property and thereby of classes themselves.[45]

B. *The Function of Equality in Historical Materialism*

Primitive Equality: The First Thesis

Viewing now this Marxian theory from the standpoint of equality, we perceive in the state of primitive communism, into which men first emerged on their evolution from the animal world, a state of natural equality. The means of production being communally owned, and private property being as yet unknown, there was no distinction between a possessing and a non-possessing

44. Karl Marx, "Contribution to the Critique of Political Economy," pref. *op. cit.*, p. 372.
45. Chang, *op. cit.*, p. 41.

group. Nature abundantly supplied the needs of the small number of individuals who were just beginning to people the earth. In such a state men were as yet imperfect, and were at the mercy of nature's forces, before which they stood timid and afraid. If there was an abundance of life's necessities, that was only because the race was still in its infancy. Here was the first *thesis* in the dialectical process of history. There was needed an *antithesis,* an opposing state, before men could reach a higher level.

Period of Private Property: The Antithesis

As the race grew and the necessities of life began to dwindle, the antithesis appeared. Property began to be individually owned and the means of production were gradually accumulated in the hands of the few, while the vast majority found themselves in economic subjection. The period of history, or as Marx prefers to call it, the period of "prehistory,"[46] emerged as the opposing state to primitive equality. This *antithesis* in the historical process is a stage of gross inequality, a period during which mankind fights a grim battle, as rulers and ruled, rich and poor, possessing and non-possessing, to secure in each succeeding era the means of production, and build a society in harmony with their interests.

It is during this second stage that the State makes its appearance as the political instrument necessary to subdue the struggle between the classes and preserve order in society.

> The state, then, did not exist from all eternity. There have been societies without it, that had no idea of any state or public power. At a certain stage of economic development, which was of necessity accompanied by a division of society into classes, the state became the inevitable result of this division.[47]
> The state, then, is by no means a power forced on society from the outside. . . . It is simply a product of society at a certain stage of evolution. It is the confession that this society has become hopelessly divided against itself, has entangled itself in irreconcilable contradictions which it is powerless to

46. Karl Marx, "Contribution to the Critique of Political Economy," pref. *op. cit.,* p. 373.
47. Engels, *The Origin of the Family,* p. 24.

banish. In order that these contradictions, these classes with conflicting economic interests, may not annihilate themselves and society in a useless struggle, a power becomes necessary that stands apparently above society and has the function of keeping down the conflicts and maintaining "order." And this power, the outgrowth of society, but assuming supremacy over it and becoming more and more divorced from it, is the state.[48]

Though the State is but the product of a society torn asunder in class conflict, it is essentially an instrument in the hands of the dominant class to preserve its property, and keep in subjection the masses who would despoil it of its ill-gotten possessions.

The state is the result of the desire to keep down class conflicts. But having arisen amid these conflicts, it is, as a rule, the state of the most powerful economic class that by force of its economic supremacy becomes also the ruling political class and thus acquires new means of subduing and exploiting the oppressed masses.[49]

Classless Society: The Synthesis

This conflict of classes, however, this period of turbulent inequality, is doomed to disappear. As the productive forces take on a more and more social character and become incompatible with the system of private ownership and distribution, then will emerge the *synthesis* or final stage of history, the classless society of the communist social order, in which full and perfect equality will be enjoyed by all men. The dialectic of class struggle, thus becomes the dialectic of equality, for the conflict of classes has no other purpose than the attainment on a higher plane of the equality it experienced to an imperfect degree in the state of primitive communism, before private property divided men into warring classes.

C. Material Production and Historical Epochs

The progress from this first and imperfect state of equality until the attainment of a full and complete equality in the classless

48. *Ibid.*, p. 206.
49. *Ibid.*, p. 208.

society of the future, Marx traces through the various periods that mark the stages of human history. He divides history into four epochs distinguished by four different modes of production, the gens, the slave, the feudal, and the capitalist. Each of these was simply the peculiar formation of society called into existence by the prevailing mode of economic production. The dialectical forces functioning within each regime brought about the evolution of the succeeding epoch.

Gens Society: Classless Equality

In the gens society the means of production were communally owned. Hence there were no classes, no private property, and therefore no State.[50] Men were on a footing of equality as regards each other, because as yet nature's resources were held in common. But as private property, and the division of labor, made their appearance, the first class division of society sprang into being.[51]

Ancient Society: Freeman vs. Slave

Slavery, which first matured in the womb of the gens society, soon became the

> predominant form of production among all people who were developing beyond the primitive community. . . . It was slavery that first made possible the division of labour between agriculture and industry on a considerable scale, and along with this, the flower of the ancient world, Hellenism. Without slavery, no Greek state, no Greek art, and science; without slavery, no Roman Empire. But without Hellenism and the Roman Empire as a basis, also no modern Europe. We should never forget that our whole economic, political and intellectual development has as its presupposition a state of things in which slavery was as necessary as it was universally recognized.[52]

Slavery was the medium through which society based on class antagonisms emerged on a higher level than the gens society of

50. Bober, *op. cit.*, p. 277.
51. Engels, *The Origin of the Family*, p. 119.
52. Engels, *Anti-Dühring*, p. 195.

primitive communism. In the ancient world the class struggle was carried on between freeman and slave, patrician and plebeian.[53] New productive forces ripening in the decadent Roman Empire brought on the dissolution of slave production and called forth the feudal structure of the Middle Ages.

Medieval Society: Lord vs. Vassal

In the medieval framework, lord and vassal, guild-master and journeyman, apprentice and serf, made up the new class alignments.[54]

> From the serfs of the middle ages sprang the chartered burghers of the earliest towns. From these burgesses the first elements of the bourgeoisie were developed.
>
> The discovery of America, the rounding of the Cape, opened up fresh ground for the rising bourgeoisie. The East Indian and Chinese markets, the colonization of America, trade with the colonies, the increase in the means of exchange and in commodities generally, gave to commerce, to navigation, to industry, an impulse never before known, and thereby, to the revolutionary element in the tottering feudal empire a rapid development.
>
> The feudal system of industry, under which industrial production was monopolized by the closed guilds, now no longer sufficed for the growing wants of the new markets. The manufacturing system took its place. The guild-masters were pushed on one side by the manufacturing middle-class; division of labor between the different corporate guilds vanished in the face of division of labor in each single workshop.[55]

Just as slavery developed in the womb of the gens society, so there developed in the womb of the feudal order the class which was destined in the future course of its evolution to be the stand-ard-bearer of the modern demand for equality. This class, the bourgeoisie,[56] originally one of the "estates" of the feudal order, was recruited from the serfs and villeins who were bound by

53. Marx & Engels, *The Communist Manifesto,* p. 59.
54. *Ibid.,* p. 60.
55. *Ibid.,* pp. 60-61.
56. Engels, *Anti-Dühring,* p. 118.

obligation to the ruling nobles. From its birth, therefore, it was an oppressed class. Nevertheless, it was this very condition of subjection that formed it into the revolutionary class that was to bring about the transition into modern society. Through its labor the handicraft industry and exchange of products within the feudal society were brought to a high degree of development. Then came the great maritime discoveries of the fifteenth century when whole continents were thrown open to the trade of Europe. This brought within its wake a need for a great increase in material productivity. Handicraft industry was unable to meet this need and, as a consequence, there sprang up in the leading industries of Europe the new system of manufacture, which revolutionized the whole economic conditions of society. This revolution in industry soon outgrew the feudal political structure in which it had its birth, and the incompatibility of the economic and political orders gave rise to the bourgeois revolutions whose demand for equality Engels described in the following passages:

> But this mighty revolution in the economic conditions of society was not followed by any immediate corresponding change in its economic structure. The state order remained feudal, while society became more and more bourgeois. Trade on a large scale, that is to say, international and, even more, world trade, requires free owners of commodities who are unrestricted in their movements and have equal rights as traders to exchange their commodities on the basis of laws that are equal for them all, at least in each separate place. The transition from handicraft to manufacture presupposes the existence of a number of free workers—free on the one hand from the fetters of the guild and on the other from the means whereby they could themselves utilize their labor power: workers who can contract with their employers for the hire of their labor power, as parties to the contract have equal rights with his. And finally equality and equal status of all human labor, because and in so far as it is *human* labor, found its unconscious but clearest expression in the law of value of modern bourgeois economy, according to which the value of a commodity is measured by the socially necessary labor embodied in it. But where economic relations required freedom and equality of rights, the political system opposed them at every step with guild restrictions and special privileges. Local privileges, differential duties, exceptional laws

of all kinds in trade affected not only foreigners or people living in the colonies, but often enough also whole categories of the nationals of each country; the privileges of the guilds everywhere and ever anew formed barriers to the path of development of manufacture.   Nowhere was the path open and chances equal for all the bourgeois competitors—and yet this was the first and ever more pressing need.

The demand for liberation from feudal fetters and the establishment of rights by the abolition of feudal inequalities was bound soon to assume wider dimensions from the moment when the economic advance of society first placed it on the order of the day.   If it was raised in the interests of industry and trade, it was also necessary to demand the same equality of rights for the great mass of peasantry who, in every degree of bondage from total serfdom upwards, were compelled to give the greater part of their labor time to their lord without payment and in addition to pay innumerable dues to him and to the state.   On the other hand, it was impossible to avoid the demand for the abolition also of feudal privileges, the freedom from taxation of the nobility, the political privileges of the various feudal estates.   And as people were no longer living in a world such as the Roman Empire had been, but in a system of independent states dealing with each other on an equal footing and at approximately the same stage of bourgeois development, it was a matter of course that the demand for equality should assume a general character reaching out beyond the individual state, that freedom and equality should be proclaimed as human rights.[57]

The struggle of the bourgeoisie to gain emancipation from the restrictions of the feudal order was at first a struggle against the ruling nobles who held political power.   To break this power the Crown first enlisted the aid of this growing middle class.   But as the latter gained in economic power, the Crown, seeing its own power menaced, joined forces with the nobility, thereby precipitating the great bourgeois revolutions, first in England and then in France.[58]   The "glorious revolution" in England in 1688 brought into power the landlord and the capitalist.   The former class seized not only the Crown lands and the Church estates, but by a form of

57. *Ibid.*, pp. 118-120.
58. *Ibid.*, p. 184.

parliamentary robbery in the passing of the Enclosure Acts
granted themselves the communal property of the people, thereby
building up the great capitalist farms and setting free the agricultural population, from which were recruited the proletariat or
new exploited class for the manufacturing industry.[59]   In France,
where the classic example of the feudal structure of society hem-
ming in the new economic order is best illustrated, the struggle
of the bourgeoisie against the privileges of the nobles ended in
another great bourgeois revolution, the French Revolution of 1789,
which brought the political order in line with the economic.

> Not, however, by adjusting the economic order to suit the
> political conditions . . . but by doing the opposite, by casting
> aside the old mouldering political rubbish and creating political
> conditions in which the new "economic order" could exist and
> develop.   And in this political and legal atmosphere which
> was suited to its needs it developed brilliantly, so brilliantly
> that the bourgeoisie already almost occupies the position filled
> by the nobility in 1789; it is becoming more and more not
> only socially superfluous, but a social hindrance; it is more
> and more becoming separated from productive activity, and
> becoming more and more like the nobility in the past, a class
> merely drawing its revenues; and it has accomplished this
> revolution in its own position and the creation of a new class,
> the proletariat, without any hocus-pocus of force whatever,
> and in a purely economic way.[60]

Modern Society: Bourgeois vs. Proletarian

With the victory of the bourgeoisie came the establishment of
the bourgeois State in which freedom and equality were set up as
the natural rights of man.   However, from the moment when, "like
a butterfly from the chrysalis, the bourgeoisie arose out of the
burghers of the feudal period, when this 'estate' of the Middle
Ages developed into a class of modern society, it was always and
inevitably accompanied by its shadow, the proletariat."[61]

59. Karl Marx, *Capital* (trans. by Samuel Moore and Edward Aveling;
Chicago: Charles H. Kerr & Co., 1906), I, pp. 795-796.
60. Engels, *Anti-Dühring*, p. 185.
61. *Ibid.*, p. 120.

The bourgeoisie begins with the proletariat which is itself a relic of the proletariat of the feudal times. In the course of its historical development, the bourgeoisie necessarily develops its antagonistic character, which at first is more or less disguised, existing only in a latent state. As the bourgeoisie develops, there develops in its bosom a new proletariat, a modern proletariat; there develops a struggle which, before being felt, perceived, appreciated, understood, avowed and proclaimed aloud by the two sides, expresses itself to start with, merely in partial and momentary conflicts, in subversive acts.[62]

The freedom and equality idealized by the new State became, therefore, only the freedom and equality of the bourgeoisie to produce and exchange unhampered by political fetters, and to enjoy for itself alone the new political ideals it created. The prophets of the Enlightenment, who paved the way for the great French bourgeois revolution, visioned a kingdom of reason in which:

> superstitution, injustice, privilege and oppression were to be superseded by eternal truth, eternal justice, equality grounded in nature and the inalienable rights of man.
> We know today that this kingdom of reason was nothing more than the idealized kingdom of the bourgeoisie; that eternal justice found its realization in bourgeois justice; that equality reduced itself to bourgeois equality before the law; that bourgeois property was proclaimed as one of the essential rights of man; and that the government of reason, the Social Contract of Rousseau, came into existence and could only come into existence as a bourgeois-democratic republic. No more than their predecessors could the great thinkers of the eighteenth century pass beyond the limits imposed on them by their own epoch.[63]

The rational State and the rational society with which the eighteenth century philosophers hoped to replace the superstitious and unreasonable order of things in the Middle Ages, turned out to be "bitterly disillusioning caricatures."[64]   As in the epochs that

---

62. Marx, *The Poverty of Philosophy*, p. 104.
63. Engels, "Socialism, Utopian and Scientific," *op. cit.*, pp. 141-142.
64. *Ibid.*, p. 146.

preceded them, the new ruling class, the bourgeoisie, gathered into its hands the means of production, and society once more found itself hopelessly divided into rich and poor, exploiting and exploited. The freedom of property which was to be enjoyed once the abolition of the guild and other feudal fetters brought to an end hampering restrictions, proved to be for the small bourgeois and small peasant merely the freedom to sell their property to their crushing competitors, as the great landed capitalists forced them from the *open* market.[65] The feudal proletariat, as soon as he was freed from attachment to the soil, and no longer bound as serf or bondsman to another, soon realized that his new freedom only permitted him to become a free seller of his labor power wherever he was fortunate enough to find a market. Robbed of whatever small holdings the feudal regime permitted him, and stripped of the guarantees of existence which the feudal arrangement afforded him, his emancipation from serfdom became the freedom to sell himself into wage-slavery.[66]

(1). *Social production* vs. *Individual appropriation.* The new bondage and the new exploited class, the proletariat, are the necessary products of the capitalist mode of production which developed under the aegis of the bourgeois regime. The distinguishing characteristic of the bourgeoisie is the ownership of property, that is, the ownership of money, land, or the instruments of production. The proletariat possesses nothing but his labor power, which, because of the invention of the new industrial techniques transforming handicraft industry into the large-scale industry of the modern factory, he has been forced to sell for his bare subsistence. Although in the course of a day, he may produce far more than is needed for his actual subsistence, he by no means reaps the benefit of this surplus product. Rather, it is appropriated by the capitalist owner, who looks upon human labor as one more tool in the transformation of the raw material into the finished product.

It is this theory of surplus value that Marx offers as the explanation of the growing wealth of the capitalists and the increasing

65. *Ibid.*, p. 145.
66. Marx, *Capital*, I, p. 786.

misery of the poor. It is his explanation of the new form of exploitation that has superseded the exploitation by the feudal aristocracy. But along with the appropriation of the surplus product on the part of the commodity owners, there is the added feature of the social character of labor resulting from concentration of production in the great factories that were necessary to house the new machinery, the invention of which brought on the Industrial Revolution. Production for individual use, which characterized much of the handicraft industry of the medieval era, now becomes the social production of commodities, that is, the coöperative production of goods by a group of workers, not for their individual use, but for purposes of exchange. Nevertheless, these new forces of social production were negated by the old form of individual appropriation. It is this contradiction between social production and capitalist appropriation that lies at the base of the struggle of the two classes of modern society, the bourgeoisie and the proletariat.

> Then came the concentration of the means of production in large workshops and manufactories, their transformation into means of production that were in fact social. But the social means of production and the social products were treated as if they were still, as they had been before, the means of production and the products of individuals. Hitherto, the owner of the instruments of labor had appropriated the product because it was as a rule his own product, . . . now the owner of the instruments of labor continued to appropriate the product, although it was no longer *his* product, but exclusively the product of *others' labor.* Thus, therefore, the products now socially produced, were not appropriated by those who had really set the means of production in motion and really produced the products, but by the *capitalists.* Means of production and production itself had in essence become social. But they were subjected to a form of appropriation which has as its presupposition private production by individuals, with each individual owning his own products. . . . In this contradiction which gives the new mode of production its capitalist character *the whole conflict of today is already in germ.* . . . *The contradiction between social production and capitalist appropriation became manifest as the antagonism between proletariat and bourgeoisie.*[67]

67. Engels, "Socialism, Utopian and Scientific," *op. cit.,* pp. 168-170.

(2). *Organization* vs. *Anarchy.* This struggle is further accentuated by the fact of another contradiction, "the antithesis between the organization of production in the individual factory and the anarchy of production in society as a whole."[68]   Here the struggle for markets, carried on by rival capitalists and rival industries, had reached national proportions. It has thrown whole countries into competing positions, thereby fostering national hatreds and international wars. The contradiction between social production and individual appropriation has thus taken on an international scope. In addition there has ensued social anarchy in production—the mad rush on the part of factories, industries, and countries to secure an outlet for their surplus goods; all of which has resulted in a cruel competition that kills off smaller industrial units and centralizes the control of industry into fewer and fewer hands.

The result of such concentration is threefold: a virtual collectivization of industry; the substitution for free competition of its opposite, economic despotism;[69] and the accumulation of larger and larger amounts of capital necessary for operations of such gigantic proportions. Of this accumulation is born finance capitalism, the control not only of industry, but of money, by a few financial overlords.[70]

(3) *Political Equality* vs. *Economic Oligarchy.* When this stage of capitalism has been reached, the State has already passed into the control of the small financial oligarchy, whose ownership of the means of production, and whose appropriation of the surplus products, is in distinct contradiction to the social production it has engendered. In its endeavors to secure the control of raw materials, wherever situated, and to command the markets of the world, this small group of industrial and financial super-capitalists enlists the aid of the State,[71] and embarks on the highest and final

68. *Ibid.*, p. 173.

69. V. I. Lenin, "Imperialism and Imperialist War," *Selected Works* (New York: International Publishers, n.d.), V, pp. 14-26.

70. *Ibid.*, pp. 42-45.

71. Marx & Engels, *The Communist Manifesto*, p. 62.   Cf. Karl Marx, "The Civil War in France," *Handbook of Marxism*, pp. 141-143.

stage of capitalism, the period of capitalist imperialism, which Lenin describes as follows:

> Imperialism is capitalism in that stage of development in which the domination of monopolies and finance capital has established itself; in which the export of capital has acquired pronounced importance; in which the division of the world among the international trusts has begun; in which the partition of all the territories of the globe among the great capitalist powers has been completed.[72]

> Imperialism in particular—the era of banking capital, the era of gigantic capitalist monopolies, the era of transformation of monopoly capitalism into state monopoly-capitalism—shows an unprecedented strengthening of the "state machinery" and an unprecedented growth of its bureaucratic and military apparatus, side by side with the increase of repressive measures against the proletariat, alike in the monarchial and the freest republican countries.[73]

Socialism: Proletarian Dictatorship

(1). *The Proletariat awakens.* Side by side with this expanding system of capitalism, there developed the ever-increasing misery of the proletariat. The frenzied struggle on the part of commodity owners to realize greater and greater profits demanded of the workers greater and greater efficiency, and the execution of their tasks with machine-like precision. The mechanization of factories and increased skill were everywhere followed by technological unemployment and the flooding of the market with surplus labor.[74] The declining purchasing power of the workers, and the improved techniques in the factories brought on over-production and periods of industrial stagnation. Into this milieu of misery there is injected the bitterness of class struggle. As the proletariat sinks deeper and deeper into poverty and want, it becomes conscious of its exploitation by the capitalist owners. Trade associations, formed to increase proletarian resistance to capitalist oppression, foster the realization by the workers of the nature of their

72. Lenin, "Imperialism and Imperialist War," *op. cit.,* V, p. 81.
73. V. I. Lenin, *The State and Revolution* (New York: International Publishers, 1932), p. 29.
74. Marx, *Capital,* I, p. 470.

degradation. With this realization comes the recognition of the solution of the economic anarchy into which the contradictions within the capitalist system have thrown society. This solution is none other than the appropriation by society as a whole of the means of production.[75]   Only in a system of social ownership can the social forces of production operate, and since these social forces have outgrown the capitalist framework in which they are imprisoned, only the destruction of that framework will permit their free play and harmonious development. The emancipation of these forces from their capitalist fetters is the historic rôle of the proletarian class. The conditions for the enactment of that rôle having fully developed within the capitalist regime, there remains but the forceful action on the part of the awakened proletariat to break the capitalist integument and set free these fettered powers.

> Centralization of the means of production and socialization of labour at last reach a point where they become incompatible with their capitalist integument. This integument is burst asunder. The knell of capitalist private property sounds. The expropriators are expropriated.[76]

(2). *The Proletariat seizes the State.* The destruction of capitalism, however, can only be accomplished by the overthrow of the bourgeois State. So long as political power remains in the hands of the overlords of industry and finance, so long will the capitalist system continue to oppress the masses and strangle the productive forces of society. As the State is the weapon of the bourgeois class by which it maintains its control over production,[77] so the conquering class must first seize State power and use it to demolish the existing social order. That is why Marx insists that "every class struggle is a political struggle,"[78] and that the organization of the proletariat into a class is at the same time their organization into a political party. The capture of the bourgeois

75. Engels, "Socialism, Utopian and Scientific," *op. cit.*, p. 180.
76. Marx, *Capital*, I, p. 837.
77. Marx, "Civil War in France," *op. cit.*, pp. 141-144.
78. Marx & Engels, *The Communist Manifesto*, p. 69.

State by the proletariat is no mere parliamentary winning of political control, but the violent overthrow of all the political paraphernalia which have helped the appropriators to exploit the nation. "Force," says Marx, "is the midwife of every old society pregnant with a new one."[79]

> In depicting the most general phases of the development of the proletariat, we traced the more or less veiled civil war, raging within existing society, up to the point where that war breaks out into open revolution, and where the violent overthrow of the bourgeoisie, lays the foundation for the sway of the proletariat.[80]

> If the State is the product of the irreconcilable character of class antagonisms, if it is a force standing *above* society and "increasingly separating itself from it," then it is clear that the liberation of the oppressed class is impossible not only without a violent revolution, *but also without the destruction* of the apparatus of state power, which was created by the ruling class and in which this "separation" is embodied.[81]

The violent seizure of State power does not mean that the working class simply lays hold of the ready-made State machinery, and wields it for its own purposes.[82]   The social forces of production can no longer function within the bourgeois State.   This latter must be converted into the proletarian State.

> After the bourgeois State has been overthrown the proletariat will become the ruling class. Hence, the State will be a proletarian State in which socialism . . . replaces capitalism. But the political task of the proletariat is not ended here. The proletariat cannot use the bourgeois State machinery. To perform this task and to suppress the bourgeoisie, the proletariat must establish its dictatorship. Thus the proletarian State in Marxism is nothing but the dictatorship of the proletariat.[83]

79. Marx, *Capital*, I, p. 824.
80. Marx & Engels, *The Communist Manifesto*, p. 71.
81. Lenin, *The State and Revolution*, p. 9.
82. Karl Marx, "The Civil War in France," *op. cit.*, p. 141.
83. Chang, *op. cit.*, p. 88.

86	The Philosophy of Equality

(3). *It suppresses the bourgeoisie.* After the proletariat has shattered the bourgeois State,[84] and entrenched itself in political power, its "historical mission" is by no means fulfilled. There ensues a long period of transition from capitalist society to complete communism, a period designated by Marx as the dictatorship of the proletariat.

> Between capitalist and communist society lies the period of the revolutionary transformation of the one into the other. There corresponds to this also a political transition period in which the state can be nothing but the *revolutionary dictatorship of the proletariat.*[85]

This dictatorship has two prime functions: the suppression of the bourgeoisie and the establishment of socialism. For the accomplishment of the first, it pursues a relentless warfare against the bourgeoisie, crushing it under ever sterner and harsher measures. Only when it has broken the resistance of this class, only when the class has ceased to exist, will the dictatorship of the proletariat mitigate the harshness of its rule. During this period is effected the socialization of the means of production. The bourgeoisie having been "expropriated," the ownership of the means of production pass to the proletariat, that is to the majority of the population. The proletarian State is still a class State, for there still exists the division of society into classes. Only now these classes have reversed places. State power lies in the hands of the proletariat, the new owning and governing class, which uses all the force at its command to wipe out its ancient enemy.[86] With the extermination of the bourgeoisie and the disappearance of all class distinctions, the State, the organ of class domination, having no further function, "withers away," and complete communism is at last attained.

> Former society, moving in class antagonisms, had need of the state, that is, an organization of the exploiting class at each

84. Karl Marx, *Letters to Dr. Kugelmann* (New York: International Publishers, 1934).
85. Karl Marx, *Critique of the Gotha Program* (New York: International Publishers, 1938), p. 18.
86. N. Bukharin & E. Preobrazhensky, *The A B C of Communism* (trans. by Eden and Cedar Paul; Great Britain: 1922), pp. 79-80.

period for the maintenance of its external conditions of production . . . when ultimately it becomes really representative of society as a whole, it makes itself superfluous. As soon as there is no longer any class of society to be held in subjection, as soon as, along with class domination and struggle for individual existence based on the former anarchy of production, the collisions and excesses arising from these have also been abolished, there is nothing more to be repressed which would make a special repressive force, a state, necessary. The first act in which the state really comes forward as the representative of society as a whole—the taking possession of the means of production in the name of society—is at the same time its last independent act as a state. The interference of state power in social relations becomes superfluous in one sphere after another, and then ceases of itself. The government of persons is replaced by the administration of things and the direction of the processes of production. The state is not "abolished"; *it withers away.*[87]

(4). *It abolishes private property.* In the socialist revolution, the dictatorship of the proletariat is a special stage in the passage from capitalism to communism. It is a transitory period during which the ideals of communism are being gradually realized: namely, the abolition of private property, and in its place the substitution of the communal ownership of the means of production. Since class distinctions arose with the institution of private property and the individual production of *commodities,* the abolition of these will at the same time be the abolition of the class structure of society. With social production, and social ownership of the means of production, the period of prehistory will come to an end.[88]

During this period, the insufficiency of the material necessities of life demanded the division of society into exploiting and exploited classes. So long as this insufficiency continued, society would be rent by the conflict between the possessing and the non-possessing classes. But once the productive forces reach their full development and provide for human wants far in excess of bare subsistence, then such class antagonisms will disappear. Within bourgeois pro-

87. Engels, "Socialism, Utopian and Scientific," *op. cit.,* p. 182.
88. Marx, "Contribution to the Critique of Political Economy," *op. cit.,* p. 373.

ductive relationships, the vast expansion of the productive forces
reaches a point where absorption of the products by the exploiting
few is incompatible with the productive capacities that have been
called into being. For this reason Marx insists that bourgeois
productive relationships are the last antagonistic form of the social
process of production.[89] When the last exploiting class has ceased
to exist, and man, by becoming master of the natural laws of society, is no longer buffeted by the "objective, external forces which
have hitherto dominated history, then will men fashion their own
history, and humanity, leap from the realm of necessity into the
realm of freedom."[90]

(5). *Proletarian Equality.* In this realm of freedom, equality
will no longer be a mere phantasy or pious wish, no longer the
disillusioning caricature that was bourgeois equality, but a real
objective social relation, in which men, freed from the "conditions
of animal existence, enjoy conditions which are really human."[91]
The Marxian concept of equality, the perfect realization of which
is obtained only with the emergence of the classless society, is not
to be identified with the bourgeois concept of equal rights, nor the
possession of equal amounts of material goods.

> . . . the real content of the proletarian demand for equality
> is the demand for the *abolition of classes.* Any demand for
> equality that goes beyond that, of necessity passes into
> absurdity.[92]

The abolition of classes is the chief task of the dictatorship of
the proletariat. Until this task is accomplished the equality prevailing will still bear something of the taint of capitalism. Hence
Marx speaks of this period as the first or lower phase of communism,[93] a phase generally called *socialism.*

> What we have to deal with here is a communist society, not
> as it has *developed* on its own foundations, but on the con-

89. *Ibid.,* p. 373.
90. Engels, *Anti-Dühring,* pp. 309-312.
91. *Ibid.,* p. 311.
92. *Ibid.,* p. 121.
93. Lenin, *The State and Revolution,* p. 76.

trary, as it *emerges* from capitalist society; which is thus in
every respect, economically, morally, and intellectually, still
stamped with the birth-marks of the old society from whose
womb it emerges.[94]

During this period there is no private property, and no exploitation of classes. Although the dictatorship is still burdened with
class distinctions—the dying bourgeoisie and the triumphant proletariat—there is no leisure class, no class that appropriates the
products of another's labor. The principles that guide the distribution of the social product, however, have not yet been divested
of their capitalist birthmarks. The productive forces of socialism
being not yet sufficiently developed to provide according to need,
the products of these forces must be distributed according to the
amount of labor expended.[95] This, however, is merely the bourgeois principle which regulates the exchange of commodities, since
it is an exchange of equal values. "So much labour in one form is
exchanged for an equal amount of labour in another form."[96]

The amount of labor is, therefore, the standard which measures
the reward, and all who perform equal amounts of labor have an
equal right to claim the products. Hence right is determined by
the work done. A man has a right to claim from society, not the
full product of his labor time, but exactly what he gives to society,
less certain deductions made for social uses.

> Accordingly the individual producer receives back from soci-
> ety—after the deductions have been made—exactly what he
> gives to it. What he has given to it is his individual amount
> of labor. For example, the social working day consists of the
> sum of the individual labor hours; the individual labor time
> of the individual producer is the part of the social labor day
> contributed by him, his share in it. He receives a certificate
> from society that he has furnished such and such an amount
> (after deducting his labor for the common fund), and with
> this certificate he draws from the social stock of means of
> consumption as much as the same amount of the labor costs.

94. Marx, *Critique of the Gotha Program*, p. 8.
95. "Program of the Communist International," *Handbook of Marxism*,
p. 987.
96. Marx, *Critique of the Gotha Program*, p. 9.

The same amount of labor which he has given to society in one form, he receives back in another.[97]

This same thought is expressed in Article twelve of the new Soviet Constitution, which reads in part:

In the USSR the principle of socialism is realized: "From each according to his ability, to each according to his works."[98]

Marx, in his *Critique of the Gotha Program,* which program provided that the "proceeds of labor belong undiminished with equal right to all the members of society," pointed out that the rights of producers, being proportional to the labor they supply, become in fact unequal rights for unequal labor. Men are not equal mentally or physically, consequently the amount of labor expended during equal portions of time varies. To reward each, therefore, according to his labors is not genuine social democracy nor justice, but it is the best attainable

in the first phase of communist society as it is when it has just emerged after prolonged birth-pangs from capitalist. Right can never be higher than the economic structure of society, and the cultural development thereby determined.[99]

This right, however, the right of each to get back from society the product of his labor (due allowance being made for certain social deductions), recognizes no class distinctions, since everyone is a worker like everyone else. But it does recognize individual differences, and, therefore, differences in productive capacities. Hence, Marx argues, the right to the product of one's labor, is a right of inequality. When unequal individuals are measured by an equal standard, one is bound to receive more than another. To avoid this rights have to be unequal. Consequently, any theory holding that men have equal rights, is nothing but the pseudo equality of the bourgeoisie. It ends, as all such rights end, in inequality.

97. *Ibid.,* p. 8.
98. Anna Louise Strong, *The New Soviet Constitution* (New York: Henry Holt & Co., 1937), p. 124.
99. Marx, *Critique of the Gotha Program,* p. 10.

However, the first phase of communism, being still too close to the source of its capitalist parentage, must be characterized by a certain inequality. There still exist remnants of class antagonisms, for the division of society into classes, while dying, is not yet wholly dead. The entire conversion of all the members of society into workers is not yet complete, and there is lacking that full development of productive forces that would permit the members of society to share in the social wealth according to their needs. Nevertheless, the advance over bourgeois equality is a real though partial gain. Stalin in his report to the seventeenth Congress of the Russian Communist Party, sums up these gains in the following propositions:

> By equality Marxism means, not equality in personal requirements and personal life, but the abolition of classes, i. e., (a) the equal emancipation of all toilers from exploitation after the capitalists have been overthrown and expropriated; (b) the equal abolition for all of private property in the means of production after they have been transformed into the property of the whole of society; (c) the equal duty of all to work according to their ability and the equal right of all toilers to receive according to the amount of work they have done.[100]

(6). *The State withers away.* When the dictatorship of the proletariat has finally eradicated from society all class distinctions, and when there is no longer any class to suppress, then, the foundations of Socialism having been laid, the proletarian State will wither away. The State being the special instrument for the suppression of one class by another, it will disappear in proportion as classes disappear. Violation of the rules of social life find their chief cause in the exploitation of the masses, and in the poverty and suffering which such exploitation entails. But when the exploitation of one class by another no longer exists, then such violations will cease. People will become so accustomed to the observance of the elementary rules of social life that any special apparatus to enforce such observance will no longer be necessary.

100. Joseph Stalin, "Report at the Seventeenth Congress of the Communist Party of the Soviet Union," *Handbook of Marxism*, p. 938.

The expression "the state *withers away*," is very well chosen,
for it indicates both the gradual and the elemental nature of
the process. Only habit can, and undoubtedly will, have such
an effect; for we see around us millions of times how readily
people get accustomed to observe the necessary rules of life
in common, if there is no exploitation, if there is nothing that
causes indignation, that calls forth protest and revolt and has
to be *suppressed*.[101]

Communism: Classless Equality

(1). *Conditions of its emergence.* All the negative conditions
for the emergence of the highest phase of communism are now
present. But there is needed, in addition, certain positive requirements. These are had when all the members of society have been
so trained, that each can assume the management and direction of
the affairs of society, and each feels it his compelling duty to deal
swiftly and severely with the social parasites and all who violate
the rules of social life.[102] When the productive forces operating
to their fullest capacity cause an unlimited supply of wealth to be
constantly pouring into the social channels, then the impulse to
private accumulation will die out, and men will voluntarily take
from the common supply, only what their present need demands.

> In the higher phase of communist society, . . . the productive
> forces have also increased with the all-round development of
> the individual, and all the springs of coöperative wealth flow
> more abundantly—only then can the narrow horizon of bour-
> geois right be fully left behind and society inscribe on its
> banners: from each according to his ability, to each according
> to his needs.[103]

Through the development of such a social conscience there is
bred a new race of men,[104] men who know nothing of private
property and its baneful effects, and who have no experience of
exploitation and selfish accumulation. Imbued with the principle
of coöperation and consideration for the common good, they know

101. Lenin, *The State and Revolution*, p. 74.
102. *Ibid.*, p. 105.
103. Marx, *Critique of the Gotha Program*, p. 10.
104. Lenin, *The State and Revolution*, p. 80.

nothing of the restraining force of law. These are indeed *free* men, men who direct their lives without any of the trammels of political authority and with the complete absence of any subjection to another.

(2). *Its Principle of Equality.* Equality in such a society reaches its fullest perfection. It provides for that material and economic equality, the absence of which made the formal equality before the law of the bourgeois democracies, a mere juridical fiction.[105] Democracy being a form of the State, it is nothing but the special instrument of the bourgeoisie for defending and strengthening the monopoly of the capitalist and landlord classes. The equality it conceded, namely, the equality of all citizens before the law, and the equal rights of all to determine the structure and administration of the State,[106] was equality for the ruling class alone. With the abolition of classes, and the passage of the means of production into the hands of the community as a whole, this formal equality passes into real equality.

> Democracy implies equality. . . . But this equality of Democracy is formal equality—no more; and immediately after the attainment of equality of all the members of society in respect of the ownership of the means of production, that is of equality of labour and equality of wages, there will inevitably arise before humanity the question of going further from equality which is formal to equality which is real, and of realizing in life the formula: "From each according to his ability; to each according to his needs."[107]

This new principle of distribution is a distinct gain over the principle prevailing in the dictatorship. Then production according to ability and reward according to work, was still tainted with the capitalist habit of punishing the weak in favor of the strong. This higher principle, taking cognizance of the unequal capabilities of men, more truly equalizes their condition. Rights are no

---

105. "Program of the Communist International," *Handbook of Marxism,* pp. 992-993.

106. Lenin, *The State and Revolution,* p. 83.

107. *Ibid.,* p. 102.

longer grounded on any fictitious equality of human endowments, but on human needs. They are, therefore, as Marx said, unequal, for men's needs are not identical. Nevertheless, the right to receive according to one's need is a more equitable distribution, and one which prevents appropriation at the expense of another. When, to the total of social production, each contributes labor according to his capacity, and receives in return products proportional to his needs, social antagonisms can have no ground in which to take root.

(3). *Division of labor abolished.* The operation of this principle permits the development of men's capacities to their fullest perfection. When men no longer have to work beyond their physical strength in order to secure the necessities of life, when these necessities are provided in accordance with the normal operation of one's powers, then men, freed from the drudgery of excessive toil, have time to secure an all-round development of their capacities. With this all-round development, division of labor, which lay at the basis of the division of society into classes, disappears. Men can pass from one form of employment to another, and the experience gained from the variety of functions performed, still further develops the human faculties.

> Under communism, for example, there will not be permanent managers of factories, nor will there be persons who do one and the same kind of work throughout their lives. Under capitalism, if a man is a bootmaker, he spends his whole life in making boots; . . . if he is a pastrycook, he spends all his life baking cakes; if he is the manager of a factory, he spends his days in issuing orders and in administrative work; if he is a mere laborer, his whole life is spent in obeying orders. Nothing of this sort happens in communist society. Under communism people receive a many-sided culture, and find themselves at home in various branches of production; today I work in an administrative capacity, I reckon up how many felt boots or how many French rolls must be produced during the following month; tomorrow I shall be working in a soap factory, next month, perhaps in a steam laundry, and the month after in an electric station. This will be possible when all the members of society have been suitably educated.[108]

108. Bukharin & Preobrazhensky, *op. cit.,* pp. 71-72.

(4). *Distinction between mental and physical labor ceases.* When division of labor has been abolished, then also will disappear the distinction between mental and physical labor.[109] This distinction was one of the principal sources of modern social inequality. With intellectual work regarded as the special prerogative of the bourgeois class, and manual work as the badge of the proletariat, the one naturally became regarded as a superior function, the other as the sign of inferiority. In the classless society of the future, such distinctions will be unknown. Intellectual development will no longer be a special privilege but an opportunity afforded to all, so that mental and manual tasks will be equally shared by all members of society. When every member of society is equally free to receive the benefits of an all-round education, human culture will reach such lofty heights, that specialists in any one field will no longer be necessary. Science as a productive force distinct from labor was the curse of capitalism.[110] When the intellect becomes the handmaid of labor, when "in principle a porter differs less from a philosopher than a mastiff from a greyhound,"[111] when all exercise their capacities to the full—today in an administrative bureau, tomorrow in an iron factory—when human productive forces reach the maximum output, then will human culture reach its zenith.

> The communist method of production will signify an enormous development of productive forces. As a result, no worker in communist society will have to do as much work as of old. The working day will grow continually shorter, and people will be to an increasing extent freed from the chains imposed on them by nature. As soon as man is enabled to spend less time upon feeding and clothing himself, he will be able to devote more time to the work of mental development. Human culture will climb to heights never attained before. It will be no longer a class culture, but will become a genuinely human culture.[112]

(5). *Town and country distinctions abolished.* Along with the disappearance of the division of labor, and the eradication of dis-

---

109. Marx, *Critique of the Gotha Program*, p. 10.
110. Marx, *Capital*, p. 397.
111. Marx, *The Poverty of Philosophy*, p. 109.
112. Bukharin & Preobrazhensky, *op. cit.*, p. 77.

tinctions between the mental and the manual worker, there will also be effected the abolition of any distinctions between town and country worker. The concentration of manufacture in the cities, and the relegation of agriculture to the country, will be superseded by an equitable distribution of the population throughout the country.[113] Manufacture, instead of being concentrated in the cities will be strategically placed in country districts. In this way men can pass from the factory to the field, and the farmer and the factory-hand will fuse into the village worker.

> Accordingly, abolition of the antithesis between town and country is not merely possible. It has become a direct necessity of industrial production itself, just as it has become a necessity of agricultural production and, moreover of public health. The present poisoning of the air, water and land can only be put to an end by the fusion of town and country; . . . The abolition of the separation between town and country is therefore not utopian, even in so far as it presupposes the most equal distribution possible of large-scale industry over the whole country. It is true that in the huge towns civilization has bequeathed us a heritage to rid ourselves of which will take much time and trouble. But this heritage must be got rid of, however protracted the process may be.[114]

(6). *The universality of plenty.* When the foul air of the cities will no longer be the special lot of the slum inhabitant, and the invigorating air of the countryside the special benefit of the agricultural worker, then all alike will enjoy strong and virile health, and the productive forces will no longer be curtailed by the limited output of weak and puny physiques. When the race as a whole is in possession of keen minds and strong bodies, when male and female, child and adult are all engaged in productive functions, when the whole of society has become one gigantic mass of producers, then such a torrent of wealth will be constantly realized, that plenty, far from being the property of any superior class, will become the happy lot of every member of the community.

113. Marx & Engels, *The Communist Manifesto*, p. 81.
114. Engels, *Anti-Dühring*, pp. 325-326.

(7). *Universal equality.* When the world becomes one vast workshop, and the participation by all in prodigious abundance an established fact, then the principle of equality will be extended beyond the just distribution of material goods, to include the abolition of distinction in all the other phases of life. Occupations, sexes, races, nations, which under previous modes of production were established in a hierarchical order, will no longer occupy fixed positions of preëminence or subordination. Women, freed from subjection to their husbands and the discrimination of capitalist society, will enter upon a complete comradeship with men. Freed from the drudgery of domestic life, they will take their place in social production on a footing of complete equality with men, possessing exactly the same rights and enjoying an equal status with their male companions, whether in marriage, in the family, in political affairs, or in any productive enterprise.[115]

The same application of the principle of equality extends to races and nationalities.[116] In the struggle of the proletariat against the bourgeoisie, Marx urged in the closing sentence of the *Manifesto,* that all the workers of the world unite.[117] But workers are not only brothers in oppression, they are brothers in the enjoyment of earth's wealth as well.

> It is essential that the working class should overcome all national prejudices and national enmities. This is requisite, not only for a world-wide attack upon capital and for the organization of a single world-wide economic system. . . . The bourgeoisie has found itself unable to organize a world economy, and the bourgeois system has been ship-wrecked upon this difficulty. The proletariat is alone competent to organize such a system with success. To this end, however, it must proclaim the watchword, "All the world and all the wealth that it contains, belong to the whole world of labor."[118]

115. Bukharin & Preobrazhensky, *op. cit.,* p. 74.
116. *Ibid.,* pp. 177-179.
117. Marx & Engels, *The Communist Manifesto,* p. 94.
118. Bukharin & Preobrazhensky, *op. cit.,* p. 194.

D. *Summary of Communist Equality*

In summing up the condition of equality that will obtain in the classless society of the future, we find that equality is essentially and before all else the absence of social classes. There is only one social grade, that of producer, whether by hand or brain. The universal duty of all is socially productive labor, and no exemptions from that duty will be made in favor of wealth or rank, race or sex. The reward of such universality of production is a universality of plenty. In contrast to the prevailing conditions of former modes of production which permitted the advantages of a civilization to reach only the top-most crest of society, in the communistic classless society, such advantages and benefits as well as even the luxuries, will be showered on all alike with no disqualifying reservations as to birth, wealth, race, sex, occupation, or nationality. "From each according to his ability, to each according to his needs," will recognize no distinctions as between brain and brawn, rural and urban, black, white, and yellow, male and female, or any other antithetic feature that has heretofore provided a basis for discrimination. When all work according to their abilities, and take only according to their needs, the superabundance yielded by the smooth functioning of productive forces will obliterate the need for discriminatory measures. To realize the complete operation of this principle, there is needed a race of men with a radically modified human nature. To form in men the habit of directing their lives in accordance with the communist principles will require generations of training. Marxian theorists, however, have not despaired. When classes have been abolished, and the chief cause of social malefactions obliterated, when the universality of plenty is afforded, and all the resources of education are at the disposal of every member of the community, then it is hoped that

> the present man in the street, capable of spoiling, without reflection, . . . the stores of social wealth and of demanding the impossible[119]

119. Lenin, *The State and Revolution*, p. 80.

will cease to exist. His place will be taken by a man, who, stripped of the animal conditions of prehistory, will enter upon truly human ones. Master of his social organization, he becomes the real conscious lord of nature. The laws of his own social action, no longer confronting him as unknown forces of nature, he will use with understanding and mastery. The dialectics of social revolution will cease to work, for men will have ascended from the kingdom of necessity to the kingdom of freedom.[120]

E. *Communist Equality and the Two Traditions*

The political equality of men achieved through the three great modern revolutions did not succeed in erasing the remaining differences among men. Indeed, through the philosophy of Liberalism, which made natural equality the basis of the atomic liberal State, and through the revolution in industry, which ushered in a new economic order, political equality became a positive hindrance to the economic equality into which it was expected by theorists to issue. When, therefore, its admirers sought to justify it on the grounds that it offered an equality of opportunity and a career open to talent, the palpable inequalities engendered ushered in a violent reaction. To Marxian theorists it was nothing more than a "bourgeois equality," aiming only at erasing any social or legal distinctions between the ancient aristocrat, with his halo of hereditary privilege, and the new class of exploiters, blessed not with birth but with wealth. To the mass of mankind, political equality was a chimera, for at the bar of civil law what practical equality could there be between the mill-hand and the millionaire; between an individual laborer and the corporation; between wealth that can hire the best legal talent and poverty that must be content with the merest tyro in law?

Was it not the bitterest satire to be told that "everybody must count for one, and no one for more than one," when the economic baron could control the legislature, while the humble citizen, whose energy he drained as he threw him a pittance, could lift but a feeble voice in the body politic? No, political equality was a sham. It

120. Engels, *Anti-Dühring*, pp. 311-312.

was dust thrown into the eyes of the worker. Nature never meant men to be politically equal because nature never meant man to be politic. He is an economic animal, and the only equality natural to him, the only equality that is practical, is an equality in the field of economics. It was thus in the state of nature, the thesis in the material dialectic. Only in the antithesis, the period of private property does the dialectic of nature push man through the thraldom of inequality. But when the basic law of nature completes its dialectic cycle in the synthesis of the future, then will a true and permanent equality erase all class distinctions, because it will have erased all economic differences in a regime crowned with a universality of plenty.

Such in brief is the communist theory. With the truth or falsity of its premises, and the validity of its conclusions we shall deal in a later chapter. It will suffice here to locate its equalitarian doctrine in the two traditions already outlined.

Communism is Liberalism at its last logical conclusion; for the Communist, like the Liberal, begins with a *state of nature,* and following in the Liberal's footsteps, views civilized institutions as artificial creations, needful perhaps, but certainly not nature at its best. Thus the State is a negation of nature, an instrument to protect private property, which private property itself was unknown when man lived the *natural* life.

In concurring on these points, Locke, Rousseau and Marx have unquestionably traveled a long way together. But the English and the French Liberals stopped mid-way in the journey. Only the Father of Dialectical Materialism completed it and reached again the golden age of the Stoics, now permanently enhanced with the human purification wrought in man's nature at the hands of the great dialectic purge.

Locke confined State action to the barest minimum necessary for social peace and individual justice. Marx dispensed with the State altogether when man reached the peak of human beatitude. In the classless society of the future, like the golden age of the past, men will not need the State, for they will have returned again to a community of possession. But whereas life in the golden age remained golden only when the race was young and small in numbers, in the golden age of the future, the *classless society,* the universality of plenty will obviate the restraint of civil laws. Men will again be free, and equally so, but their freedom will be of a more exalted character; for, whereas men of the golden age of the past were ruled alike by the instinctive forces of nature, men of the future golden age will have attained to a new and more glorious freedom, the *freedom of necessity*. In this new freedom man will know once more only the rule of nature's laws. But no longer blindly subject, he will understand how they apply to the social life of men, and knowing the *reason* of their operation he will freely submit, for does not knowledge beget freedom? Verily Zeno and Marx have met!

PART II

Metaphysical Foundations of Equality and Inequality

CHAPTER III

PERSONALITY AND INDIVIDUALITY

The preceding section of the present study was concerned with the exposition of the modern notion of equality, namely, the political equality of the modern liberal State, and the economic equality of the classless society. Both were shown to be the modern version of the Stoic concept, which viewed human equality as natural to man because such was his condition in a primitive state of nature. This Stoic-liberal notion provided the key for the nature of political society and its effect on economic life, as these were understood by the Liberal and the Communist. It was the foundation on which were erected those political philosophies which gave birth to the atomic liberal State. It likewise functioned in the dialectical process which will end when the classless society has emerged from the womb of private property, thus restoring to men their ancient equality now purified of its primitive ignorance.

Gradually this newer view overshadowed the older Augustinian-medieval concept so vitally operative in the English and American Revolutions, and which for centuries before was fundamental to the Christian understanding of civil society. This Augustinian-medieval concept has become a stranger to the modern mind. So completely has it disappeared from the political stage that modern thinkers are either unaware of its existence, or so confuse it with the Stoic-liberal view, as to negate its separate and characteristic content. It is the task of the present section to set forth this content, and thus to unfold a third view of human equality, the specific and spiritual equality of men. In this view, born of Augustine and enhanced by the brilliant mind of Aquinas, we shall seek the principles with which to appraise critically the notion of equality that is basic to the philosophies of Liberalism and Communism.

1. MAN AS INDIVIDUAL

An adequate understanding of the sense in which men are or are not equal demands a close study of human nature. That nature through its spiritual component, the soul, has the perfection of rationality; through its material component, the body, it has the limitations of individuality. In the union of body and soul is to be found, therefore, man's individual and personal character, as well as the source of his equality or inequality as regards other men.

Body and soul are to each other as matter and form, the primary constituents of any corporeal substance.[1] Matter is a potential principle, and needs for its actualization to be united to a substantial form. Potentiality implies an imperfection, a limitation, a restriction of some kind. It is the *power* of being, rather than being in the full and primary sense of the term. Form, on the other hand, is the principle of actuality. It is that which perfects and completes a being, and determines it to be of a certain kind.[2] Substantial forms, as such, are universal in character. They give to a being its specific nature, the nature it holds in common with others of the same species. But common natures, as such, do not exist; they have reality only in the realm of thought. What exists is individual, concrete, incapable of being communicated to another.

How, then, can a substantial form, with its character of communicability to many, exist as incommunicable in the individual? And, as our problem is concerned with man, how can the spiritual soul, which gives to man his specific nature, at the same time constitute him an individual in that species? Here is an important problem in philosophy, the intricacies of which need not detain us here. It is sufficient to say that it is the consistent teaching of St. Thomas that matter is the principle of individuation.[3] Apply-

1. Joseph Gredt, *Elementa Philosophiae* (Friburg: 1932), I, pp. 212-221.

2. P. Coffey, *Ontology* (New York: Longmans, Green & Co., 1926), pp. 52-60.

3. *De Princ. Indiv.*, c. 3: "Et ideo materia sub quantitate determinata est principium individuationis; materia enim sola est principium individuationis. . . ." *Summa Theol.* III, q. 77, art. 2: "Materia est individuationis principium omnibus formis inhaerentibus." Cf. *De Ente Essentia. De Natura Materiae.*

ing this doctrine to the human soul, it may thus be asserted that
the soul is individuated because it has a transcendental relation to
this particular body.[4]

This teaching is of far-reaching importance to the problem of
human equality, for if the numerical diversity of human souls is
occasioned by the diversity of bodies, so that "this soul is adapted
to this and not to that body, and that soul to another body,"[5] then
it is evident that as individuals men are not equal. It is a fact of
every day experience that men are distinguished one from another
by a host of individual differences. Is this difference, however, to
be located merely in the body, or does it enter into the very constitution of the soul itself? St. Thomas answers this question with
unmistakable clarity. Souls not only differ, but they differ with
a "twofold inequality, one intrinsic to the soul itself, the other
extrinsic on the part of the sensitive powers."[6]

> For it is plain that the better the disposition of a body, the
> better the soul allotted to it; which clearly appears in things
> of different species: and the reason thereof is that act and
> form are received into matter according to the matter's capac-
> ity: thus because some men have bodies of better disposition,
> their souls have a greater power of understanding, wherefore
> it is said . . . *that it is to be observed that those who have
> soft flesh are apt of mind.* Secondly, this occurs in regard to
> lower powers of which the intellect has need in its operation:
> for those in whom the imaginative, cogitative and memora-

---

4. John of St. Thomas, *De Generatione:* q. 2, cited by R. J. Slavin,
The Philosophical Basis for Individual Differences (Washington: The
Catholic University, 1936), p. 72, n. 74: "Notandum est quod principium individuationis animae humanae est ordo transcendentalis ad hoc
corpus. Individuatio animae non pendet a corpore causaliter sed quasi
occasionaliter. Multiplicatio corporum est occasio in fieri multitudinis
animarum. Ordo transcendentalis ad hoc corpus est principium intrinsecum
individuationis animae, et hic ordo semper in anima remanet etiam destructo
corpore, hoc vero non est causa proprie dicta, sed conditio individuationi
animae intellectivae necessaria, qua conditione desinente non desinit individuatio."

5. *Con. Gen.*, II, c. 81, ad. 2: ". . . haec enim anima est commensurata
huic corpori et non illi, illa autem alii et sic de omnibus."

6. R. J. Slavin, O. P., *The Philosophical Basis for Individual Differences*
(Washington: The Catholic University, 1936), p. 80.

tive powers are of better disposition, are better disposed to understand.[7]

Although St. Thomas holds that the diversity of souls arises primarily from the diversity of bodies, he does not mean by this that there is any direct action of the body upon the soul. Were such the case the inferior would be the cause of the perfection of the superior, a patent violation of the principle of causality. Whatever perfections or imperfections a soul may have, these come to it through the direct creation of God, Who fashions the soul with a view to the particular body which it is destined to inform.

> Now the proximate end of the human body is the rational soul and its operations; since matter is for the sake of the form, and instruments for the action of the agent. I say, therefore, that God fashioned the human body in that disposition which was best, as most suited to such a form and to such operations. If defect exists in the disposition of the human body, it is well to observe that such defect arises as a necessary result of the matter, from the conditions required in the body, in order to make it suitably proportioned to the soul and its operations.[8]

7. *Summa Theol.*, I, q. 85, art. 7: "Manifestum est enim quod quanto corpus est melius dispositum, tanto meliorem sortitur animam: quod manifeste apparet in his quae sunt secundum speciem diversa. Cuius ratio est, quia actus et forma recipitur in materia secundum materiae capacitatem. Unde cum etiam in hominibus quidem habeant corpus melius dispositum, sortiuntur animam majoris virtutis in intelligendo: unde dicitur in II *de Anima* quod *molles carne bene aptos mente videmus.* Alio modo contingit hoc ex parte inferiorum virtutem quibus intellectus indiget ad sui operationem: illi enim in quibus virtus imaginativa et cogitativa et memorativa est melius disposita, sunt melius dispositi ad intelligendum." Cf. *II Sent.*, d. 32, q. 2, art. 3.

8. *Summa Theol.*, I, q. 91, art. 3: "Finis autem proximus humani corporis est anima rationalis et operatione ipsius: materia enim est propter formam, et instrumenta propter actionis agentis. Dici ergo quod Deus instituit corpus humanum in optima dispositione secundum convenientiam ad talem formam et ad tales operationes. Et si aliquis defectus in dispositione humani corporis esse videtur, considerandum est quod talis defectus sequitur ex necessitate materiae, ac ea quae requiruntur in corpore ut sit debita proportio ipsius ad animam et ad animae operationes."

The same thought is brought out more explicitly in another text, where diversity of body is shown to be the occasion, but not the cause of formal diversity.

> Although the individuation of the soul is brought about by the body it does not depend upon the body in such a way that when the body ceases to exist the soul loses its individuality. The reason for this is, that since every perfection with which matter is endowed, is modified by the capacity of the matter which receives it, the nature of the soul is infused into different bodies in a different degree of excellence and purity. Hence, in each body the soul will possess being determined in accord with the capacity of the body. And although this determinate mode of existence is acquired by the soul in the body, it does not receive it from the body, nor through dependence on the body. When bodies perish, there will remain in each soul its determinate being, according to the conditions and dispositions which have accrued to it so far as it was the perfection of a particular body.[9]

It is clear from the above texts that man's individuality, while proceeding from the body as a principle, reaches into the very substance of the soul itself,[10] so that the individuality of the composite is derived from the fact that it is informed by *this* soul.[11] Here is an extremely important fact bearing on man's personality, for the individuality of the human soul entering into its very substance

9. *I Sent.*, d. 8, q. 5, art. 2, ad. 6: "Quamvis individuatio animarum dependeat a corpore quantum ac suum principium, non tamen quantum as suum finem, ita quod cessantibus corporibus cessit individuatio animarum. Cujus ratio est quia, cum omnis perfectio infundatur materiae secundum capacitatem suam, natura animae infunditur diversis corporibus non secundum eandem nobilitatem et puritatem. Unde in unoquoque corpore habebit esse terminatem secundum mensuram corporis. Hoc autem esse terminatem, quamvis acquiratur animae in corpore non tamen ex corpore, nec per dependentiam ad corpus. Unde remotis corporibus, adhuc remanebit unicuique animae esse suum terminatum, secundum affectiones vel dispositiones quae consecutiae sunt ipsam, prout fuit perfectio talis corporis."

10. *Con. Gen.*, II, c. 81, ad. 2: "Multitudo igitur animarum consequitur diversitatem formarum secundum substantiam quia alia est substantia hujus animae et illius et ista diversitas est secundum diversam commensurationem animarum ad corpora; haec enim anima est commensurata huic corpori et non illi, illa autem alii, et sic de omnibus."

11. Slavin, *op. cit.*, p. 76.

provides the source of human personality, the discussion of which will follow subsequently.

Though the commensuration and coaptation of this soul to this body enters into the very substance of the soul, thereby constituting it a *human*[12] soul, this does not bring about any specific distinction. The reason for this is the twofold character of formal diversity: the one, touching the form in its very essence, results in specific diversity; the other, entering the form in an accidental manner, may change it substantially, though leave the essence untouched.[13] An illustration may make this clear. If, of two wooden chairs, one is subsequently painted red and the other blue, there is brought about an accidental diversity, though without any change in the essence or substance of either. They are still chairs, and still wooden. But if one chair is made of wood and the other of steel, the diversity, while still accidental, leaves the "chairness" intact, but changes the substance. However, reduce one chair to ashes, and the diversity brought about, is not only substantial but specific as well.

Applying this twofold character of formal diversity to human souls, we come to the root of human equality and inequality. Human souls are incomplete rational substances, with an exigency for informing bodies, and while this exigency is found in the individual in the commensuration and coaptation of *this* soul to *this* body, it is the fact of the exigency for informing a body that constitutes the soul a human soul, not the particular exigency realized in *this* commensuration and *this* coaptation. This is a very important distinction for the subject of human equality. For the substantial inequality of souls flowing from the commensuration and coaptation of *this* soul to *this* body, is the ultimate explanation of individual inequality. But since the substantial individuation is not a specific distinction, entering into the essence of the soul itself, so that one soul is not more or less human than another, then the ground for specific equality is manifest.

12. Cajetan, Com. in *De Ente et Essentia,* c. 6, q. 13: "De essentia hujus animae est commensuratio ad hoc corpus; et sic commensuratio ad corpus humanum non sequitur animam humanam sed constituit ipsam humanam."

13. Slavin, *op. cit.,* p. 78.

The substantial inequality of individuals, therefore, leaving the human essence intact and the same in all men, in no way disturbs the specific equality of men. The individuals of the human species are indeed unequal, but not in that whereby they are human. The exigency of the spiritual soul for union with matter is not more or less. Every human soul, being an incomplete substance, demands for its substantial completion, union with a body. It is in the composite that such completion is found. Hence, irrespective of the particular differences inhering in human souls, whereby they are fitting complements of bodies more or less perfect, the human composite resulting from the union of the two principles, is just as truly human in one case as in the other. It is distinction among things that gives perfection to the universe.[14] For this reason the multiplication of individuals within a species would have no meaning if all the individuals were identical. Nothing is more monotonous than the constant repetition of sameness. Unity amid variety, on the other hand, is a basic principle both of order and of beauty, and nowhere is it better illustrated than among men who in their specific perfections are one and equal, while in their individual perfections they are manifold.

2. MAN AS PERSON

It has already been intimated that the individuality of men is intrinsically bound up with their personality. The root of this connection lies in the fact that individuality penetrates into the very substance of the soul itself. Now if we recall the definition of a person, *an individual substance of a rational nature*,[15] the intrinsic connection of these two notions is made clear. The soul,

---

14. *Summa Theol.*, I, q. 47, art. 2: "Sicut ergo sapientia causa est distinctionis rerum propter perfectionem universi, ita et inaequalitatis. Non enim esset perfectum universum, si tantum unus gradus bonitatis inveniretur in rebus."

15. Boethius, *De Persona et Duabus Naturae*, cap. 2: "Naturae rationalis individua substantia." Cf. *Summa Theol.*, I, q. 29, art. 1. *De Potentia*, q. 9, art. 2. *I. Sent.*, d. 25, art. 1.

however, is not a person for it is an incomplete substance,[16] nor is the body, for it lacks rationality. Personality, therefore, resides in the composite, the union of *this* soul and *this* body.[17] Break this union and personality vanishes. Put the individuality in the body alone, or in the body and some accident of the soul, and the substantial union of body and soul will be seriously impaired, thereby destroying personality. It is, then, the union of *this* soul and *this* body into a complete substantial composite that provides the basis of personality. But though the human personality cannot be realized except in the composite, nevertheless, it takes its exalted character from the rational spiritual soul.

This soul is the direct creation of God. It is not like the forms of material things, which are educed from matter and have an intrinsic dependence on the matter they inform. The human soul is a subsistent being, a perfection which, added to the individual rational nature of man, makes him independent, autonomous, and master of his own acts. Here is the very essence of personality, a subsistence bestowing independence and self-mastery.[18] It is this independence and self-mastery that gives to the person its high dignity. Any substance subsists, in the sense that it is capable of existing *per se,* and is not, therefore, dependent on another in which to exist, as white is dependent on the subject of its inherence. But the rational natures are subsistent in a more excellent manner. They not only exist and act *per se,* as befits any substance, but they act *per se* super-eminently, since they possess complete domin-

16. *De Potentia,* q. 9, art. 2, ad. 14: "Anima separata est pars rationalis naturae scilicet humanae, et non tota natura rationalis humana, et ideo non est persona." *Summa Theol.,* I, q. 75, art. 4, ad. 2: ". . . non qualibet, substantia particularis est hypostasis vel persona: sed quae habet completum naturam speciei. Unde manus vel pes non potest dici hypostasis vel persona. Et similiter nec anima, cum sit pars speciei humanae."

17. *Summa Theol.,* I, q. 29, art. 2, ad. 3: "Sed compositum ex *hac materia* et ex *hac forma,* habet rationem hypostasis et personae: anima enim et caro et os sunt de ratione hominis, sed haec anima et haec caro et hoc os sunt de ratione *huius hominis.*"

18. R. P. Phillips, *Modern Thomistic Philosophy* (London: Burns, Oates, and Washburne, 1935), II, pp. 220-222. Cf. Coffey, *op. cit.,* pp. 265-273. E. Delaye, "La Personne Humaine," in *La Personne Humaine en Péril* (Paris: 1937), pp. 184-190. R. P. Schwalm, O.P., *Leçons de Philosophiae Sociale* (Paris: 1911), II, pp. 434-435.

ion over their own acts.[19] It is for this reason that St. Thomas speaks of a person as signifying "what is most perfect in all nature."[20]

A. *The Dignity of Personality*

As has already been pointed out, the two endowments of the human person which give to man his high dignity are intelligence and freedom. In these two perfections man becomes more than any other creature of the visible universe, "like unto God."[21] The one activity that sums up the whole of human striving is the quest for a richer and fuller life. If life is that perfection of immanence in virtue of which an agent is both the principle and term of its act, the originator and recipient of the perfection which the act brings,[22] then of no act of man is immanence more true, or *living*

19. *De Potentia*, q. 9, art. 1, ad. 3: "Sicut substantia individua proprium habet quod per se existet, ita proprium habet quod per se agat; nihil enim agit nisi actu; et propter hoc calor sicut non per se est, ita non per se agit; sed calidum per calorem calefacit. Hoc autem quod est per se agere, excellentiori modo convenit substantiis rationalis naturae quam aliis. Nam solae substantiae rationalis habent dominium sui actus; ita quod in eis est agere et non agere, aliae vero substantiae magis aguntur quam agant. Et ideo conveniens speciale nomen haberet."

20. *Summa Theol.*, I, q. 29, art. 3: "Persona significat id quod est perfectissimum in tota natura." *Ibid.*, ad. 2: "Quia . . . impositum est hoc nomen *persona* ad significandum aliquos dignitatem habentes." *I Sent.*, d. 23, art. 1: "Ulterius hoc nomen "persona" significat substantiam particularum prout subjicitur proprietati quae sonat dignitatem." *De Potentia*, q. 9, art. 3: "Natura autem quem persona in sua significatione includit est omnium natura dignissima."

21. *Summa Theol.*, q. 93, art. 2: "Assimilantur autem aliqua Deo, primo quidem, et maxime communiter, inquantum sunt; secundo vero, inquantum vivunt; tertio vero, inquantum sapiunt vel intelligunt. Quae, ut Augustinus dicit . . . *ita* sunt Deo similitudine proxima, ut in creaturis nihil sit propinquius."

22. St. Thomas, *Commentaria in Libros Metaphysicorum*, Lib. ix, lectio 4: "Et hoc ideo quia quando per actionem potentiae constituitur aliquod operatum, illa actio perficit operatum, et non operantum. Unde est in operatio sicut actio et perfectio ejus, non autem in operante. Sed quando non est aliquod opus operatum praeter actionem potentiae, tunc actio existit in agente et ut perfectio ejus, et non transit in aliquid exterius perficiendum; sicut visio est in vidente ut perfectio ejus, et speculatio in speculante, et vita in anima ut per vitam intelligamus opera vitae." *Summa Theol.*, I, q. 19, art. 3, ad. 1: "Sicut dicitur in IX *Metaphys.*, duplex est actio: una, quae transit in exteriorem materiam, ut calefacere et secare; alia, quae manet in agente, ut intelligere, sentire et velle. Quarum haec est differentia: quia prima actio non est perfectio agentis quod movet, sed ipsius moti; secunda autem actio est perfectio agentis."

more fittingly predicated, than the act of intelligence, which remains
within and perfects the intellect which generates it, by uniting it
with the form of the being it contemplates.[23]   Intelligence is none
other than the contemplation of being,[24] and since the form is the
principle of being in anything,[25] the union of this form with the
intellect is the essence of knowing.[26]   Because the object of the
intellect is being in general, there is no being beyond the power
of the human intellect to grasp, however feebly it may do so.[27]
Not only can it encompass and bring within itself the whole of the
universe, so that man is truly a microcosm, but its capacity for
being will never be fully realized until it is united with the Infinite
Being of God.   Only in God is there perfect life, for only in God
is there perfect immanence, in whom intelligence and being are
one.[28]   Here is supreme life that needs no determination from

23. *Con. Gen.*, IV, c. 11: "Est igitur supremus et perfectus gradus vitae
qui est secundum intellectum; nam intellectus in seipsum reflectitur, et
seipsum intelligere potest." *Summa Theol.*, I, q. 14, art. 2: "Ex hoc enim
aliquid in actu sentimus vel intelligimus, quod intellectus noster vel sensus
informatur in actu per speciem sensibilis vel intelligibilis."
24. *Summa Theol.*, I-II, q. 94, art. 2: "Nam illud quod primo cadit in
apprehensione, est ens, cuius intellectus includitur in omnibus quaecumque
quis apprehendit."
25. *Con. Gen.*, II, c. 54.
26. *Summa Theol.*, I, q. 55, art. 1, ad. 2: ". . . ita et intellectus in actu
dicitur esse intellectum in actu, non quod substantia intellectus sit ipsa
similitudo per quam intelligit, sed quia illa similitudo est forma eius.   Idem
est autem quod dicitur, in his quae sunt sine materia, idem est intellectus
et quod intelligitur, at si diceretur quod intellectus in actu est intellectum in
actu." Cf. *Ibid.*, q. 87, art. 1, ad. 3.
27. Although the proper object of the human intellect is the being of
material things, nevertheless, man can know spiritual beings, and even the
Infinite Being, by way of analogy. Cf. Fulton J. Shean, *Philosophy of
Science* (Milwaukee: The Bruce Publishing Co., 1934), p. 142: "It is the
Scholastic position that there is a way of understanding something of the
nature of God . . . and that is by the analogy of being." Garrigou La-
grange, *God, His Existence and His Nature* (St. Louis: B. Herder, 1936),
I, p. 236: "For us the concept of being denotes a perfection without any
admixture of imperfection, it is an analogical concept, which means that
it is capable of existing according to essentially different modes.   And
from this point of view an infinite mode is not beyond the scope of being."
Cf. *Summa Theol.*, I, q. 13, art. 5. *Ibid.*, q. 13, art. 3, ad. 1. *De Veritate*,
q. 23, art. 7, ad. 9.
28. *Con. Gen.*, IV, ch. 11: "Ultima igitur perfectio vitae competit Deo, in
quo non est aliud intelligere et aliud esse. . . ."

without, for Infinite Intelligence contemplating Infinite Being, with which it is identical, is ever the term and perfection of its act.[29] This is the peak of life, Perfect Life, indeed the very Life of all living, Divine Intelligence contemplating the Divine Being.

It is thus that man is like unto God, for the human intellect contemplating being can find its perfection, not in contemplating that which has being by participation, but that which *is* Being;[30] not in the contemplation of finite being, but only in the contemplation of Divine Being. Only here will the quest for life end, for here alone is had life in all its fulness.

Having led man to the summit of life in his quest for truth, we may follow him along the same path in his pursuit of good. Knowledge is for the sake of desire. The intellect knows that the will may seek,[31] and in proportion as the intellect knows being, the will loves it as good. If, then, the intellect seeks its perfection in the contemplation of Divine Being, the will ends its quest only in the presence of Infinite Good, which is God.

The nobility and high dignity of the person consists, therefore, not only in the fact that it is the direct handiwork of God, but in the endowment of those twin capacities for God-like action, whose fruition results in what St. Thomas rightly calls *that which is noblest in all nature*,[32] a creature participating in the perfection which is Divine Life. This is the exalted destiny of all persons, whether angelic or human. In the realm of earthly experience it places man in a position of preëminence. But though the human

---

29. *Summa Theol.*, I, q. 18, art. 3: Illud igitur cuius sua natura est ipsum eius intelligere, et cui id quod naturaliter habet, non determinatur ab alio, hoc est quod obtinet summum gradum vitae. Tale autem est Deus."

30. *Summa Theol.*, I, q. 3, art. 4: "Oportet igitur quod ipsum esse comparetur ad essentiam quae est aliud ab ipso, sicut actus ad potentiam. Cum igitur in Deo nihil sit potentiale, . . . sequitur quod non sit aliud in eo essentia quam suum esse . . . sicut illud quod habet ignem et non est ignis est ignitum per participationem, ita illud quod habet esse et non est esse, est ens per participationem."

31. *Summa Theol.*, I, q. 82, art. 4, ad. 1: "Ex his ergo apparet ratio quare hac potentiae suis actibus invicem se includunt: quia intellectus intelligit voluntatem velle, et voluntas vult intellectum intelligere." *Ibid.*, ad. 3: "Omnem enim voluntatis notum necesse est quod praecedat apprehensio. . . ."

32. *Summa Theol.*, I, q. 29, art. 3.

person owes its nobility to the source and end of its being, namely
God, it owes its mastery of all creation below it, to the self-domination through which it is master of its own acts.

Only the immediate perception of Infinite Good can compel the
human will,[33] for only Infinite Good can exhaust the power of
the will to love. Finite good leaves the will indifferent,[34] free to
choose or reject. This is freedom of choice, the foundation of all
freedom.[35] It is the freedom of man enroute to his end, and the
basis of human autonomy, but it does not constitute the perfection
of freedom. It is rather the means of freedom, the inheritance of
nature, through the proper use of which true autonomy is achieved.
Man becomes master of himself, not merely because he chooses to
do this or that, but in proportion as he chooses wisely. Self-
mastery is progressive. It is the gradual rule of reason over the
lower powers of the nature, so that man is directed not by his lower
appetites, but by his rational appetite or will. Reason indicates
among the manifold goods presented to the will those capable of
assuaging man's thirst for the Infinite, for the choice of those things
conformable to the laws of right conduct and the ideals of human
living develops character and leads to the perfection of the whole
man. Partial goods which solicit the will are declared unworthy,
for they induce man to quench his insatiable yearning for the Absolute in things of the sense, and thereby bind his spirit to what is
below it. But let the will choose what reason declares to be a good

33. *Summa Theol.*, I, q. 82, art. 2: "Sed voluntas videntis Deum per
essentiam de necessitate inhaeret Deo, sicut hunc ex necessitate voluntas
esse beati."

34. *Summa Theol.*, I-II, q. 10, art. 2: "Unde si proponatur aliquod
objectum voluntati quod sit universaliter bonum et secundum omnem considerationem, ex necessitate voluntas in illud tendet, si aliquid velit: non
enim poterit velle oppositum. Si autem proponatur sibi aliquod objectum
quod non secundum quamlibet considerationem sit bonum, non ex necessitate
voluntas feretur in illud. Ex quia defectus cuiuscumque boni habet rationem
non boni, ideo illud solum bonum quod est perfectum et cui nihil deficit, est
tali bonum quod voluntas non potest non velle: quod est beatitudo. Alia
autem qualibet particularia bona, inquantum deficiunt ab aliquo bono, possunt
accipi ut non bona: et secundum hanc considerationem, possunt repudiari
vel approbari a voluntate, quae potest in idem ferri secundum diversas
considerationes." Cf. *De Veritate*, q. 24, art. 7, ad. 6. *De Malo*, q. 6, art. 1.

35. *Summa Theol.*, I, q. 83, art. 3: "Proprium liberi arbitrii esse dicimur
quod possumus unum recipere, alio recusato, quod est eligere."

for the totality of his being, and man is free to follow the lead of
the spirit. Then does reason rule, and man, truly free, truly autonomous, is master of all below him. This is the freedom of autonomy,
the perfection of freedom of choice.[36] In it the human person
attains his exalted character. He is complete, autonomous, independent, the master, not only of the irrational universe, but master
of himself as well. Here is the pinnacle of personality, a life-long
task to achieve, but in so far as man achieves it, he participates in
the act of his own creation, and verifies the words of Christ, "You
shall know the truth and the truth shall make you free."

Rational freedom is then the impregnable fortress of personality.
Let man become anything less, and his nature is violated, the
noblest and highest in him being put under the dominion of what
is lowest. When man is ruled by his lower nature, spirit becomes
subject to matter, person subservient to thing, and man, no longer
king of the universe, is enslaved by that which is base.

B. *Equality of Personality*

The personality of man is, then, his greatest prerogative,[37] an
endowment that lifts him into the realm of spiritual beings, and
makes him a little less than the angels. Is it a prerogative in which
men share equally, or has one more of personality than another?
A distinction must be made. The individual person may achieve
greater self-mastery than another, and so develop his personality
to a higher degree.[38] But does that initial personality that derives
from the individuation of human nature, admit of diversity? We
have seen that men differ individually, that the particular endowments of one are not the particular endowments of another. But
as the rational natures of men make them specifically equal,[39] no

36. Jacques Maritain, *Freedom in the Modern World* (New York:
Charles Scribner's Sons, 1936), pp. 29-39.

37. Virgil Michel, "Ownership and the Human Person," *Review of Politics,* I (1939), pp. 155-177.

38. *II Sent.,* d. 44, q. 1, art. 3, ad. 1: ". . . quod natura omnes homines
aequales in libertate fecit, non autem in perfectionibus naturalibus, liberum
enim; secundum Philosophum, in I *Metaphysic.,* cap. iii, est quod si causa
est."

39. *II Sent.,* d. 6, q. 1, art. 4, ad. 5: ". . . quod homines non sunt sibi
invicem prae-eminentes secundum ordinem naturae. . . ."

one sharing more or less in that nature than another, so man's
personality, the individual realization of that nature, with its gift
of freedom of choice, does not admit of more or less.

All men are equally persons, because all are individual substances of a rational nature, possessing an equal capability of
self-domination, and an equal exigency to realize the fulness of
their being in union with the Divine. Generically every man has
the same end,[40] the contemplation and love of Divine Being, the
face to face vision of God. In the realization of that end, no one
may become the means of another, and whether the person be that
of an angel or a man, he stands in relation to his end, complete,
autonomous, independent, the master of his own destiny.[41] This
does not mean that every individual person in the attainment of
his final perfection, is the exact counterpart of every other. The
particular capacities differ, but to the realization of those capacities
all are equally called, and no one may give way or renounce that
complete fulfillment which his nature demands, that union with
Divine Life, in order that another may not be impeded in that
possession of God which is his due. Here is the sanctity of the
human person. Whatever be his individual capacity for knowing
and loving God, it is equally sacred, equally inviolable, because
equally willed by God the End and Author of his being.

3. MAN AS SOCIAL

Aristotle and St. Thomas never tire of repeating that man is
by nature both a political and social animal.[42] If we seek the
reason for this social urge we shall find it in the natural tendency

40. *Summa Theol.*, I-II, q. 3, art. 8: "Ultima et perfecta beatitudo non
potest esse nisi in visione divinae essentiae. . . . Ad perfectum igitur beati-
tudinem requiritur quod intellectus pertingat ad ipsam essentiam primae
causae. Et sic perfectionem suam habebit per unionem ad Deum sicut ad
objectum in quo solo beatitudo hominis consistit." Cf. *Ibid.*, q. 1, art. 7.

41. *II Sent.*, d. 44, q. 1, art. 3: "Sed creatura rationalis, quantum est
de se, non ordinatur ut ad finem ad aliam, ut homo ad hominem."

42. St. Thomas, *Ethicorum*, lib. 1, lectio 1: "Homo naturaliter est animal
sociale." Cf. *Politicorum*, lib. 1, lectio 1. *De Regimine*, lib. 1, c. 1.
Summa Theol., I, q. 96, art. 4. *Ibid., Suppl.*, q. 41, art. 1. *Ibid.*, II-II,
q. 61, art. 5. Aristotle, *Politica*, lib. 1; *Perihermenias*, lectio 2, prin. 0.

to self-perfection inherent in every man.[43] This self-perfection, as has been shown, is a movement toward the good that is conformable to man's nature.[44] To the degree that this rational good is possessed, man becomes autonomous, the master of his acts, and the "creator" of his person. But to secure this good perfective of his nature, and so constitutive of his person, man stands in need of the corporative action of others like unto himself. Out of the urge to self-perfection, therefore, comes the urge to social life. Man is ordered to society solely because he is a person. His social nature is embedded in his personality.

Life below the level of the person is not social. The gregarious tendency of certain animals is only a herd instinct, a pattern stamped on their natures impelling them into a crowd, an aggregate, a mere numerical grouping, without any internal principle of unity.[45] For man, society is an ordered whole, a thing of reason. It is not the sum of individuals, but a totality directed to an end. That end is the common good, something distinct from the individual good of the single person, yet a necessary condition for the fulfilment of his personal capabilities, and the attainment of the end for which he was created.[46]

A. *The Person is Social*

Because of his relation to Infinite Good, the human person has a relation to the common good. Toward the former, man is ordered as to an end; toward the latter, as to a necessary means. The demand for social life springs from two vital needs, the basic needs of human existence plus that sufficiency of life without which devel-

43. Desmond Fitzgerald, *Preface to Statecraft* (New York: Sheed & Ward, 1939), p. 11.

44. *Summa Theol.*, I-II, q. 94, art. 2: "Tertio modo in est homini inclinatio ad bonum secundum naturam rationis, quae est sibi propria: sicut homo habet naturalem inclinationem ad hoc quod veritatem cognoscat de Deo, et ad hoc quod in societate vivat. Et secundum hoc, ad legem naturalem pertinent en quae ad huiusmodi inclinationem spectant."

45. *De Regimine Principum*, lib. 1, c. 1. Cf. *Politicorum*, lib. 1, lectio 1.

46. *De Regimine*, lib. 1, c. 1: "Ad hoc enim homines congregatur ut simul bene vivant quod consequi non posset unusquisque singulariter vivens." Cf. Schwalm, *Leçons de Philosophie Sociale*, II, p. 422. Michel, *op. cit.*, p. 163.

opment would be impossible; and that mutual interchange among men through which the growth of personality is fostered.[47]   The condition best conducive for securing these needs is the common good.   It may be defined as:

> a perfect good, a good of full sufficiency for human life; *ad vitae sufficientiam perfectum.*[48]

Man is, therefore, ordered to two ends, an ultimate end, which is Infinite Good, and a proximate end or common good.   The first claims the full totality of his being, the second does not.   In relation to the former he is an autonomous substance; in relation to the latter he is a part.   But since the ultimate end embraces the proximate end, that is, the Infinite Good is achieved through the common good, man plays in society a double rôle.   He functions both as a part ordered to a whole, and as an autonomous substance to whom society is subservient as a means for personal development.   This double rôle is clearly outlined by St. Thomas who, though he speaks in unmistakable language of man's character as a member and as a part ordered to a whole, never loses sight of the fact that man has a rôle outside society with which society may never interfere.

Now it is evident that all who are included in a community stand in relation to that community as parts to a whole; while

47. *Ethicorum*, lib. 1, lectio 1: "Sciendum est autem quod quia homo naturaliter est animal sociale, ut pote qui indiget ad suam vitam multis, quae sibi ipse solus praeparare non potest; consequens est quod homo naturaliter sit pars alicujus multitudinis, per quam praestetur sibi auxilium ad bene vivendum.   Quo quidem auxilio indiget ad duo.   Primo quidem ad ea quae sunt vitae necessaria, sine quibus praesens vita transigi non potest; et ad hoc auxiliatur homini domestica multitudo cujus est pars. . . . Alio modo juvatur homo a multitudine, cujus est pars, ad vitae sufficientiam perfectam; scilicet ut homo non solum vivat, sed et bene vivat, habens omnia quae sibi sufficiunt ad vitam: et sic homini auxiliatur multitudo civiles, cujus ipse est pars. . . ." Cf. *De Regimine*, lib. 1, c. 14. *Politicorum*, lib. 1, lectio 1. *Con. Gen.*, III, c. 85.

48. Schwalm, *op. cit.*, II, p. 430: "le bien commun est un bien parfait, un bien de pleine suffisance pour la vie humaine; *ad vitae sufficientiam perfectam.*"

a part as such belongs to the whole, so that whatever is the good of a part can be directed to the good of the whole.[49]

Now every part is directed to the whole as imperfect to perfect, wherefore every part is naturally for the sake of the whole. . . . Now every individual person is compared to the whole community as part to whole.[50]

Man is not ordained to the body politic according to all that he has; and so it does not follow that every action of his acquires merit or demerit in relation to the body politic.[51]

Man is subject to God simply as regards all things, both internal and external. Wherefore he is bound to obey Him in all things. On the other hand, inferiors are not subject to their superiors in all things, but only in certain things and in a particular way, in respect of which the superior stands between God and his subjects, whereas in respect to other matters the subject is immediately under God by Whom he is taught either by the natural or by written law.[52]

In his function as a part, man has a duty to coöperate with his fellowmen in order that through peaceful intercourse, such a condition of general well-being is brought about that each individual

49. *Summa Theol.*, II-II, q. 58, art. 5: "Manifestum est autem quod omnes qui sub communitate aliqua continentur comparantur ad communitatem sicut partes ad totum. Pars autem id quod est totius est; unde et quodlibet bonum partis est ordinabile in bonum totius." Cf. *Ibid.*, I, q. 60, art. 5; II-II, q. 64, art. 5; II-II, q. 65, art. 1.

50. *Summa Theol.*, II-II, q. 64, art. 2; Con. Gen., III, c. 17: "Omnis autem pars ordinatur ad totum ut imperfectum ad perfectum. Et ideo omnis pars naturaliter est propter totum. . . . Quaelibet autem persona singularis comparatur ad totam communitatem sicut pars ad totum."

51. *Summa Theol.*, I-II, q. 21, art. 4, ad. 3: ". . . homo non ordinatur ad communitatem politicam secundum se totum, et secundum omnia sua: et ideo non oportet quod quilibet actus eius sit meritorius vel demeritorius per ordinem ad communitatem politicam."

52. *Summa Theol.*, II-II, q. 104, art. 5, ad. 2: "Deo subiicitur homo simpliciter quantum ad omnia, et interiora et exterioria: et ideo in omnibus ei obedire tenetur. Subditi autem non subiiciuntur suis superioribus quantum ad omnia, sed quantum ad aliqua determinate. Et quantum ad illa, medii sunt inter Deum et subditos. Quantum ad alia vero, immediate subduntur Deo, a quo instruuntur per legem naturalem vel scriptam."

person in his rôle as member in the social totality, receives from the totality that which he would not be able to attain alone.[53] This duty is encumbent on every person in virtue of the moral law of self-perfection.

But though the common good is a necessary prerequisite for individual development, nevertheless, it does not belong totally to any one member as his private and particular good. It is the common possession of all the members of society in which each shares in proportion to his function in the whole.[54] To that common good all individual and particular goods must be ordered.[55] Man must, therefore, sacrifice certain private goods to the general well-being of the social whole, and society can legitimately make demands on the human person, demands, not only that he forfeit the enjoyment of certain material goods, but even life itself if the common good is menaced.[56] And society can demand that man so act, because he is obliged to use the means necessary for the attainment of the ultimate good of his own nature, to which the common good stands as that necessary means. In his office as part or member, therefore, man has certain functions ordered to the social whole, functions to which he is obligated by society, and which may be determined by society in so far as it sees them as necessary for the maintenance of the common good. But though man as a person is ordered to society, and has certain functions subordinate to it, nevertheless society does not exhaust the whole of his personality. His rôle as member is always subordinate to his rôle as autonomous substance. Society may claim certain of his functions, but not all of them. Beyond society man is ordered to God, and so cannot be encompassed by society wholly. Because his social being

---

53. *Summa Theol.*, II-II, q. 58, art. 9, ad. 3: "Bonum communi est finis singularum personarum in communtate existentium, sicut bonum totius est bonum cujuslibet partium."

54. *Summa Theol.*, II-II, q. 26, art. 3, ad. 2: "bonum totius diliget quidem pars secundum quod est sibi conveniens: non autem ita quod bonum totius ad se referat, sed potius ita quod seipsam referet in bonum totius."

55. *Summa Theol.*, II-II, q. 26, art. 4, ad. 3: "Semper autem commune bonum est magis amabile unicuique quam proprium bonum: sicut etiam ipsi parti est magis amabile bonum totius quam bonum partiale sui ipsius."

56. *Summa Theol.*, II-II, q. 65, art. 1. *Ibid.*, q. 26, art. 3.

does not equate his whole being, but only a part of it, so society may not absorb him totally. Man is an absolute with a vocation toward the Infinite. Society may claim him only to the degree that his functions in society produce that sufficiency of life and mutual interchange, without which his vocation would fail or fall short of realization.[57]

Beyond this, society may make no demands. Its authority ceases with the realization of the common good, which is its *raison d'être*. If it exceeds this, man's autonomous nature intervenes, and asserts its independence. Should it demand of man anything contrary to the ultimate good of his nature, or make any claims on man at variance with the law imposed on him by the Author of his nature, such claims are automatically invalid, and in no sense partake of the nature of a law.[58]

> . . . there are two reasons for which a subject may not be bound to obey his superior in all things. First on account of the command of a higher power. . . . Therefore, if the emperor command one thing and God another, you must disobey the former and obey God. Secondly, a subject is not bound to obey his superior, if the latter commands him to do something wherein he is not subject to him, for Seneca says . . . It is wrong to suppose that slavery falls on the whole man: for the better part of him is excepted.[59]

There is, therefore, between the individual person and society a bi-polar relation; "a mutuality in the order of ends characterized

---

57. Fitzgerald, *op. cit.*, pp. 15-18. Cf. Michel, "Ownership and the Human Person," *op. cit.*, p. 164.

58. *Ibid.*

59. *Summa Theol.*, II-II, q. 104, art. 5: "Ex similiter ex duobus potest contingere quod subditis suo superiori non teneatur in omnibus obedire. Uno modo, propter praeceptum maioris potestatis. . . . Ergo, si aliud imperator, aliud Deus iubeat, contempto illo, obtemperandum est Deo.

"Alio modo, non tenetur inferior suo superiori obedire, si ei aliquid praecipiat in quo ei non subdatur. Dicit enim Seneca. . . . Errat si quis existimat servitutem in totum hominem descendere. Pars eius melior excepta est."

as the relation between potency and act."[60]   As the potential is actualized by the form, and the form limited by potency, so man's end is actualized through society, which is in turn limited by the end it seeks to realize.   This relationship stems from the fact that though man is part of society, he is a substantial part, receiving from society, not his substantial nature, but only its integral perfection.[61]   That is why St. Thomas always speaks of man as *ordered to* society, never subordinate to it.[62]

The part that man plays in society cannot be equated with that played by the parts of an organism.   These latter receive their substantial being from the organism, and have no existence as such apart from the organism.   Man, on the other hand, has a substantial existence outside of society, and though St. Thomas compares the person to society as part to whole, he is using here the analogy of proportionality.[63]   Society, therefore, cannot be called an organism in the literal sense.   It is an analogically organic whole.   Its existence is bound up with the existence of its substantial parts.

B. *The Person and the State*

The failure to recognize the exact relationship between the individual person and society has resulted in three erroneous conceptions of the State.   Two of these are outside the tradition of the *philosophia perennis* and one within.   The recognition of man as a substantial unit, but the inability to comprehend how a multitude of such units can be at the same time both one and many, has given rise to the concept of the State as atomic.   Society is only the sum of its members, each of which is a complete and inde-

---

60. Eberhard Welty, *Gemeinschaft und Einzelmensch* (Leipzig, 1935), p. 282: "Der Gliedschaftscharakter bedeutet nicht dass die Einzelnen zu Nutzwerten der Gemeinschaft werden und werden sollen; weder das selbstangeordnete noch das gemeinschaftsbestimmte Tun des Menschen muss vielmehr gekennzeichnet werden als das Verhältnis von Potenz und Akt in der zielhaften Ordnung.   Thomas spricht meist von 'Hinordnung', nicht von 'Unterordnung'."   Cf. *Summa Theol.*, I-II, q. 21, art. 4, ad. 3: "Homo non ordinatur ad communitatem politicam secundum se totum et secundum omnia sua."
61. Schwalm, *op. cit.*, II, p. 424.
62. Welty, *op. cit.*, p. 282.
63. *Summa Theol.*, II-II, q. 61, art. 1.

pendent unit, an atom, which added to other atoms equal to itself, gives the aggregate, or social whole. Such a State, lacking any genuine principle of unity is bereft of continuity. It vanishes with each succeeding generation, and must be re-created as each new generation comes into being. The one having been lost in the multitude, the common good so necessary for the perfection of the human person, is replaced by the individual good of each of the members. Such a State is nothing more than political anarchy. Its inability to function gives rise to its antithesis, the notion of the State as organic. Here the recognition of society as possessing a genuine unity, over and above the sum of its members, but the denial of the substantial character of its parts has resulted in the concept of the State as organic. The autonomous and independent character of the members has thus been sacrificed to the unity of the whole. The multitude has been merged with the one. Of necessity man becomes wholly subordinate to the State with no end or function beyond it. The particular good vanishes, and the common good is magnified. The State is no longer a means but an end. Man's quest for Infinite Good is reduced; the common good must satisfy. The State must be man's God.[64]

But neither the common good of the organic State, nor the particular good of the atomic one, can ever quench man's thirst for the Infinite. Only in the synthesis of the two will man reach his final end. The attempt to make this synthesis, and to explain how man in his relation to society is both a part and a substantial whole has produced an unsound solution within the Scholastic fold. The sacrifice of social unity to the substantial being of man was the error of atomic Liberalism. The sacrifice of man's substantial being to social unity was the error of Hegelian organicism. The solution of some Scholastics has not been a happy one. Not only has social unity been sacrificed, but man's substantial being as well. What we have been offered is the dichotomy of man.

The attempt to explain how man is a part of society, and at the same time transcendent to it, on the basis of the distinction between man's individuality and personality, is, to say the least, hazardous.

64. Charles C. Miltner, "Social Unity and the Individual," *Thomist*, I (1939), pp. 31-34.

The identification of man's individuality with his body, and his personality with his soul, is not valid; neither is the identification of man's individuality with his character as social member, and his personality with his substantial independence. Such a splitting up of the human person is both metaphysically and morally unsound. The proponents[65] of this view will no doubt seriously object to the charge that they are destroying man's substantial unity. Real distinction, it may be granted, is not separation. Nevertheless the objection will not hold. There is no quarrel with the position that maintains a real distinction between man's individuality and his personality. The quarrel lies, rather, with the attempt to identify man's individuality with his body, and his personality with his soul, and the transference of such identification to the immanent and transcendent character of man's relation to the State.

The metaphysical unsoundness of such a theory is not hard to establish. Man is not a member of society because he is an individual, nor transcendent to it because he is a person, for the simple reason that he is not an individual because he has a body, nor a person because he has a soul. Man is a substantial composite, a unity of body and soul. It is man's substantial unity that is identified with his personality. And though the body is the principle of individuation, it must be remembered that no positive act of the body gives individuation to the soul. It is not the cause of individuation, but the occasion. That individuation is brought about by the direct action of God, Who forms the soul with a view to the body that it is to inform. It is *this* soul that brings individuation to the composite, and this composite that makes the person.

That such is the Thomistic doctrine has already been shown in the earlier pages of this chapter. The bald identification of individuality with body and personality with soul, will find no corroboration in Thomistic teaching. Man's individuality is embedded in his personality, and his personality in his individuality. The very definition of a person confirms this: "a complete individual sub-

65. Jacques Maritain, *The Three Reformers* (London: Sheed & Ward, 1929), pp. 19-24. Jacques Maritain, *L'Humanisme Integral* (Paris: 1936), pp. 145-147. J. Vialatoux, "Reflexions sur l'Individu et la Personne," *Chronique Social de France* (1936), t. 45, pp. 335-358.

stance of a rational nature." Put man's individuality in his body and his personality in his soul, and you destroy the substantial unity of man, and leave the door open for those immoral attempts that would divorce man from the State on the one hand, or absorb him in it on the other. This is the moral unsoundness of such a dichotomy. The modern world is not interested in man's soul. It is satisfied if it possesses his body. Give man's body to the State, and you give man, the human person. Take man's soul out of the State, and you have left a society of animals. To order the lower part of man's nature to the State, and his higher nature beyond the State is to deprive society of the saving grace of the spirit. Either anarchy or loss of freedom is the result.[66]

The solution of the problem of man's relation to the State lies not in the consideration of the double aspect of man's individuality and personality. It lies rather in the consideration of his double circle of obligations, the twofold functional rôle of the human person—the obligation to attain his end, and the obligation to secure the means necessary for that attainment.[67] The one directs him beyond society, the other directs him to society. But to both he is ordered as a person, a complete substantial unity. Substantial completeness, however, does not mean self-sufficiency. Because he is not self-sufficient, man needs society; because he is substantially complete, man can never be wholly subordinate to society. He is ordered to society, not as a part to an organism, taken in its literal

66. Welty, *op. cit.*, p. 138: "Zum Verständnis des Gesagten behalte man: wir haben uns ausdrücklich gewahrt gegen eine Gleichsetzung von Individualität und sinnenhafter Sphäre. Darum trifft uns der Vorwurf nicht; wir ordneten den Menschen nach seinem niederen Teile dem sozialen Leben zu und unter, ordneten ihn aber nach seinem höheren Teile dem sozialen Leben schlechthin über. Wäre das richtig, dann würden allerdings der Gemeinschaft die Kräfte des Geistes entzogen. Individualität und Personalität sind nicht zwei Stücke, sondern der Doppelbetracht des Menschen. Beide haben ihre Funktion im Sozialen und für das Soziale. Aber beide sind nicht vollkommen aus dem Sozialen zu erklären und nicht ausschliesslich dem Sozialen zugewandt. Darum wollen unsere letzten Ausführungen keineswegs besagen alles den Menschen als Individuum Betreffende gehe in Gemeinschaft auf, und alles den Menschen als Person Betreffende rage über Gemeinschaft hinaus. Wir wollten nur den formalen Seinsgrund ersichtlich machen, der eine doppelte soziale Stellung und einen doppelte sozialen Aufgabenkreis fundiert."

67. *Ibid.*

sense, but as a substantial being functioning in an ordered whole. Here is the secret of true social unity that does not deny the substantial and autonomous nature of the parts. It is a unity that cannot be solved either in the subordination of parts to an organism, or in the disintegration of parts in an aggregate; and it is definitely not solved by splitting man into twin halves. The unity of society and the substantial character of the parts is preserved by a unity of order. To this St. Thomas plainly agrees.

> It is to be noted that the whole whether it be the domestic family or the multitude of citizens has only a unity of order, which is incapable of rendering a thing absolutely one; hence each part of the whole can have its own proper operations, as the soldier in an army.[68]

Since the end of man is external to society, its principle of unity can only be that of external order. Such a unity leaves intact the substantial character of the parts, while directing their functions to the common good. It thus conserves society in its proper being, and the human person in his sacred character.

---

68. *Ethicorum,* lib. 1, lect. 1: "Sciendum est autem quod hoc totum quod est domestica familia vel civilis multitudo habet solum unitatem ordinis, secundum quam non est aliquid simpliciter unam. Et ideo pars hujus totius potest habere operationem quae non est operatio totius, sicut miles in exercitu habet operationem quae non est totius exercitus."

CHAPTER IV

SPIRITUAL EQUALITY OR HIERARCHICAL SOCIETY

1. METAPHYSICAL EQUALITY

The problem of human equality is complex. The failure to reach its adequate solution lies not only in the fallacy of over-simplification that would deny equality on the one hand, and inequality on the other, but more fundamentally in the failure to trace the problem to its metaphysical roots. There is a basic reason why men are both equal and unequal, and that reason must be sought not on the surface of appearances too often deceptive, but in the inner nature of the human individual. In the numerical multiplicity of the human species lies the answer. Man is both an individual and a member of a species. As the former he differs from others of his kind; as the latter he stands on a footing of equality with his fellow members within the species.

We have seen that the specific form to exist needs to be in-dividuated. This is true of all forms essentially disposed for union with a material principle.[1] Before union with matter they have only a logical existence, and, as such, are communicable, capable of indefinite multiplication by reason of the fact that it is their nature to actuate a material principle which is itself indefinitely determinable.[2] Herein lies their universality. Being communicated to every individual which they actuate, thereby giving to that individual its specific nature, they unify all the beings in which

---

1. *Con. Gen.* Bk. II, c. 93: "Ad hoc sunt plura individua in una specie in rebus corruptibilibus, ut natura speciei quae non potest perpetuo con-servari in uno individuo conservetur in pluribus, unde, etiam in corporibus incorruptibilibus, non est nisi unum individuum in una specie. Substantiae autem separatae natura potest conservari in uno individuo, eo quod sunt incorruptibiles, ut supra (c. 55) ostensum est. Non igitur oportet esse plura individua in illis substantiis, ejusdem speciei." *De Spiritualibus Creaturis,* q. 1, art. 8. Etienne Gilson, *The Philosophy of St. Thomas Aquinas* (St. Louis: B. Herder, 1924), ch. 8. P. Coffey, *Ontology* (New York: Longmans, Green & Co., 1926), p. 129.

2. Coffey, *op. cit.,* p. 129.

they are numerically repeated by giving to each the same specific essence or nature. Take, for example, a radio. Before it has real existence, it is only an idea in some mind. As such it is universal and communicable, that is, capable of being communicated to matter in an innumerable number of ways. Thus it may be communicated to mahogany and form a beautiful cabinet radio in some tastefully appointed living-room. Or it may be communicated to metal and become the crude but proud possession of some youthful experimenter. Lastly, there is the communication to the exquisite little set that gives the final touch of daintiness to some feminine boudoir. All three are very different, yet all three are equal in that they are radios. They share in the same essential nature. Mahogany, tin, and rosewood receive the *form* or idea *radio*. Yet it is indifferent to *radio* whether it be concretized in these three materials or receive its particular existence in walnut, chromium, or oak. The essential fact is, that regardless of the media that reduces the universal notion or *form* to the singular object, the multiplicity of individuals resulting receives that form, and is unified by it. Each bears to the other a relation of equality because each possesses the same essential nature; each is a radio.

Every individual, therefore, possessing the same form is the equal of every other individual actuated by that form. Here is the basis of specific or essential equality. Such equality consists simply in this, that every individual of a species, in its nature, is the equal of every other individual of the same species because it owes its being to the same specific form.

This is not to deny individual differences within the species. It is simply to assert that despite individuation and the numerical diversity which it entails, such diversity even though entering into the very substance of the form, in no way changes its essential nature. It merely adds to the essential nature a reality by which it is distinct from every other individual possessing that nature.[3]

3. Joseph Gredt, *Elementa Philosophiae Aristotelico-Thomisticae* (Fribourg: 1932), I, p. 125: "Haec in substantiis corporeis consistit in aliquo positivo superaddito quidditati, quod est relatio seu ordo transcendentalis (quasi modus naturae) unius individui ad aliud eiusdem speciei secundum prius et posterius. . . ."

Essentially, therefore, every individual of the same species bears to every other individual of that species a relation of equality.

There is a Scholastic aphorism, *Omne agens agit propter finem*,[4] which throws further light on this problem of essential equality. The intrinsic end of every being, the *finis operis*, determines its nature and implants within it those activities proper to the being and through which its end is realized.[5] This is an elementary truth of everyday life. The architect is limited in his design by the use to which the building is to be put. So it is with specific natures. Each such nature has a determinate end, and the manifold realizations of that nature in no way change the generic character of its end. It is the end which gives to the nature the activities proper to it, through which it is perfected and the end realized. It is thus that St. Thomas says, "the first of all causes is the final cause."[6] Now since the end determines the nature, wherever that nature is realized, it is always for the sake of the same end. Hence, the specific nature of each individual member of a species being the same, every individual in that species tends to the same generic end.

Essential equality is, therefore, twofold, equality of nature, and equality of end. Indeed, the equality of finality is the very basis of equality, since two natures possessed of the same end cannot be subordinated one to another in the attainment of that end. No one member of a species may, therefore, be subordinated to another member of the same species. Both stand on a footing of equality in the pursuit of their specific ends. Thus an acorn is never

4. *Summa Theol.,* I, q. 44, art. 4.

5. *Summa Theol.,* I, II, q. 1, art. 2c: "Prima autem inter omnes causas est causa finalis. Cuius ratio est, quia materia non consequitur formam, nisi secundum quod movetur ab agente: nihil enim reducit se de potentia in actum. Agens autem non movet nisi ex intentione finis. Si enim agens non esset determinatum ad aliquem effectum, non magis ageret hoc quam illud: ad hoc ergo quod determinatum effectum producat, necesse est quod determinetur ad aliquid certum, quod habet rationem finis." Cf. *Con. Gen.,* Bk. III, chs. 1, 2. *De Veritate,* q. 22, art. 2.

6. *Summa Theol.,* I, II, q. I, art. 1, ad. 1: "Quod finis, etsi sit postremus in executione, est tamen primus in intentione agentis. Et hoc modo habet rationem causae." *Con. Gen.,* Bk. III, ch. 17: "Est igitur finis ultimus prima omnium causa."

subordinated to another acorn. Both having their natural fulfillment in an oak tree, the specific tendency of one cannot be
realized through the specific tendency of the other. There may be
subordination of acorn to squirrel, but never of acorn to acorn.

What is true of a member of any species, is necessarily true of
the members of the human species. Men are equal in their specific
natures.[7] No one is more or less a man than another. Human
nature is complete in every individual member of the human race,
and each member is capable of realizing the fullest perfection of the
nature. But since every specific nature is ordered to a definite
end, human nature is ordained to its end. Consequently, every
individual man partaking of that nature, of necessity tends to the
same end.[8] This fact precludes the subordination of one to another. Each tends to his end directly, no man being conditioned in
achieving the goal of his nature by the prior achievement of any of
his fellows.[9] Plato does not reach his end on condition that
Socrates first attain his, anymore than one acorn becomes an oak
only on condition that another acorn first sends out roots and
branches. Nor may anyone forfeit his end that another's end be
gained. The law of one's nature is adamant. Though it can be
violated, it can never be abrogated.[10] The myth of racial superiority or inferiority is thus exploded, not because science fails to offer
empirical evidence in support of it, but because it has struck the
rock of metaphysical impossibility.

7. *Summa Theol.*, II, II, q. 104, art. 5: "In quibus tamen etiam, secundum
ea quae ad naturam corporis pertinent, homo homini obedire non tenetur,
sed solum Deo, quia omnes homines natura sunt pares." *II Sent.*, d. 6, q. 1,
art. 4, ad. 5: "Quod homines non sunt sibi invicem praeeminenter secundum
ordinem naturae, et etiam non ordinantur damnati in exercitium aliorum
vel in punitionem."

8. *Summa Theol.*, I, II, q. 1, art. 7: "Quantum igitur ad rationem ultimi
finis, omnes conveniunt in appetitu finis ultimi: quia omnes appetunt suam
perfectionem adimpleri, quae est ultimus finis, ut dictum est."

9. *II Sent.*, d. 44, q. 1, art. 3, ad. 1: "Quod natura omnes homines aequales
in libertate fecit, non autem in perfectionibus naturalibus; liberum enim,
secundum Philosophum in I *Metaphysic.*, cap. iii, est quod sui causa est.
Unum enim homo ex natura sua non ordinatur ad alterum sicut ad finem."

10. *Summa Theol.*, I, II, q. 94, art. 5.

2. Spiritual Equality

We have seen that specific nature takes its being from the form, and the nature of the form is determined by the end of the being it actuates. In the case of man the form is the spiritual soul.[11] This not only determines that men be equal in their specific natures, but that such equality be spiritual. Inequality, as we shall later explain, comes from the soul's relation to a material principle. The spiritual soul is the direct creation of God,[12] Who, in accordance with the principle of finality, fashioned it for an end. That end is the perfection of man's two highest powers, the intellect and the will, flowering into a perfect natural knowledge and love of God. The attainment of this perfection is the work of man's autonomy, for in him is no impelling necessity directing him to the goal of his nature. That nature, bearing the stamp of rationality and free choice, is the nature of a person. Equality of nature, therefore, means that men are equally autonomous in relation to their end and destiny. The origin, nature, and final goal of every man being the same, in relation to all three man is the equal of his fellowman. Yet since it is a spiritual principle, the human soul, which is the determining factor in such equality, men bear to one another an equality that is spiritual.

It is this spiritual equality that gives to men their equal dignity. The perfect independence and self-mastery, the perfect knowledge and love of God, which is man's end, are but the flowering of the spiritual soul. To this all men are obligated by the law of their nature. But that nature being the nature of a person whose high dignity derives from a spiritual principle, the autonomy with which it vests men partakes likewise of a spiritual character. It is the perfection of this autonomy to which every man is directed by the natural law, and since no one man may take precedence over another in its achievement, there is to that extent an equality of persons.

---

11. *Summa Theol.*, I, q. 76, art. 1 c. Cf. *Con. Gen.*, Bk. II, ch. 87.
12. Summa Theol., I, q. 90, art. 3.

3. Metaphysical Inequality

It was Shailer Mathews who warned against the inference that because all men are brothers they are therefore to be twins.[13] While human inequality is too stark a reality to permit denial there are not wanting those devotees of equality who would explain away inequality by its origin. It is all so simple. Men are by nature equal. Their inequality is the work of environment. Equalize the environment and mankind will become one vast set of identical twins. Wishful thinking has solved more than one difficult problem, but the hitch in this solution lies in the fact that, whereas human equality is an endowment of man's nature, human inequality is not less so. Environment is not without its effect on the human individual, but distinctions among men flow from an inner more than from an outer principle. Like equality, inequality must be traced to its metaphysical roots. Only in the inner constitution of things lies their ultimate explanation. This held good for equality, and it likewise holds good for inequality. Both are rooted in the ultimate constituents of the corporeal nature. That nature, it may be recalled, is a composite of matter and form. As it is the latter that unifies the species by giving to the members the same specific nature or essence, thereby generating specific equality, so it is the former that diversifies the species by adding to the essential nature those differentiating notes, by which comet, cow, or canary, becomes *this* comet, *this* cow, or *this* canary. Such differences, issuing not from the formal principle which unifies, but from the material principle which diversifies, are limited to *one*. They add to the essential nature the character of *more* or *less*.

Because form is the principle of unity, and matter the principle of diversity, the union of the two makes corporeal reality both one and manifold, creating thereby unity amid variety and beauty amid order. In the universality of the form, and the individuality of matter lies the ultimate explanation of specific unity on the one hand, and individual diversity on the other. Because of the one,

13. Shailer Matthews, *Jesus on the Social Institutions* (New York: The Macmillan Co., 1928), p. 39.

members of a species can claim an equality of nature; because of the other they must admit individual inequality. Here is the last reason why in their specific nature things are equal, as individuals they are not. The oak, the elm, and the birch shading the lawn below are all equally trees, because in each is realized the idea or *form* of tree. It is thus the three are unified in the class *tree* in spite of their manifest differences. But as their unity springs from the common idea incorporated in them, so their diversity springs from the matter in which that idea takes real existence. No one oak will ever exhaust all that is contained in the idea *tree*, or even in the idea *oak*, because the material can never exhaust the spiritual, nor the particular the universal.

Just as matter is the principle of inequality among the members of any species, so the body brings to the members of the human species their inequality. Just how this is done has already been explained. The substantial union of spiritual soul and material body does not destroy the real distinction between the two. In the human composite they both retain their characteristic function, the one bestowing the specific nature, the other conferring those individual differences by which each of the possessors of that nature is distinguished from the rest of humanity. It is the one that actuates and the other that individuates. And since the actual must be singular,[14] the form or principle of actuality must sum up or exhaust the perfection of the specific type in its single existence, or undergo repeated realizations of itself in order to fully and adequately express the exemplar in the Divine Mind of which it is the created reflection.[15] Only in God is there Pure Actuality.[16]

---

14. St. Thomas, *De Veritate*, q. 1, art. 1. *Summa Theol.*, I, q. 11, art. 1.

15. Coffey, *op. cit.*, p. 129.

16. *Con. Gen.*, II, c. 52: "Perfectius est quoque in actu quod est ipse actus quam quod est habens actum; hoc enim propter illud actum est. His ergo positis constat . . . quod Deus solus est primum agens. Sibi ergo soli competet esse in actu perfectissimo modo, ut scilicet sit Ipse actus perfectissimus." Cf. *Summa Theol.*, I, q. 3, art. 1, art. 4. *Ibid.*, q. 50, art. 2, ad. 3. *Ibid.*, q. 75, art. 5, ad. 4. *De Spiritualibus Creaturis*, q. 1, art. 1.

Everything else, enjoying but a conferred actuality,[17] must be limited by some principle, for the creature cannot be equal to God. That principle is potentiality.[18] In created natures it distinguishes the being of a thing from its substance,[19] thereby differentiating the creature from the Creator, in Whom being and substance are one.[20]   Every created nature is, therefore, a composition of act and potency, because its essence is distinct from its existence. *What a thing is,* is a reality quite distinct from that *whereby it is.*[21] To know what Pithecanthropus Erectus *is,* is not necessarily to know that Pithecanthropus Erectus *was.*   The first reveals the nature or essence; the second, its existence.

Now it is potentiality that limits the created nature to one.   This potentiality is of two kinds: that which distinguishes the being of a thing from its substance, thereby preventing it from being pure

17. St. Thomas, *De Spiritualibus Creaturis,* q. 1, art. 1: "Et ideo invenitur aliquis purus actus absque omni potentia; numquam tamen invenitur in rerum natura potentia quae non sit perfecta per aliquem actum; et propter hoc semper in materia prima est aliqua forma. A primo autem plentitudinem perfectionis, causatur esse actu in omnibus." Cf. *Con. Gen.,* II, c. 52.

18. St. Thomas, *De Ente et Essentia,* cap. 4: "Omne autem quod recipit ab alio, est in potentia respectu illius; et hoc quod receptum est in eo, est actus ejus.   Ergo oportet quod ipsa forma vel quidditas quae est intelligentia, sit in potentia respectu esse quod a Deo recipit; et illud esse receptum est per modum actus; et ita invenitur actus et potentia in intelligentiis, non tamen forma et materia, nisi aequivoce." Cf. *Con. Gen.,* II, ch. 53. Coffey, *op. cit.,* p. 102.

19. *Con. Gen.,* II, ch. 52: "Illud igitur quod est subsistens non potest esse nisi unum tantum.   Ostensum est autem quod Deus est suum esse subsistens. Nihil igitur aliud praeter Ipsum potest esse suum esse; oportet igitur, in omni substantia quae est praeter Ipsum aliud esse ipsam substantiam et aliud ejus esse."

20. *Summa Theol.,* I, q. 3, art. 4: "Cum igitur Deo nihil sit potentiale, . . . sequitur quod non sit aliud in eo essentia quam suum esse. Sua igitur essentia est suum esse."

21. *Con. Gen.,* Lib. II, cap. 54: "In substantiis autem intellectualibus, quae non sunt ex materia et forma compositae, (sed in eis ipsa forma est substantia subsistens), forma est quod est, ipsum autem esse actus et quo est; et propter hoc in eis est unica tantum compositio actus et potentiae, quae scilicet est ex substantia et esse, quae a quibusdam dicitur ex 'quod est et esse' vel ex 'quod est et quo est'." *Con. Gen.,* II, ch. 54: "In substantiis autem compositis ex materia et forma, est duplex compositio actus et potentiae: prima quidem ipsius substantiae, quae componitur ex materia et forma; secunda vero, ex ipsa substantia jam composita et esse; quae etiam potest dici ex *quod est et esse* vel ex *quod est* et *quo est.*"

actuality, or God; and that which distinguishes matter from form.[22] In substances which are "pure forms," such as the angelic natures, the only potentiality present, and hence the only composition present, is that between being and substance, or existence and essence.[23]

In corporeal natures, on the other hand, both types of potentiality are present, that within the substance itself, which is composed of matter and form; and that of essence and existence. The latter is common to all created natures, the former is peculiar to the corporeal nature. Here matter, the principle of potentiality, puts a second limitation upon the actuality of the divine exemplar, thereby preventing the specific nature from totally expressing that exemplar in a single existence. Only by an infinite number of repetitions can the divine type be exhaustively expressed. And since matter is corruptible, only an infinite number of repetitions can preserve the species. Were each of these repetitions identical, the divine ideal would remain forever only partially realized. Though God may never be encompassed by numbers, neither should He be hemmed in by matter. Such would be the case were the divine ideal adequately expressed in one corporeal realization. The reason why matter diversifies, and must remain forever indefinitely determinable is evident: were the individuals of a species equal, the divine ideal would be frustrated; were the specific repetitions determined, God could be computed by numbers. That is why individuals must be unequal, and inequality limited only by infinity.[24] Inequality is, therefore, not a fact contingent on environment, but granted the act of creation, a reality of strict necessity.

---

22. *Ibid.* Cf. *De Spirit. Creat.*, q. 1, art. 1.

23. *Ibid.* Cf. *Summa Theol.*, I, q. 50, art. 2, ad. 3. *De Spirit. Creat.*, q. 1,

24. *Summa Theol.*, I, q. 47, art. 3, ad. 2: "quia materialis multitudo non habet certum terminum, sed de se tendit in infinitum; . . ." *Summa Theol.*, I, q. 50, art. 2, ad. 4: "Creaturae autem materiales habent infinitatem ex parte materiae. . . ." *Summa Theol.*, I, q. 50, art. 4, ad. 4: "Quod multiplicatio secundum numerum, cum in infinitum protendi possit. . . ." Cf. *Ibid.*, q. 47, art. 2.

In the corporeal world below man, the individual guarantees the
continued existence of the species.[25]   But man is something more
than matter. The human form being a spiritual soul, man is a
compound of matter and spirit. He plays, therefore, a double
functional rôle. He preserves the species with his body, and
transcends it with his soul. In his chemical and biological functions man is ordered to the specific good; in his spiritual functions
he commands the service of the species. That is why the family,
though primarily for the good of the individual, is nevertheless
ordered to the race because the race is at the service of the human
person.[26]   As man's body ministers to his soul and is subordinate
to it, so in his chemical and biological functions man ministers to
the race, but the race in turn ministers to the human person.

Just as men are unequal as individuals but equal in nature, so
races, the fruit of man's chemical and biological functions, are
unequal as societies of individuals,[27] but never as societies of men.
Indeed such societies are but the extensions of human personality,
and as such are called moral persons. That is why races may
never be denied autonomy, and why that autonomy must be
increased in proportion as the race develops and reaches a higher
cultural level.   Just as the individual person is never lacking in
that initial autonomy wherein it is human and grows in freedom
in proportion as it attains self-mastery, so it is with races.   This

25. *Con. Gen.,* Bk. II, ch. 93: "Ad hoc sunt plura individua in una specie
in rebus corruptibilibus, ut natura speciei quae non potest perpetuo con-
servari in uno individuo conservetur in pluribus." Cf. *Summa Theol.,* I,
q. 98, art. 1.
26. *Summa Theol.,* I, q. 98, art. 1: "Quia igitur in rebus corruptibilibus
nihil est perpetuum et semper manens nisi species, bonum speciei est de
principali intentione naturae, ad cuius conservationem naturalis generatio
ordinatur. . . . Sic igitur homini ex parte corporis, quod corruptibile est
secundum naturam suam, competit generatio. Ex parte vero animae, quae
incorruptibilis est, competit ei quod multitudo individuorum sit per se intenta
a natura, vel potius a naturae Auctore, qui solus est humanarum animarum
creator."
27. St. Thomas, *Politicorum,* III, lect. 15: "Si contingat unum totum
genus, vel unum inter alios sic differre in genere ab aliis secundum virtutem, ut virtus ejus excedat virtutem omnium aliorum, justum est hoc
genus esse regale, vel illum si sit unus, et regnum et dominium esse unum
omnium: hoc enim est secundum naturam quod ille qui excedit secundum
virtutem sit dominus aliorum."

is not to deny that races may suffer the tutelage of more capable human groups, anymore than it denies that a child may suffer obedience to his parents. But as the parent's right to youthful obedience stops short of whatever injures the child's person, so the domination of one racial group by another must never jeopardize the persons of the subjugated race. As the child on reaching autonomy of manhood is given greater freedom, so the race on attaining racial maturity must be permitted an autonomy that corresponds to its cultural growth.[28]

What is true of races is likewise true of classes. Inequality of social classes follows inequality of individuals. In general men tend to group themselves in accordance with their respective capacities, each one approximating the social class that best fits his individual talents. But though the hierarchy of classes results from individual differences, it is with classes as it is with races, the sacredness of the human person must never be sacrificed for the cultural level.

4. Spiritual Inequality

Though the inequality of the members of a species is in the last analysis attributed to the material constituent of the nature, that is not to say that in their formal principle all these members are identical. It will be recalled that between matter and form there must be commensuration, not only essentially but accidentally. As the form of a mountain cannot give being to the matter of a mouse, so the soul of a great dane is not fitting to the body of a pekingese. The constituents of the corporeal nature must be finely matched if there is to be compatibility in the substantial union. Whether the Creator calls into existence mountains, mice, or men, He never makes the mistake of putting the square peg in the round hole.

Human inequality is the result, therefore, not only of bodies more or less perfect, but of souls as well. Though it may never touch the essence, it need not stop short of the substance. Men differ not only physically but spiritually, not only in their bodies but in their souls. Spiritual inequality, however, halts at the threshold of

28. *Ibid.,* III, lect. 2. Cf. Michael Cronin, *The Science of Ethics* (Dublin: M. H. Gill & Son, 1929), II, pp. 509-513.

the human essence. Men are never more or less men, never more
or less persons, anymore than H_2O is more or less water, regardless of whether it form the fluid content of limpid pool or mighty
ocean.

But if as individuals men are not equal, neither are they equal
in their individual ends. The razor and the ax were never meant
for the same purpose even though they both cut. But since one
trims beards and the other fells trees, their functions are everlastingly different. And so it is with men. Every single man brought
into existence is meant to know and love God, but that knowledge
and that love is the fruit of individual capacity and voluntary
effort. In these, men differ. Are they, then, for all eternity to
know and love God with the same clarity and desire? Is individual
perfection of the nature to end in a dead level of unvarying sameness? Not if the principle of contradiction has any meaning. If
individual differences can beget men the exact counterpart of every
other, to what purpose this inequality? Since nature's acts are
never meaningless, the conclusion is evident: individuals are unequal because their eternal role is unequal.

5. Equality and Social Hierarchy

As it is a fundamental exigency of human nature that man live
in society, the equality of nature and the inequality of individuals
exercise important functions in man's social universe. Man's personality demands society, but because the person is also an individual it likewise demands that such society be a hierarchy.
While man is an autonomous being acquiring self-perfection by
freely conforming to the law of his nature, he is by no means self-
sufficient in the exercise of that autonomy. Indeed his very
individuality puts a limitation upon his personality, forcing him
into dependence upon other persons for that temporal well-being
necessary for self-development.[29]   It is as an individual of a

29. St. Thomas, *De Regimine*, Lib. I, cap. 1: "Naturale autem est homini
ut sit animal sociale et politicum in multitudine vivens maius etiam quam
omnia alia animalia: quod quidem naturalis necessitas declaret. . . . Ad
quae praeparanda unus homo non sufficit; nam unus homo per se sufficienter
vitam transigere non potest. Est igitur homini naturale quod in societate
multorum vivat." Cf. *Ethicorum*, Lib. I, lect. 1. *Con. Gen.*, III, ch. 85.

species that man is most helpless, and most dependent upon his fellow members within the species for the necessities of his very existence. The limitation placed on the spiritual soul by its relation to matter puts man under the necessity of developing his personality by uniting with other persons like unto himself. Were man only an individual of a species directed to the preservation of a specific nature he might very well dispense with the services of his fellows once he becomes sufficiently mature to permit independent action. Were physical maturity and specific reproduction the goal of his being, man could well suffice with the transitory society of sex.[30] But man is more than a member of a species. He is a person ordered to an end beyond the species, an end for which the species constitutes a necessary means. Yet it is his membership within the species that by limiting his person curtails his self-sufficiency and necessitates a community of action by which the person can surmount the handicap of a material principle.

Man is a member of society not only through the force of instinct, but by the command of reason, for society is a necessary means to a divinely imposed goal.[31] Yet though it is as a person that man is ordered to society, it is because as a person he is also an individual that such ordering becomes imperative. The limitation placed on the nature by its individuation creates individual differences resulting in one having what another lacks. Here is the root of interdependence. They err, therefore, who make man social by either the individual or personal aspect of his nature. Man enters society through the function of his personal nature, and this for the simple reason that man becomes a person by becoming an individual. That person is at birth, as it were, in an embryonic stage. It must grow and develop, until it attains that full autonomy

---

30. St. Thomas, *De Regimine,* Lib. I, cap. 1: "Nam medicus curam gerit ut vita hominis conservetur in sanitate; oeconomous, ut suppetant necessaria vitae; doctor autem curam gerit ut veritatem cognoscat, institutor autem morum ut secundum rationem vivat. Quod si homo non ordinaretur ad aliud exterius bonum, sufficerent homini curae praedictae."

31. *Ethicorum,* I, lect. 1: "Alio modo jurator homo a multitudine, cujus est pars, ad vitae sufficientiam perfectam; scilicet ut homo non solum vivat, sed et bene vivat habens omnia quae sibi sufficiunt ad vitam." *De Regimine,* Lib. I, cap. 15: "Sicut autem ad vitam quam in caelo speramus beatam ordinatur sicut ad finem vita quia hic homines bene vivant."

of which the initial gift of freedom is but the seed. Such growth and development demands that betwen man and his fellows there be a mutual interchange of services, the one complementing and perfecting the other. And since the specific act of the person is intellectual and moral, man is not only dependent on his fellowmen for help in securing those physical needs of his nature which condition intellectual growth, but for his very intellectual and moral formation as well.[32]

This mutual aid is a strict necessity for in no other way can man attain the full perfection of his person. Now since it is in their specific natures that men are equal, but as individual members of a species that they are unequal, these two facts are not without significance in man's relation to society. Society being necessary for the perfection of the person, it is a means for the realization of man's potentialities. In their need for such perfection men stand on a footing of equality, hence society is equally a means for all. The common good achieved through personal union is, therefore, at the disposal of one no more than another. Since to perfection of nature all are equally bound, all stand in equal need of the means necessary to fulfill that obligation. It is in the society of his fellows that man's vocation is realized, yet he may never become so submerged in the collectivity as to lose his autonomy. Indeed, it is by his autonomous action that he contributes to the perfection of his person. Though society is a necessary means to the use of that autonomy, it is never an end. It provides men with that sufficiency of well-being best conducive to their personal development. To the creation and maintenance of that sufficiency all have an obligation since it stands to the attainment of man's end as a necessary means. Since all men have the same end, all have a claim to the enjoyment of the benefits of the common good. Be-

---

32. *De Regimine*, Lib. I, cap. 1: "Homo autem horum quae sunt vitae necessaria, naturalem cognitionem habet solum in communi quasi eo per rationem valente ex universalibus principiis ad cognitionem singulorum quae necessaria sunt humanae vitae pervenire. Non est autem possibile quod unus homo ad omnia hujusmodi per suam rationem pertingit. Est igitur necessarium homini quod in multitudine vivat, ut unus ab alio adjuvetur, et diversi diversis inveniendis per rationem occuparentur, unus in medicina, alius in hoc, alius in alio."

cause men are persons, therefore, they stand in need of society; because as persons they have the same end, society is equally a means for all with which to fulfill their potentialities.

It is, however, in these potentialities that men differ. Such potentialities springing from that which individuates the nature, are at once the root and source of inequality. Because of them men differ in their relation to the common good, and such differences entail that men fall into diverse social levels. It is thus that society becomes a hierarchy. Such social organization is not only in keeping with the individual differences of the members, but it is also in keeping with the strain of unity that pervades mankind, as it is in keeping with the notion of society as a means to an end. If men as individuals are unequal, a union of such individuals must reflect the fact. If in their personal natures men bear to each other a relation of equality, should not their social ordering be based on a principle of unity? Finally, if society is a means whereby man reaches his end, should not that ordering of society which implies relationship to an end be most natural to it? Now hierarchical order is a grouping of unequals according to a principle of unity that directs to an end.[33] It is, therefore, the social ordering most fitting to human society.

As men are unequal in their individual ends, though tending alike to the same generic end, so they are unequal in their relation to the end of society. It is in proportion as man is more or less immediately concerned with his end, that he takes his place above or below his fellows on a scale of preference. The more a man directs his action to the perfection of his whole being, the greater the superiority of his manhood. As we judge a doctor in proportion

33. Mercier, *Manual of Modern Scholastic Philosophy* (St. Louis: B. Herder, 1919), p. 557, V. I: "Now order implies: (1) several things distinct from one another; (2) certain relations of succession between them; (3) some single principle which governs these relations—'*Ordo nihil aliud dicit quam rationem prioris et posterioris in distinctis sub aliquo uno principio.*' . . . If we inquire what is this principle of unity necessary for order we see that it is the purpose for which the work is 'ordained' or set about. . . . In a word, the first principle of unity of order is the *end* of the work into which the order is introduced. Hence St. Thomas has the further definition: Order is the adaptation of things to their end— *Recta ratio rerum ad finem.*"

as he attains the goal of his profession, soundness of health, so we grade men in relation to their end. But what is true of man in relation to the end of his nature, is likewise true of his relation to the end of society. That end being the common good, the more immediately a man is directed to it, the higher his rank in the social hierarchy. *Dignitas in ordine ad finem*,[34] is the consistent teaching of St. Thomas for whom the teleological principle is basic whether in the realm of politics[35] or in any other realm.[36] Now it is through their individual potentialities that men are more or less apt in realizing the common good, and, therefore, more or less the recipients of social power. As Aristotle has pointed out, and St. Thomas confirms, political society is not only for the purpose of men living together, but for living as men ought. Hence, those who contribute most to this end are deserving of the greater power in the State.[37]

Now power is always for the sake of an end, and is derived from the end it serves. Since there is a hierarchy of ends, the more proximate for the sake of the more ultimate, there is also a hier-

34. *Politicorum*, Lib. III, lect. 7: "Ex quo apparet, quod si justum est aequale aliquarum rerum aliquibus personis secundum *dignitatem in ordine ad finem*, quod in politia illa in qua ponitur rectus finis, est justum simpliciter. Justum enim ut dictum est, attenditur secundum *dignitatem in ordine ad finem*, sicut in regno et politiis rectus universalite." Cf. Desmond Fitzgerald, *Preface to Statecraft* (New York: Sheed & Ward, 1939), pp. 74-80.

35. Edouard Crahay, *La Politique de Saint Thomas D'Aquin* (Louvain: 1896), p. 149: "Cette philosophie (La philosophie politique de Saint Thomas d'Aquin) git tout entière dans le principe de la *finalité*, c'est à dire dans l'affirmation d'une destinée essentielle de la personalité humaines, et dans la necessité des l'adaptation des moyens à la fin."

36. Mathieu Robert, "Hierarchie Necessaire Des Fonctions Economiques, D'après Saint Thomas D'Aquin," *Revue Thomiste*, XXI (1913), pp. 419-431. Cf. *II Sent.*, d. X, q. 1, art. 3, ad. 1.

37. *Politicorum*, Lib. III, lect. 7: "Et dicit quod, cum finis civitatis sit feliciter vivere practice, feliciter autem vivere sit operari secundum optimam virtutem practicam, quae est prudentia, et communicatio politica consistit in hujusmodi actionibus; manifestum est quod illi qui plus addunt ad talem communicationem plus addunt ad civilitatem, et plus civitatis pertinet ad istos quam ad illos qui sunt aequales in libertate vel genere, et quam ad illos qui sunt majores in genere, tamen minores et inaequales secundum virtutem politicam. Iterum plus attinet illis de eis quae pertinent ad vivitatem quam illis qui excedunt alios in divitiis, sed exceduntur ab aliis in virtutibus. Ex quo apparet, quod si justum est aequale aliquarum rerum aliquibus personis secundum dignitatem in ordine ad finem."

archy of powers, that power being supreme which serves a supreme end.[38]   This is true of the individual man and it is likewise true of man in relation to the family.   The individual man is a microcosm in whom the physical and chemical elements exist for the biological, the biological for the sense, and the sense for the rational. Now these hierarchical elements are unified in the rational soul, which is the principle of the whole man.   It is thus that the rational powers direct the whole man to his supreme goal, and, therefore, exercise over the lower powers a supreme authority.[39]

This hierarchy of powers in the individual man is reflected in the first social group of which he becomes a member.   For the family is likewise a hierarchy wherein the child in his capacity as a member is obedient to the parent, and the father as the principle of family life has care of that domestic well-being for which the family was called into existence to serve as a means for youthful development.   As the father is thus directed to the end of the family, he exercises within the domestic group supreme authority.[40] Just as the family is indispensable for the personal perfection of the individual, so civil society is indispensable for the welfare of the family.   If the individual must seek his end through the medium of the family, so the family must seek its end through the medium of the State.   And as the end of the family is individual well-being, so the end of the State is domestic well-being.   If the individual cannot realize his well-being except in an environment fostered by the family, neither can the family realize its well-being except in an environment fostered by the State.[41]   Hence as the hierarchy

38. *De Regimine,* Lib. I, cap. 14: "Semper enim invenitur ille ad quem pertinet ultimus finis imperare operantibus ea quae ad finem ultimum ordinantur."

39. *Summa Theol.,* I, II, q. 72, art. 4: "Triplex autem ordo in homine debet esse.   Unus quidem secundum comparationem ad regulam rationis: prout scilicet omnes actiones et passiones nostrae debent secundum regulam rationis commensurari."

40. Pope Pius XI, *Casti Connubi* (1931).   Cf. Pope Leo XIII, *Arcanum Divinae Sapientiae* (1880).   *Summa Theol.,* I, II. q. 104, art. 4: "Quadruplex autem ordo in aliquo populo invenire potest: . . . quartus autem, ad domesticos, sicut patris ad filium, uxoris ad virum, et domini ad servum."

41. *Politicorum,* Lib. II, lect. 1: "Manifestum est enim quod una domus vel familia tota magis est sufficiens ad vitam quam unus homo; et civitas est magis sufficiens quam domus."

of powers in the individual is reflected in the family, so the hierarchy of powers in the family must be reflected in the State. As in
the individual, equality of powers would end in its dissolution "if
all had the dignity of an eye"[42] so in the family, if all exercised the
authority of the parent there would be no family, and in the State
if all the citizens possessed an equal authority there would be no
State.[43]

So indigenous is order to human society that without it social
life would become impossible; for where many are tending to one
end there must be one at the head directing, otherwise chaos would
result. Not only is this a truism of everyday life, as all traffic laws
attest, but it is evident in the world of nature where physical laws
maintain a most marvelous order. Whether among planets in their
celestial orbits, or electrons in their atomic ones, the principle of
order is most manifest.

No one more clearly saw the application of such a principle to
social life than St. Thomas, for whom it was so natural and so
necessary that he held that even in a "state of innocence man would
have been master of men."

> But a man is master of a free subject, by directing him either
> towards his proper welfare, or to the common good. Such a
> kind of mastership would have been in the state of innocence
> between man and man, for two reasons. First, because man
> is naturally a social being, and so in the state of innocence he
> would have led a social life. Now a social life cannot exist
> among a number of people unless under the presidency of one
> to look after the common good; for many as such seek many
> things, whereas one attends only to one. Wherefore, the Phil-
> osopher says in the beginning of the *Politics*, that wherever
> many things are directed to one, we shall always find one at
> the head directing them.[44]

42. *Summa Theol.*, I, q. 47, art. 2, ad. 1: "tolleretur enim bonitas animalis,
si quaelibet pars eius oculi, haberet dignitatem." St. Paul, I *Cor.*, xii, 19.
43. *Politicorum*, Lib. II, lect. 1: "Sic igitur patet quod cum de ratione
civitatis sit quod civitas ex dissimilibus construatur . . . quia si tollatur
dissimilitudo civium jam non erit civitas."
44. *Summa Theol.*, I, q. 96, art. 4: "Tunc vero dominatur aliquis alteri
ut libero, quando dirigit ipsum ad proprium bonum eius qui dirigitur, vel
ad bonum commune. Et tale dominium hominis ad hominem in statu innocentiae fuisset, propter duo. Primo quidem, quia homo naturaliter est

If civil society is impossible without the preëminence of one directing the whole, it is also impossible without a scale of preëminence whereby men fall into levels in accordance as there exists a proportion between their individual capacities and their contribution to the common good.[45] Political society is not just a multitude under the leadership of one. Life on the animal level frequently manifests the herd and its leader. Only when such a feature is given human status does it become an anomaly.[46] Because civil society is a thing of reason, it is a thing of order, the adaptation of things to their end. But that order is not something extrinsically imposed. It is the natural result of individual differences. These individual differences, as we have seen, are the endowments of nature. They exist wherever a multiplication of the species exist, effecting man in his function as a member, in order that his function as a person be more fully realized. Consequently, man takes his place in civil life in accordance as his function contributes to the well-being of the civic whole.[47] Because these functions are determined largely by inherent capabilities, social order is neither arbitrary nor extrinsic, but natural. The dictum of St. Thomas is here very much to the point:

> Men are not made by society, but are accepted in it as generated by nature, and used accordingly.[48]

animal sociale: unde homines in statu innocentiae socialiter vixissent. Socialis autem vita multorum esse non posset, nisi aliquis praesideret, quid ad bonum commune intenderet: multi enim per se intendunt ad multa unus vero ad unum. Et ideo Philosophus dicit in principio *Politic.* quod quandocumque multa ordinantur ad unum, semper invenitur unum ut principali et dirigens."

45. *Summa Theol.*, I, q. 108, art. 2, ad. 2: "Et quanto perfectius donum aliquis communicare potest, tanto in perfectiori gradu est."

46. *Summa Theol.*, I, q. 108, art. 2: "Una hierarchia est unus principatus, id est una multitudo ordinata uno modo sub principis gubernatione. Non autem esset multitudo ordinate, sed confusa, si in multitudine diversi ordines non essent."

47. *Summa Theol.*, III, *Suppl.*, q. 41, art. 2: "Quod natura inclinat ad aliquid duplicitis. Uno modo sicut ad id quod est necessarium ad perfectionem unius. . . . Alio modo inclinat ad aliquid quod est necessarium multitudini . . . sed inclinationi naturae satisfit cum per diversos diversa complentur de praedictis."

48. *Politicorum*, Lib. I, lect. 8: "Homines autem non facit politica sed accipit eos a natura generatos, et sic utitur ipsis."

Now men as generated by nature do exhibit varied capabilities, hence their place on the scale of social preference should be determined by the adjustment of function to capacity. As St. Thomas expresses it:

> . . . diversity of order arises from diversity of offices and actions, as appears in one city where there are different orders according to different actions.[49]

Society, however, is not just a succession of bewildering differences stretching vertically across the chart of time. The normal curve of distribution is woven into the social fabric, and the weaving has been done by natural forces on the loom of nature.

Social life is like a tapestry which portrays a three-tier structure of human society, forming a pyramid of ascending functions, the reverse of which shows a pyramid of native abilities. Nor is the pattern static. There is a center toward which men gravitate, as they tend toward the level of their intellectual gifts. For a few the point of gravity will fall within the higher reaches of the social zone; for the bulk of mankind it will hold a medial position; while the remaining minority will gravitate to a point below. This natural distribution of abilities is the loom for the natural distribution of classes. The mass of the common people will gravitate around the base of the pyramid; the middle class, the *populus honorabilis,* will cluster around the center; while the gifted few forming the highest class, will move upward toward the apex. Yet between these three there exists no clear cut division, for within each class there are always the minority, the *infimi* who tend below, the majority the *medii* who take a mid position, and the few *supremi* who seek their level near the class above.

A modern writer on social hierarchy who explains this social structure very well, quotes Leonardi da Vinci as saying:

> There are three classes of people: Those who do not see; those who see when they are shown; and those who see by themselves.[50]

---

49. *Summa Theol.,* I, q. 108, art. 2: "Quae quidem diversitas ordinum secundum diversa officia et actus consideratur. Sicut patet quod in una divitate sunt diversi ordines secundum diversos actos."

50. S. de Madariaga, *Anarchy or Hierarchy* (New York: The Macmillan Company, 1937), p. 155.

Those who do not see are the men of weaker intellects, the more concrete-minded who form the base of human society. To these fall the manual tasks of life, humble but not unimportant. They are like the roots of a tree, hidden but life-giving. As Madariaga aptly says, they are the men of Mother Earth, "flowers sprung from the ancestral loam."[51] They may not envision the end of the society they so strongly support, and, therefore, contribute not so directly to the common good, but they are a nation's backbone. They dig the foundations of the social structure. Those who see when they are shown, are men of average intelligence. They form the great middle class of society, the men of skill who perform their tasks efficiently and well. They are the executors who understand the relation of their functions to the social good when shown. They build the social structure. Those who see by themselves are the master minds, the men of giant intellects, the architects who super-vise the building of the social structure according to patterns of their own making. These are the leaders of society, men of the ruling caste, whose function is to contribute immediately to the formation of the common good.

How closely does all this approximate St. Thomas? Suppose we let him speak for himself:

> Now there should be a threefold order in men:—one in relation to the rule of reason, in so far as all our actions and passions should be commensurate with the rule of reason:—another order is in relation to the rule of Divine law, whereby man should be directed in all things: and if man were by nature a solitary animal, this twofold order would suffice. But since man is naturally a civic and social animal, as is proved in *Polit.* i, 2 a third order is necessary whereby man is directed in relation to other men among whom he has to dwell.[52]

51. *Ibid.*, p. 160.
52. *Summa Theol.*, I, II, q. 72, art. 4: "Triplex autem ordo in homine debet esse. Unus quidem secundum comparationem ad regulam rationis: prout scilicet omnes actiones et passiones nostrae debent secundum regulam rationis commensurari. Alius autem ordo est per comparationem ad regu-lam divinae legis, per quam homo in omnibus dirigi debet. Et si quidem homo naturaliter esset animal solitarium, hic duplex ordo sufficeret: sed quia homo est naturaliter animal politicum et sociale, ut probatur in I *Polit.* ideo necesse est quod sit tertius ordo, quo homo ordinetur ad alios homines, quibus convivere debet."

Now in every people a fourfold order is to be found: one, of the people's sovereign to his subjects; a second, of the subjects among themselves; a third, of the citizens to foreigners; a fourth, of members of the same household, such as the order of father to son; of the wife to her husband; of master to his servant.[53]

But although one city thus comprises several orders, all may be reduced to three, when we consider that every multitude has a beginning, a middle, and an end. So in every city, a threefold order of men is to be seen, some of whom are supreme, as the nobles; others are the last, as the common people, while others hold a place between these as the middle class.[54]

Again, in all arts and positions of authority they are more worthy of praise who rule others well than those who live well under others' direction. In speculative matters, for instance, it is greater to impart truth to others by teaching than to be able to grasp what is taught by others. So, too, among the crafts an architect who plans a building is more highly esteemed and paid a higher wage than the builder who does the manual labour under his direction; also in warfare the strategy of the general wins greater glory from victory than the bravery of the soldier. It is the same for the ruler of a multitude in regard to things which each individual according to his powers has to do, as it is for the teacher in regard to the matters taught, the architect in regard to buildings, or the general in regard to warfare.[55]

53. *Summa Theol.*, I, II, q. 104. art. 4: "Quadruplex autem ordo in aliquo populo invenire potest: unus quidem principum populi ad subditos; alius autem, subditorum ad invicem; tertius autem eorum qui sunt de populo ad extraneos; quartos autem, ad domesticos, sicut patris ad filium, uxoris ad virum et domini ad servum."

54. *Summa Theol.*, I, q. 108, art. 2: "Sed quamvis multi sint unius civitatis ordines omnes tamen ad tres possunt reduci, secundum quod quaelibet multitudo perfecta habet principium, medium, et finem. Unde et in civitatibus triplex ordo hominum invenitur: quidam enim sunt supremi, ut optimates; quidam autem sunt infimi, ut vilis populus; quidam autem sunt medii, ut populus honorabilis."

55. *De Regimine*, Lib. I, cap. 1: "Adhuc: in omnibus artibus et potentiis laudabiliores sunt qui alios bene regunt, quam qui secundum alienam directionem bene se habent. In speculativa enim majus est veritatem aliis docendo tradere, quam quod ab aliis docetur, capere posse; in artificiis etiam majus aestimatur, majorique conducitur pretio architector qui aedi-

In the same way, we find order among men. For those who excel in intelligence, are naturally rulers; whereas those who are less intelligent, but strong in body, seem made by nature for service, as Aristotle says in his *Politics.* The statement of Solomon is in agreement with this: *The fool shall serve the wise;* as also the words of *Exodus* (xviii, 21, 22): *Provide out of all the people wise men such as fear God . . . who may judge the people at all times.*[56]

But he adds that it is better for the political community be so arranged that it is possible that the same should rule always. For this is possible when in any state men are found more excellent than others, through whom it will be best that the state is always ruled.[57]

And since the counsellor rules him who receives his counsels and in a sense governs him, it is said (Prov. xvii, 2) that *a wise servant shall rule over foolish sons.*[58]

The Angel of the Schools was certainly no devotee of leveling. For him society was graded because the universe was graded. From the inert clod which was lifeless matter, to Pure Act which

ficium disponit, quam artifex qui secundum ejus dispositionem manualiter operatur; et in rebus bellicis majorem gloriam de victoria consequitur (1) prudentia ducis quam militis fortitudo. Sic autem se habet rector multitudinis in his quae a singulis secundum virtutem sunt agenda, sicut doctor in disciplinis, et architector in aedificiis, et dux in bellis."

56. *Con. Gen.,* Lib. III, cap. 81: "Ex eadem ratione, et inter ipsos homines ordo invenitur; nam illi qui intellectu praeeminent naturaliter dominantur; illi vero qui sunt intellectu deficientes, corpore vero robusti, a natura videntur instituti ad serviendum, sicut Aristoteles dicit in sua *Politica,* I, c. v; cui etiam concordat sententia Solomonis, qui dicit: Qui *stultis est serviet sapienti,* Proverb. xi, 29; et dicitur; *Provide de omni plebs viros sapientes et timentes Deum . . . qui judicent populum omni tempore,* Exod. xviii, 21-22."

57. *Politicorum,* Lib. II, lect. 1: "Subjungit autem quod melius est quod ita disponatur civitas, politica, si possibile sit quod iidem semper principentur. . . . Hoc enim dicit esse possibile quando in aliqua civitate inveniuntur aliqui viri multum aliis excellentiores per quos optimum erit ut semper civitas regatur."

58. *Con. Gen.,* III, cap. 81: "Et, quia consilians regit eum qui consilium accipit et quodammodo si cominatur, dicitur quod *servus sapiens dominabitur filiis stultis."* (Prov. xvii, 2.)

was God, rose the hierarchy of creation,[59] a vast structure of bewildering beauty wherein the imperfect was for the sake of the perfect,[60] the less noble for the sake of nobility,[61] and diversity for the sake of perfection.[62] To Aquinas, multiplicity never meant mass, but beauty, for variety was always unified.[63] Subordination never meant subjection, nor service imperfection, because inequality was never a defect.[64] It was creation beautified. To St. Thomas contemplating the Divine, creation was the overflow of Divinity. As such it could be none other than *being*, perfected.[65]

59. *Summa Theol.*, I, q. 108-109.

60. *Summa Theol.*, II, II, q. 64, art. 1: "In rerum autem ordine imperfectiora sunt propter perfectiora: sicut etiam in generationis via natura ab imperfectis ad perfecta procedit."

61. *Summa Theol.*, I, q. 65, art. 2: "Sic igitur et in partibus universi, unaquaeque creatura est propter suum proprium actum et perfectionem. Secundo autem, creaturae ignobiliores sunt propter nobiliores; sicut creaturae quae sunt infra hominem, sunt propter hominem. Ulterius autem, singulae creaturae sunt propter perfectionem totius universi."

62. *Summa Theol.*, I, q. 65, art. 2, ad. 3: "Sicut enim artifex eiusdem generis lapides in diversis partibus aedificii ponit absque iniustitia, non propter aliquam diversitatem in lapidibus praecedentem, sed attendens ad perfectionem totius aedificii, quae non esset nisi lapides, diversimodi in aedificio collocarentur; sic et Deus a principio, ut esset perfectio in universo, diversas et inaequales creaturis instituit, secundum suam sapientiam, absque iniustitia, nulla tamen praesupposita meritorum diversitate."

63. *Summa Theol.*, I, q. 108, art. 2: "Non autem esset multitudo ordinata, sed confusa, si in multitudine diversi ordines non essent. Ipsa ergo ratio hierarchiae requirit ordinum diversitatem."

64. *Summa Theol.*, I, q. 96, art. 3, ad. 3: "Causa disparitatis poterat esse et ex parte Dei, non quidem ut puniret quosdam et quosdam praemiaret; sed ut quosdam plus, quosdam minus sublimaret, ut pulchritudo ordinis magis in hominibus reluceret. Et etiam ex parte naturae poterat disparitas causari absque aliquo defectu naturae."

65. *Con. Gen.*, Lib. III, cap. 71: "Perfecta bonitas in rebus creatis non inveniretur, nisi esset ordo bonitatis in eis, ut scilicet quaedam sint aliis meliora; non enim implerentur omnes gradus possibiles bonitatis, neque etiam aliqua creatura Deo assimilaretur quantum ad hoc quod alteri emineret; tolleretur etiam summus decor a rebus, si ab eis ordo distinctorum et disparium tolleretur, et quod est amplius, tolleretur multitudo a rebus, inaequalitate bonitatis sublata, quum, per differentias quibus res ab invicem differunt, unum altero melius exsistat, sicut animatum inanimato et rationale irrationali, et sic, si aequalitas omnimodo esset in rebus, non esset nisi unum bonum creatum, quod manifeste perfectioni derogat creaturae. Gradus autem bonitatis superior est ut aliquid sit bonum quod non possit deficere a bonitate; inferior autem eo est quod potest a bonitate deficere. Utrumque igitur gradum bonitatis perfectio universi requirit." Cf. *Summa Theol.*, I, q. 47, art. 2.

6. HIERARCHY DEMANDS COMPENSATION

But though inequality adds beauty and perfection to the universe it must ever play in the human hierarchy an accidental role. There may be grades of offices but there are never grades of men. Men differ only in externals, and though that difference may never be lightly cast aside, neither may it rank men according to their substantial nature. Substantially men form one hierarchy, and though that hierarchy admits of diverse orders,[66] those orders relate to function and never to substance. If inequality demands that human society be a hierarchy, equality demands that such hierarchy submit to compensation. And rightly so. For if the social hierarchy is built of social function, social function in turn is meant for service. "Unto whomsoever much is given much shall be required,"[67] was meant for time as well as eternity.

In the hierarchy of creation the imperfect may exist for the perfect, the less honorable for the sake of high dignity, but there must always be the reverse order. As every ascending scale must have its corresponding descent, nobility would not be noble, and honor would be truly base, were the ministrations of the lowly not transformed into ennobling services by those of high degree. As the chemical serves the plant only to be lifted to the biological, and the plant serves the animal only to be raised to the sensitive, and the animal serves man only to be elevated to the rational, so men of lesser gift and function minister to those of high degree, only to be in turn benefited by the overflow of richer capabilities. Reciprocity permeates all creation. From the creature in adoration before the Creator, from Whom flows the plentitude of all being and goodness, down through the angelic hierarchies into the human and corporeal levels, preëminence of being and richness of gift were lavished only to be shared. Human pride and arrogance, human selfishness and disdain are but the barriers of the creature blocking the ministrations of the Divine.

---

66. *II Sent.*, d. 9, q. 1, art. 3, ad. 2-ad. 3: "Omnes homines sunt unius speciei; et ideo in omnibus est unus modus communis recipiendi divinas illuminationes, et propter hoc omnium est hierarchia una . . . in nostra hierarchia distinguuntur ordines secundum tres actiones hierarchicas."
67. *St. Luke*, xii, 48.

God made the world diverse, because no one grade of goodness could sufficiently manifest the Infinite.[68] And He made the diverse greater and less not only to unify and show forth the perfection of His handiwork, but in order that from nothingness to the Infinite there might stretch a ladder of creation, a symbol of the creature's ascent to the Creator. Those at the bottom reach God through those above, and in return, through those above, God reaches those below. Thus is creation unified and made interdependent. Those of greater gift are given high place that they may bring the "little ones" to God, and God to the "little ones," never for their own glorification.

What is true of all degrees of being is likewise true of man. Himself, a compound of ascending powers, wherein the vegetative and the sense serve the rational that the rational may direct the whole to its end, man must fall into a like relation with his fellows. In the family, the parent holds to the child a place of honor, only that his superiority may compensate for the feeble powers of youth. In the economic world, the employer ranks above the employee, only that his greater acumen directing the business as a whole, may bring the worker's powers to fruition. The professions rank above commerce, only that superior wisdom may spiritualize the material pursuits of men. In civil society, the ruler merits the high esteem of his subjects, only that his far-seeing vision may bring social peace to the rank and file of mankind. High dignity must always be compensated for by greater duty. It is the recognition of this fact that makes the great truly humble. Such is the divine plan of creation, and such is the teaching of its most brilliant exponent:

> If one man surpassed another in knowledge and virtue, this would not have been fitting unless these gifts conduced to the benefit of others, according to I Pet. iv, 10, *As every man hath received grace, ministering the same one to another.*

68. *Summa Theol.*, I, q. 47, art. 1: "Unde dicendum est quod distinctio rerum et multitudo est ex intentione primi agentis, quod est Deus. Produxit enim res in esse propter suam bonitatem communicandam creaturis, et per eas repraesentandam. Et quia per unam creaturam sufficienter repraesentari non potest, produxit multas creaturas diversas, ut quod deest uni ad repraesentandam divinam bonitatem, suppleatur ex alia: nam bonitas quae in Deo est simpliciter et uniformiter, in creaturis est multipliciter et divisim."

Wherefore Augustine says (de Civ. Dei xix, 14): Just men command not by the love of domineering, but by the service of counsel; and thus did God make man.[69]

But whereas superiority of office based on greater endowment begets humility and service, inferiority in high places breeds arrogance and contempt. Lacking the gifts that befit the office, such occupants cannot serve, and cannot as a consequence command respect from those below. Turning subordination into subjection they are compelled to force honor from the subjected by feigning a superiority they do not possess. Thus is disorder introduced into the social hierarchy and reciprocity thrown out of balance. The "fool set in high dignity,"[70] drew from the pen of Aquinas these words:

And just as in the works of one man there is disorder through the intellect being obsequious to the sensual faculty; while the sensual faculty, through the indisposition of the body, is drawn to the movement of the body, as instanced in those who limp; so, too, in human government disorder results from a man being set in authority, not on account of his excelling in intelligence, but because he has usurped the government by bodily force, or has been appointed to rule through motives of sensual affection.[71]

True greatness, on the other hand, though fully aware of its superior talents, recognizes them as gifts entailing heavier responsibilities and greater services to those less plenteously endowed.

69. *Summa Theol.*, I, q. 96, art. 4: "Si unus homo habuisset super alium supereminentiam scientiae et iustitiae, inconveniens fuisset nisi hoc exequeretur in utilitatem aliorum; secundum quod dicitur I *Pet.* iv: Unusquisque gratiam quam accepit in alterutrum illam administrantes. Unde Augustinus dicit, XIX *de Civ. Dei*, quod *iusti non dominandi cupiditate imperant, sed officio consulendi: hoc naturalis ordo praescribit, ita Deus hominem condidit*.

70. *Eccles.*, x, 6.

71. *Con. Gen.*, Lib. III, cap. 81: "Sicut autem, in operibus unius hominis, ex hoc inordinatio provenit quod intellectus sensualem virtutem sequitur, sensualis vero virtus, propter corporis indispositionem, trahitur ad corporis motum ut in claudicantibus apparet; ita, et in regimine humano, inordinatio provenit ex eo quod non propter intellectus praeeminentiam aliquis praeest, sed vel robore corporali dominium sibi usurpat, vel propter sensualem affectionem aliquis ad regendum praeficitur."

Such men are filled, not with the sense of their own importance, but of their lowliness. They thus minister to those below them, not condescendingly but humbly, comparing themselves with those whom they serve, not with an eye to their own superior endowments, but to their own emptiness. The truly great possess a humility, which in the words of a modern writer, "does not fly great deeds but strengthens magnanimity in making men tend to sublime actions humbly."[72]

Humility and service are thus the factors that compensate for the social differences of men. Those differences owing their origin to the human inequalities out of which the social hierarchy has been constructed, demand compensation. Nor is the demand unjust. Human inequalities touch men only in their accidentals, never in their essential nature. If then men are essentially equal, accidental inequality cannot grade men without in some way compensating them for the offense suffered by their nature. In humble service is such compensation offered, and the offering helps to usher in the reign of justice.

7. THE SOCIAL HIERARCHY AND JUSTICE

Though the social hierarchy may grade men according to their inequalities, such grading is based only on man's relation to the social whole. That relation connects man with his fellows along the vertical plane. Man, however, is related to his fellowmen horizontally as well as vertically; but whereas, vertically man is linked with other men in virtue of the relation of inequality, horizontally such linking is effected by means of the relation of equality. In the social structure, therefore, man stands at the intersection of two planes. On the one he treats with the community on the basis of legal and distributive justice; on the other he treats with the individual members as equals on the basis of commutative justice.

72. R. Garrigou Legrange, "Humility According to St. Thomas," *Thomist*, I (1939).

Now justice is a kind of equality.[73] St. Thomas defines it as "the perpetual and constant will to render each one his right."[74] It is, therefore, essentially a virtue "ad alterum."[75] It implies two terms, two extremes, creditor and debtor. When these two are made equal there is a relation of justice between them. When the relation is unequal injustice is said to prevail. Now right, the object of justice, is a sort of medium or mean in regard to both extremes. It is the *just* because it holds between them a middle position.[76] It is that which is due the creditor on the one hand, and that which is owed by the debtor on the other. When relations between these two are so adjusted that the *debitum* equals the *acceptum,* equality or justice prevails.[77]

Now equality is twofold, equality of quantity, and equality of proportion.[78] The former is effected when the medium of equality falls within an arithmetical series; it is exactly measurable. The latter requires that equality be mediated through a geometrical series. It is determined, not by an exact value, but by a relationship of proportion.[79] Arithmetical equality obtains when each of the parties concerned receives his exact due, that is, the equal of

73. *Summa Theol.,* II, II, q. 57, art. 1: "Justitiae proprium est inter alias virtutes ut ordinet hominem in his quae sunt ad alterum. Importat enim aequalitatem quandam, ut ipsum nomen demonstrat. . . ." Cf. *Ethicorum,* Lib. V, lect. 4. *IV Sent.,* d. 44, q. 1, art. 1.

74. *Summa Theol.,* II, II, q. 58, art. 1.

75. *Summa Theol.,* II, II, q. 58, art. 2: ". . . cum nomen iustitiae aequalitatem importat ex sua ratione iustitia habet quod sit ad alterum: nihil enim est sibi aequale, sed alteri."

76. *Summa Theol.,* II, II, q. 57, art. 1: "Et propter hoc specialiter iustitia prae aliis virtutibus determinatur secundum se obiectum quod vocatur iustum. Et hoc quidem est ius." *Ibid.,* art. 2: "Ius, sive iustum, est aliquod opus adaequatum alteri secundum aliquem aequalitatis modum." Cf. P. N. Zammelt, "The Concept of Right According to Aristotle and St. Thomas," *Angelicum* (1939).

77. Joseph McSorley, "Christian Ideas of Justice and Equality," *Catholic University Bulletin,* IV (1898), pp. 88-114.

78. *II Sent.,* d. 27, q. 1, art. 3: "Est enim duplex aequalitas, scilicet aequalitas quantitatis et aequalitas proportionis."

79. *IV. Sent.,* d. 32, q. 1, art. 3: ". . . duplex est aequalitas; scilicet quantitatis et proportionis. Aequalitas quidem quantitatis est quae attenditur inter duas quantitates eiusdem mensuris, sicut bicubiti ad bicubitum; sed aequalitas proportionis est quae attenditur inter duas proportiones eiusdem speciei, sicut dupli ad duplum."

what he has given.[80] Geometrical equality, or equality of proportion, on the other hand, does not consist in a strict mathematical equality, as when the *debitum* equals the *acceptum,* but only in a proportional equality. One receives, not the equal of what he has given, but in proportion either to his merits or his needs.[81]

Now since justice implies equality, these two types of equality constitute two modes of justice. Arithmetical equality is involved in commutative justice, and geometrical equality is involved in legal and distributive justice.[82] The first governs the relations between individuals and is effected by the exchange of equivalent values. It is, in the words of St. Thomas, the justice "necessary to equalize thing with thing, so that one person should pay back to the other just so much as he has become richer out of that which belonged to the other."[83] Legal and distributive justice, on the other hand, operate on a proportional basis. The former obliges the individual to contribute according to his ability to the common good; the latter obliges the State to distribute its benefits among the citizens in proportion to their needs and functions.

Now since the function of justice is to render to every one his due, thereby equating obligation and right, or *debitum* and *jus,* such equation may involve relations of man with other men taken singly, or to society as a whole. If the former, the equation falls on the horizontal plane of human relations; if the latter, it will be found on the vertical one. Since horizontally man is related to

---

80. *Summa Theol.,* II, II, q. 61, art. 2: "Et ideo oportet adaequare rem rei: ut quanto iste plus habet quam suum sit de eo quod est alterius, tantundem restituat ei cuius est. Et sic fit aequalitas secundum *arithmeticam* medietatem. . . ." Cf. *Ethicorum,* Lib. V, lect. 6.

81. *Summa Theol.,* II, II, q. 61, art. 2: "Et ideo in iustitia distributiva non accipitur medium secundum aequalitatem rei ad rem, sed secundum proportionem rerum ad personas: ut scilicet, sicut una persona excedit aliam, ita etiam res quae datur uni personae excedit rem quae datur alii. Et ideo dicit Philosophus quod tale medium est secundum geometricam proportionalitatem, in quae attenditur aequale non secundum quantitatem, sed secundum proportionem. Sicut si dicamus quod sicut se habent sex ad quattuor, ita se habent tria ad duo, quia utrobique est sesquialtera proportio. . . ." Cf. *Ethicorum,* Lib. V, lect. 5.

82. *II Sent.,* d. 27, q. 1, art. 3: "Justitia commutativa respicit aequalitatem arithmeticam, quae tendit in aequalitatem quantitatis, justitia vero distributiva aequalitatem respicet geometricam, quae est aequalitas proportionis."

83. *Summa Theol.,* II, II, q. 61, art. 2.

his fellows as to an equal, and vertically as a part to the whole, the species of justice will differ for each plane. Between the whole and the part there can never be strict equality. Such equality as exists between them will have to be on the basis of geometrical proportion. Legal and distributive justice operate, therefore, on the vertical plane; but since between the parts arithmetical equality is possible, commutative justice operates on the horizontal plane.

Man stands at the juncture of these two planes because in his specific nature he is the equal of every other member of society, and in his individual nature he differs from every other member. This twofold relationship provides him with a double set of rights, making him the subject of a dual system of justice. The one regulates his contributions to and his claims upon society, thereby adjusting the relations between whole and part. The other regulates the transactions between the parts themselves. In accordance with the former, legal justice exacts from each citizen his due contribution to the common good, and distributive justice effects its proper distribution, each part receiving a share in proportion to the importance of its function in society. Instead of a parity between *debitum* and *jus,* there is substituted a proportion between the part shared and the personal importance of the one sharing. In other words, *jus* is to *debitum* as *social function* is to *common good.* Since the individual contributions to the common good differ, the individual claims upon society likewise differ. Those claims, therefore, must be regulated not only according to human need, but according to the importance of the contributing parts as well. Since the parts are persons, the equation operating in legal and distributive justice is the equation between person and thing.[84] Taparelli aptly illustrates the case as follows:

> Let us suppose two or more individuals associating in a common end, as some mariners bent on discovering a foreign land;

---

84. *Summa Theol.,* II, II, p. 61, art. 2: "In distributiva justitia datur aliquid alicui privatae personae inquantum id quod est totius est debitum parti. Quod quidam tanto maius est quanto ipsa pars maiorem principalitatem habet in toto. Et ideo in distributiva iustitia tanto plus alicui de bonis communibus datur quanto illa persona maiorem principalitatem habet in communitate." Cf. *Ethicorum,* Lib. V, lect. 4.

if they should dispute concerning preëminence, or for any office, would it be necessary to give each the same function? Would equality of quantity here be the rule of justice? That would be a ridiculous and impossible thing. In such a case equality ought to consist in a certain proportion of function to capacity, of recompense to merit, of chastisement to fault. The real order ought to correspond as nearly as possible to the ideal proportion of means to end; in this order each ought to contribute by a different means to the common good which all propose.[85]

In commutative justice, on the other hand, the commutations or transactions between the parts are regulated on the basis of strict arithmetical equality. *Jus* is to *debitum* as *part* is to *part*. Hence commutative justice is concerned with the equality of things. That given must be the equal of that received, if parity is to be obtained. Since the *jus* and the *debitum* are equal, the *debitum* and the *acceptum* must also be equal.[86]

Because of specific equality, therefore, men in their bargaining power one with another are equal. Hence justice between them must be on the basis of strict arithmetical equality. One receives from another the exact equivalent of what he gives. When this is done commutative justice is served. Because of individual inequality, on the other hand, men hold different positions in the State. Justice, therefore, must be regulated on the basis of proportional equality. Men contribute to the common good on the basis of capacity, and they partake of that good in proportion both to need and social function. When this is the case, legal and distributive justice are served. Only where a State treats with its members on the basis of legal and distributive justice, and the members treat with one another on the basis of commutative justice, does peace abide, for peace is the fruit of justice.

85. Le R. P. Taparelli D'Azeglio, *Droit Naturel* (Paris: 1857), t. 1, p. 203.

86. *Summa Theol.*, II, II, q. 61, art. 2: "Sed in commutationibus redditur aliquid alicui singulari personae propter rem eius quae accepta est; ut maxime patet in emptione et venditione, in quibus primo invenitur ratio commutationis et ideo oportet adaequare rem rei: ut quanto iste plus habet quam suum sit de eo quod est alterius, tantundem restituat ei cuius est." Cf. *Ethicorum*, Lib. V, lect. 4.

8. The Social Hierarchy and Peace

The function of equality and inequality in man's social life is evident. The one unifies men, the other grades them, thus forming the social hierarchy or civil society. The nature of that society is determined by the nature of men, but its formation is the work of man's free will. Though man is by nature social, in the fulfillment of his social urge he is free. Just as with matrimony, men do not specify its nature, but merely cause it to arise, so too with civil society. The social hierarchy, therefore, although the structure most natural to human society, is nevertheless called into being voluntarily by men. Since the obligation placed upon man to attain his end is a moral obligation, and not a physical one, the use of the means necessary for that attainment is likewise a moral necessity. Man is at all times physically free, both as regards his end, and the means thereto. And since that end lies outside society, which has only the character of a means, man is subordinated to society only to the extent that an agent is subordinated to the means necessary to achieve his purpose. Consequently, the order in human society, although hierarchic is never organic. Man submits to the order freely and in part. For that reason the unity of the social hierarchy is not the unity of a substantial being, but a unity of order.[87]

It is this unity of order that generates peace, for peace is the work of order. Indeed, St. Augustine who made peace the fundamental aim of society, defines it as the *tranquillity of order*.[88] Such definition gives to peace two elements, one negative, the absence of conflict, and one positive, the presence of order. Now order, both to St. Augustine and St. Thomas, is "the distribution which allots things equal and unequal each to its own place."[89]

87. *Ethicorum*, Lib. I, lect. 1: "Sciendum est autem quod hoc totum, quod est civilis multitudo . . . habet solam unitatem ordinis secundum quam non est aliquid simpliciter unum."

88. St. Augustine, *De Civitate Dei* (trans. by M. Dod; Edinburgh: T. & T. Clark, 1888), XIX, p. 13.

89. St. Thomas, *Matt.*, C. 5: ". . . ordo autem est parium dispariumque sua cuique loca tribuens disposito." Cf. St. Augustine, *De Civ. Dei*, XIX, p. 13.

When everything is in its own proper place, it is evident there can be neither contention nor discord, neither conflict nor opposition. Where each receives that which is his due, justice prevails, and likewise peace, the fruit of justice.[90]

Order, therefore, implies distinction of things, and *tranquillity* of order that such things be established and fixed each within the limits of its nature.[91] For a thing to be assigned a place out of due proportion to its nature, for it to be in danger of displacement by the invasion of another, may leave a certain semblance of order intact, but tranquillity will have fled. For ordered concord there must be unity. As every being is one, unless the parts function as parts and conspire to effect a single whole, there will be no whole, but only disgregate units. Tranquillity is in proportion to unity, and where there is unity there is peace.[92] True unity, however, is intrinsic. It is a oneness flowing from nature, not a union imposed from without. There is unity of a sort in flocks and herds, but though animals may congregate from an instinct of nature, oneness of place is external and contingent. Likewise, union among men can never be a thing of force. Such order as would ensue would be a pseudo order, issuing into a pseudo peace, because based on a pseudo unity. To be genuine it must be in accordance with man's free nature. It must be a thing not of compulsion, but of rational choice.

> If one man concord with another, not of his own accord, but through being forced as it were, by the fear of some evil that besets him, such concord is not really peace, because the order

90. *Summa Theol.*, II, II, q. 29, art. 3, ad. 3.
91. St. Thomas, *De Divinis Nominibus*, XI, lect. 1: "Unitas autem pacis in tranquillitate ordinis consistit, ut Augustinus dicit XIX De Civ. Dei; ad quam quidem tranquillitatem ordinis tres requiruntur. Primo quidem, ut invicem distinguantur; non potest esse ordo nisi distinctorum, et ideo dicit quod omnia definit. Secundo, necesse est ad tranquillitatem ordinis ut rerum distinctarum nulla exeat limitem suae naturae, et ad hoc pertinet quod dicit: 'Terminat.' Tertio, requiritur quae haec definitio, et terminatio stabilitur, et ad hoc pertinet quod dicit: 'et firmat.' Alioquin si rerum definitio et terminatio non esset firma, sed una res a termino suo egrediens, alterius fines invaderet, confunderetur ordo rerum, et sic non esset tranquillitas ordinis."
92. *Ibid.*: "Idem: Sic igitur ad rationem, pacem duo concurrunt: primo quidem quod aliqua sint unita; secundo, quod concordent ad unum."

of each concordant is not observed, but is distributed by some fear-inspiring cause.[93]

Tranquillity of order, or peace, entails something more than external agreement. "Concord is not peace," says St. Thomas, "for even the wicked may concur."[94] Above the union of appetites among various persons, there is needed a union of appetites in one man.[95] Social peace, therefore, has its origin and its preservation in the individual man. Man is a hierarchy of appetites and functions. Where these are rightly ordered, where the lower conforms to the dictates of reason, and the rational directs the whole, peace reigns in the human heart. But when the appetites are disordered, where feelings and emotions displace intellect and will, there ensues a conflict of desires within the human breast, and, consequently, a loss of peace. Social harmony is begotten of individual harmony, and as the latter is the concord of *rational* appetites, so also must be the former. Social unity organized on the basis of human feeling is destined for the rocks. The mob engaged in lynching is an eloquent example of oneness of feeling, but a more eloquent example of social turbulence. The peace of society must mirror the peace of the human heart if it is to be genuine and enduring. It will be so mirrored when there is a union of rational wills. Then will men take their place in society on the basis of inferiority and superiority, that is, where function in the social whole is according to capacity.

If justice is the virtue that gives to each his due, peace is the fruit of justice only when every one in his proper place acquits himself of those obligations demanded of him both by society as a whole and its manifold parts. Yet for *tranquillity* of order, justice is not sufficient. Peace demands charity as well. Peace is order, and order is unity, and love unifies. Where there is unity, there

---

93. *Summa Theol.*, II, II, q. 29, art. 1, ad. 1: "Si enim homo concordet cum alio non spontanea voluntate, sed quasi coactus timore alicuius mali imminentis, talis concordia non est pax; quia non servatur ordo utriusque concordantis, sed perturbatur ab aliquo timorem inferente."

94. *Summa Theol.*, II, II, q. 29, art. 1, *sed contra.*

95. *Summa Theol.*, II, II, q. 29, art. 1: "Haec autem unio non est de ratione concordiae. Unde concordia importat unionem appetituum diversorum appetentium: pax autem supra hanc unionem, importat etiam appetituum unius appetentis unionem."

must be something that ordains to oneness. In the individual man,
the direction of appetites to one common end, the good of the
whole man, is productive of right order; but the good of the whole
man is none other than God, and naught but love of Him orders
human desire. Hence, just as love of God brings order and peace
into the human heart, so it brings tranquillity of order to society.
Men love their fellowmen in proportion as they love God; and in
proportion as they love one another, do they give to each his due.[96]
Charity is a bond uniting hearts, and of the union is born justice,
the parent of tranquillity. The inequality of men, therefore, brings
diversity into human society. Now diversity implies order, and
order unity. But unity is begotten of love, and justice of charity.
It signifies equality for the command "Love thy neighbor as
thyself," would hardly have been imposed on men, were men not
equal. As inequality calls forth humility, equality calls forth
charity. From both come justice which gives to society tranquillity of order or peace.

That peace is the result of order is nowhere more fittingly told
than in these graphic words of St. Augustine:

> The peace of the body, then, is the ordered regulation of the
> parts. The peace of the irrational soul, the ordered repose
> of the appetites. The peace of the rational soul, the ordered
> harmony of knowledge and action. The peace of the body
> with the soul, the ordered life and safety of a living creature.
> The peace of mortal man with God, the ordered obedience in
> faith to the eternal law. The peace of men, ordered concord.
> The peace of the home, the ordered concord of those members
> of the family who rule with those who are ruled. The peace
> of the city, the ordered concord of those citizens who rule
> with those who are ruled. The peace of the celestial city, the

96. *Summa Theol.*, II, II, q. 29, art. 3: Duplex unio est de ratione
pacis . . . quarum una est secundum ordinationem propriorum appetituum
in unum; alia vero est secundum unionem appetitus proprii cum appetitu
alterius. Et utramque unionem efficit caritas. Primam quidem unionem,
secundum quod Deus diligitur ex toto corde, ut scilicet omnia referamus
in ipsum: et sic omnes appetitus nostri in unum feruntur. Aliam vero,
prout diligimus proximum sicut nosipsos, ex quo contingit quod homo vult
implere voluntatem proximi sicut et sui ipsius. Et propter hoc inter
amicabilia unum ponitur identitas electionis: ut patet in IX *Ethic.*; et Tul-
lius dicit, in libro *de Amicitia, quod amicorum est idem velle et nolle.*"

most ordered and most harmonious fellowship of enjoying God and one another in God. The peace of all things, the tranquillity of order.[97]

Such tranquillity of order is the natural consequence of social hierarchy. Not only is that hierarchy constructed by the "proper disposition of parts, both equal and unequal, each to its own place," but it is constructed with the free assent of men, who by rendering compensatory services one to another, bring about that ordered concord which is the essence of peace.

The relations of substantial equality and inequality which men bear to one another, far from bringing discord into human society, flower into social peace when men are arranged in due order. It is not, therefore, the presence of inequality in social life that foments discord, but an inequality which flows from a lack of due order. Men are unequal by nature, and inequality demands order. When that order is disarranged, when it violates the proper allocation of the parts, or is lacking in just compensations demanded by essential equality, then do discord and conflict enter into social life. When inferiority dominates, when superiority is leveled, when social organization is arbitrarily imposed, then "ordered concord" disappears, and peace vanishes from the ranks of men. When, on the other hand, men follow the dictates of nature and arrange themselves in such fashion that the less functions for the greater, and the greater aids the less, such dove-tailing of superiority and inferiority generates "ordered concord" which constitutes tranquillity of order or peace. Only when equality unifies and inequality is ordered, does peace result. And these three, unity, order, peace, constitute in human society the common good, through which men best attain their final goal.

9. LIBERTY, EQUALITY AND FRATERNITY

The modern slogan, *Liberty, Equality* and *Fraternity,* is not a mere shibboleth concocted to play upon the emotions of the unthinking. Regardless of the degree to which it may have been flaunted by its extreme advocates, or the scorn heaped upon it by

97. St. Augustine, *De Civ. Dei*, XIX, 13.

reactionaries, it is a slogan that expresses a triple endowment of human nature that cannot be denied. Men are free in the very depths of their nature, and since that nature is the same in all men, they are likewise equal in the very depths of their nature, and for that reason equally free. The common possession of a free nature is the basis of fraternity. As brothers of the same flesh are not servile one to another, but equally free as sons of a common father, so brothers of the great family of mankind, sons in truth of the eternal Father, are equally free, for He made them members of a common species possessing one and the same rational nature. Fraternity is born of the union of equality and freedom. These two are not antithetical but complementary, and they issue into brotherhood, not by external conditions imposed from without, but because natures, equally endowed with the initial gift of freedom, find in one another their fulfillment.

Though fraternity is rooted in equality, it is not divorced, therefore, from inequality. Oneness of nature and equality of end bind men together. Such bond induces men to speedily aid a less favored brother, and out of that aid there issues a stronger bond, the bond of love, for love is born of giving not of receiving. Inequality, therefore, makes giving possible; but equality makes it obligatory. In the one, brotherhood finds a reason; in the other, a bond strengthened by love.

10. POLITICAL EQUALITY

A. *The Source and Limitation of Civil Power*

The origin of civil authority is closely bound up with the fact of human equality. Save the divine right of kings, the theory of political power has always in some way taken its inception in the notion of men as equal. Leaving aside for the present the vagaries of such theory, it is safe to say that the essential equality of men lies at the foundation of civil power. No one saw this with clearer vision than St. Augustine for whom the notion of human equality provided the basis for curtailing the powers of government and upholding the supremacy of law. Among the ancients, because the doctrine of inalienable rights was unknown and law was a thing of will, political power was absolute. There was nothing to restrain either the will of the monarch or the multitude. Against this tide of absolutism there was lifted the strong pen of Augustine, who might be justly styled the Father of Democracy. Though democracy as a method flourished in ancient Athens, as a principle it was ushered in with Augustine, for whom the doctrine of human equality set a limit to governmental power. To the ancient, justice was synonymous with force. That was right which the will of the monarch or the multitude proclaimed. To the Christian all this was changed, for human law must ever bow to the precepts of the divine. Augustine was one of the first to show the divine basis of human authority, and the reason for that basis was to be had in the doctrine of human equality. To Augustine that equality referred to specific nature and its end. Since all men are equal in nature, man has only the right to command himself and creatures below him. His authority stops short of his fellowmen.[98]

> He did not intend that His rational creature, who was made in His image, should have dominion over anything but the irrational creation, not man over man, but man over the beasts.[99]

The right of man to command men, therefore, must come from outside humanity. Hence it can have its origin only in God, Who has declared, "By Me kings reign, and lawgivers decree just things."[100] That St. Augustine sees the divine origin of civil power as the necessary consequence of human equality is clear from the following passage, where in substance, he says:

> It is thus that pride in its perversity apes God. It abhors equality with other men under Him; but instead of His rule it seeks to impose a rule of its own upon its equals.[101]

98. Gustave Combes, *La Doctrine Politique de Saint Augustin* (Paris: 1927), pp. 76-81.
99. *De Civ. Dei*, XIX, 15.
100. *Prov.*, viii, 15.
101. *De Civ. Dei*, XIX, 12.

It is this teaching that gives substance to the doctrine of inalienable rights and the supremacy of law. No man can impose his will upon his equals. The right of man to command men is forfeit, unless it be given him from above. The power of man to direct and coerce men comes to him through the natural law, which is the rational expression of the divine law. That being the case, the obligation imposed on man by the natural law to pursue his end, cannot be offset by any obligation emanating from the same source, and certainly not by any obligation short of the natural law. Law is a thing of reason, not a fiat of the will. The obligation imposed on man to attain his end carries with it the obligation to use the necessary means, among which means is civil society. It follows, therefore, that civil society must itself be limited by the natural law, whose instrument it is to lead human nature to its final perfection. The profound influence of the political thought of St. Augustine is succinctly summed up in these words of Father Millar:

> Not until it was recognized that all men are equal (specifically) in the sense that, having an inherent right to pursue an end that transcends the State, they have the consequent inherent right to all the necessary means to the attainment of that end, could it become clear on any intelligible grounds that they have, antecedent to all positive laws, inalienable rights which the State is bound to respect.[102]

It was this teaching that guided the political thinking of the Middle Ages. In the long drawn-out controversy between the Papacy and the Empire, these ideas continued to be clarified, until given adequate treatment and synthesis in the writings of St. Thomas. This peerless thinker, perceiving that equality of human nature precludes the subordination of one man to another in things touching that nature, clearly lays down the rules regarding the limit of human authority and civil power:

> . . . there are two reasons for which a subject may not be bound to obey his superior in all things. First, on account of

102. M. F. X. Millar, "St. Augustine and Political Theory," *Thought*, V, p. 278.

the command of a higher power. . . . Secondly, a subject is not bound to obey his superior if the latter commands him to do something wherein he is not subject to him. . . . Consequently in matters touching the internal movement of the will man is not bound to obey his fellow-man, but God alone.

Nevertheless man is bound to obey his fellow-man in things that have to be done externally by means of the body; and yet since by nature all men are equal, he is not bound to obey another man in matters touching the nature of the body. . . .[103]

That is, man need never submit to his fellowman in things pertaining directly to his human nature. His soul and his body are his own. The internal workings of his mind and will are subject to no jurisdiction but that of self. Consequently, the right to preserve his life, to marry or not marry, are outside the pale of another man's authority. Men are equal in nature and, therefore, in things pertaining to that nature, man never bows to the authority of his fellowman.[104] As regards his nature he submits only to God. In the accidentals of life men are unequal. In those things, therefore, *that have to be done externally by means of the body, man is bound to obey his fellowman.* In other words, whatever does not touch the sanctuary of man's nature may come under the jurisdiction of other men, when the common good so requires, and when authority is duly constituted. Thus civil power may not rescind man's right to property, since that right is grounded in man's nature; but it may regulate as to its just use, when lack of regulation imperils the common good. Man has a right to material

---

103. *Summa Theol.*, II, II, q. 104, art. 5: "Et similiter ex duobus potest contingere quod subditus suo superiori non teneatur in omnibus obedire. Uno modo, propter praeceptum maioris potestatis. . . . Alio modo, non tenetur inferior suo superiori obedire, si ei aliquid praecipiat in quo ei non subdatur. . . . Et ideo in his quae pertinent ad interiorem motum voluntatis, homo non tenetur homini obedire, sed solum Deo.

Tenetur autem homo homini obedire in his quae exterius per corpus sunt agenda. In quibus tamen etiam, secundum ea quae ad naturam corporis pertinent, homo homini obedire non tenetur, sed solum Deo, quia omnes homines natura sunt pares: puta in his quae pertinent ad corporis sustentationem et prolis generationem."

104. *Summa Theol.*, I, II, q. 93, art. 4: ". . . quae vero ad naturam hominis pertinent, non subduntur gubernationi humanae. . . ."

goods necessary to sustain him in frugal comfort, and in this right all men are equal. However, since men are unequal individually, that which constitutes the frugal comfort of one, may not constitute the frugal comfort of another.

Since in such externals as the quantity of material goods men differ, the State may impose its rule on men and stipulate a just amount. In those things, in which men are equal, they are autonomous, but in those things in which they are unequal, they must submit to the authority of civil power. St. Thomas sums the whole matter up briefly in the following passage, to which Cajetan adds a significant comment:

> Man is subject to God simply as regards all things, both internal and external, wherefore he is bound to obey Him in all things. On the other hand, inferiors are not subject to their superiors in all things, but only in certain things and in a particular way, in respect of which the superior stands between God and His subjects, whereas in respect to other matters the subject is immediately under God, by Whom he is taught either by the natural law or by the written law.[105]

> When you hear that men are equal according to nature, understand this not of the equality of dignity or nobility, for one is found naturally superior to another in mind and body, but rather of the equality of power, for no man has any power over another in those things which relate to nature.[106]

This is clear and consistent teaching, and it gives the only valid grounds for the doctrine of inalienable rights. These rights are not State conferred, but they should be State respected. They are

105. *Summa Theol.,* II, II, q. 104, art. 5, ad. 2: "Deo subiicitur homo simpliciter quantum ad omnia, et interiora et exteriora: et ideo in omnibus ei obedire tenetur. Subditi autem non subiiciuntur suis superioribus quantum ad omnia, sed quantum ad aliqua determinate. Et quantum ad illa, medii sunt inter Deum et subditos. Quantum ad alia vero, immediate subduntur Deo, a quo instruuntur per legem naturalem vel scriptam."
106. *Summa Theol.,* II, II, q. 104, art. 5: "Cum autem audis homines secundum naturam esse pares, intellige non de aequalitate dignatatis seu nobilitatis, quoniam et secundum animam et secundum corpus unus alio invenitur nobilior a natura; sed de aequalitate potestatis; quia nullus homo, in his quae ad naturam spectant, habet potestatem super alium." Cf. Cajetan, *Com.* in *Summa Theol.,* II, II, q. 104, art. 5.

the corollaries of a nature upon which the State may never impinge. But rights in the concrete, rights which differ according as men differ, are subject to State control, for the individual good must always give way to the common good. Such rights do not touch man in his essentials and, therefore, by the jurisdiction of the State may become greater or less, according as men are greater or less.

The relation of human equality to civil power received its fullest expression in the polemical writings of Bellarmine and Suarez. These two Jesuit thinkers, confronted with the absolutism of the Stuart kings, reëmphasized the traditional teaching of the supremacy of law, and the inviolability of natural rights which lay at the basis of the English system of government until democratic principles were undermined through the upheaval of the Protestant Revolution.

Attacking the theory of divine right upon which the English kings based their unrestricted power, Bellarmine and Suarez presented a strong defense of the democratic principle in civil society. That principle, they contended, places a limitation on civil power, which far from being omnicompetent, is restricted by the personal end of the individual members of society. Not only may it not interfere with that end, but it has the positive obligation of actively fostering it by providing the necessary material environment. This is sound doctrine. Since human nature demands civil society for the realization of its purpose, such society is restricted in the exercise of its power by the end for which it was called into being.

> Man by his very nature leans to civil society and supremely needs it for the proper conservation of life.[107]

> Political power . . . derives from the natural law, since it does not depend upon the consent of men; for willing or unwilling they must be ruled by some one, unless they wish the human race to perish, which is against the primary in-

107. Suarez, *Defensio Fidei Catholicae,* Lib. III, cap. 1: "Homo enim natura sua propensus est ad civilem societatem, eaque ad convenientem hujus vitae conservationem maxime indiget. . . ."

stincts of nature. But natural law is Divine Law, therefore, government was instituted by Divine Law.[108]

If civil society is called into being by a mandate of the natural law, it is not an arbitrary institution; hence it cannot claim an arbitrary use of power. As its power is divine in origin, it must be exercised for a divine purpose, to lead men to the end assigned them by the Creator. This may have been new to Stuart kings, but it was not new to pre-Reformation England as Father Millar indicated in this excerpt from the *Song of Lewes:*

> Let every king understand that he is the servant of God; let him love that only which is pleasing to Him, and let him seek His glory in ruling, not his own pride by despising his equals.[109]

Bellarmine and Suarez, so far, have but echoed the mind of Augustine and Thomas. The former based the divine origin of government on the fact of human equality; the latter insisted that political society, being a need of man's nature and not something extrinsic, bears to that nature the relation of a means. It must, therefore, serve the nature and not subject it by arbitrarily imposing on it decrees of its own. Bellarmine and Suarez carried this doctrine one step further and asked this question: "If political authority comes from God to whom does He give it directly, the community or the ruler?" The answer is unmistakable. Power is vested immediately in the multitude, for says Bellarmine, "in the absence of positive law there is no good reason why in a multitude of equals one rather than another should dominate."[110] Nor is Suarez any less uncertain when he writes:

---

108. *De Laicis,* cap. 6: ". . . politicam potestatem . . . est de jure naturae, non enim pendit ex consensu hominum: nam velint, nolint, debent regi ab aliquo, nisi velint perire humanum genus, quod est contra naturae inclinationem. At jus naturae est jus divinum. . . ."

109. *Song of Lewes* (trans. by L. E. Kingsford), quoted by M. F. X. Millar, "Do Politics Make Sense?" *Commonweal,* XXI, p. 387.

110. *De Laicis,* cap. 6: "Praeteria sublato jure positivo, non est major ratio cur ex multis aequalibus unus potius, quam alius dominetur."

> By nature all men are born free and therefore no one has political jurisdiction over another nor dominion; nor is there any reason *from nature* why this is attributed to one rather than another.[111]

God respects the natures He makes, and as He made human nature free, He gives to men the power to rule themselves; as He made that nature the same in all men, He will subject no man to another unless by his own free choice. Self-government is the demand of man's freedom, but it does not give any man the right to rule his equals. The power of the individual to rule himself is not the power of the individual to rule the multitude, regardless of how many times it may be multiplied. The same power numerically repeated does not constitute a new kind of power, for the simple reason that the individual good differs in kind from the common good, as the end differs from the means. For that reason, the power to direct to the common good is of a species different from the power that directs to the individual good. The power to rule the multitude, therefore, must come from outside humanity. Yet because men are free it must be vested in humanity, and because men are equal the choice of the one who is to exercise that power cannot fall upon one man more than another, unless that choice be the decision of the free wills of men. Such choice preserves man's liberty, and respects his equality.

As far as human equality is concerned, it matters little for all practical purposes whether political power be vested directly in the multitude or in the ruler designated by the multitude. *Designation by the people* or *transfer by the people* is a disputed point, the solution of which lies outside the present study. If vested in the multitude, then it must be transferred to the ruler by the free consent of men, "for the community cannot by itself exercise this power."[112] If vested in the ruler immediately by God, that ruler must be the free choice of men, before power is conferred.

111. Suarez, *Tractatus de Legibus,* Lib. III, cap. 2: ". . . quia ex natura rei omnes homines nascuntur liberi, et ideo nullus habet jurisdictionem politicam in alium, sicut nec dominium: neque est ulla ratio cur tribuatur ex natura rei his respectu illorum potius quam e converso."

112. *De Laicis,* cap. 6: ". . . nam Respublica non potest per seipsam exercere hanc potestatem. . . ."

> If it be held that the consent of the people is always a necessary pre-requisite to the assumption of political power by any person, it is of no practical significance whether the people be conceived as handing over to the ruler authority which God has deposited with them or as designating the person upon whom God will bestow authority nor does the ruler receive it, until the people have somehow given their consent.[113]

To which we might add, that the only valid reason for awaiting the consent of the people is out of respect for human equality. Since all men are equally free, God will not subject one man to the rule of another unless by his own consent. Hence whether power be vested according to *designation by the people* or *transfer by the people,* matters little if the people have the determining voice in appointing the wielder of power. If "to order for an end is the function of the being whose end it is,"[114] then rational creatures, whose peculiar characteristic it is to adapt means to an end, can hardly be denied that function in the ordering either of their individual or communal lives. That such function is the right either of the whole people or of someone designated by the people is the clear statement of St. Thomas:

> Now to order anything to the common good, belongs either to the whole people or to someone who is the vicegerent of the whole people. And therefore the making of a law belongs either to the whole people or to a public personage who has care of the whole people; since in all other matters the directing of anything to the end concerns him to whom the end belongs.[115]

113. John A. Ryan, *Catholic Doctrine on the Right of Self-Government* (New York: Paulist Press, 1919), p. 5.

114. *Summa Theol.,* I, II, q. 90, art. 3.

115. *Summa Theol.,* I, II, q. 90, art. 3: "Ordinare autem aliquid in bonum commune est vel totius multitudinis, vel alicuius gerentis vicem totius multitudinis. Et ideo condere legem vel pertinet ad totam multitudinem, vel pertinet ad personam publicam quae totius multitudinis curam habet. Quia et in omnibus aliis ordinare in finem est eius cuius est proprius ille finis."

The relation of equality to political power may be summarized in the following principles:

1. The equality of men demands that the right of man to command men must come from outside humanity, that is, it must come from God.

2. Men have by nature only the power to rule themselves. As this power is essentially different from the power to rule the multitude, such power cannot come from men, hence must come from God.

3. Since men are endowed with freedom, the power of ordering men to their end must be conferred on humanity.

4. As all men are *equally* free, that power must be vested either in the multitude or in someone designated by the multitude.

5. Since men are equal in nature, political jurisdiction must stop short of whatever touches that nature. As inalienable rights are the means whereby the nature attains its end, political authority not only cannot interfere with those rights, but has the positive duty of protecting them.

These principles are basic to democracy. It matters little whether the method by which they function be monarchic, aristocratic, or democratic, or a combination of all three. The principles must ever remain inviolate. The method by which they are administered may change according to the conditions in which men find themselves. The lower the development of a people, the more concentrated the power that directs them; the higher the development of a people, the more widely may power be disseminated, for it is with peoples as with individuals, as they mature in virtue and wisdom, so they grow in autonomy.

B. *Equality Before the Law*

When the all-wise and omnipotent Creator called natures into being, He did so with a purpose, and that purpose determined the kind of nature created. Between the nature and the end there is a divine proportion,[116] and having established that proportion, God indicated by a law which He implanted in the nature the line of action it must pursue to achieve the purpose of its creation.[117] What is true of natures in general is true of human nature, with this exception: that while the natures on the sub-human level attain their end through physical necessity, man, being free, is under no physical compulsion. Though he knows his end, and the line of action he must pursue to attain it, that attainment is for him a matter of free choice. This does not mean that man is free of obligation as regards his end. The natural law of his nature remains, and it obliges with a strict necessity. But that necessity in no way constrains man in his physical acts. Rather it binds his will with the knowledge that being a creature of God, his being is not absolutely his own. Man is, therefore, subject to a law which is beyond human power to rescind. Though he is physically free to obey it or defy it, he possesses no freedom to render it impotent. This law, placing a bond on a moral faculty, a faculty directed to an end through knowledge, is a moral law. Once man sees the connection between an act and his end, he is obliged by the law to perform the act or omit it according as he sees that act leading him to or away from his end. There are certain acts, therefore, which he ought to omit, and others which he ought to perform, if he is to realize the purpose of his creation, the perfect development of his nature in the knowledge and love of God. The obligation imposed by the law being solely moral, the power to fulfill it must likewise be moral. The mere physical power to perform the activities perfective of man's nature must be completed by a moral power sufficient to keep another from inhibiting one's physical acts. Such a moral power constitutes in man a right. It is a means given by the Creator to fulfill a divinely imposed obligation, for God cannot will an end without willing what is needful for the attainment of that end.

---

116. *Summa Theol.*, I, II, q. 95, art. 3: ". . . uniuscuiusque rei quae est propter finem, necesse est quod forma determinetur secundum proportionem ad finem. . . ."

117. *Summa Theol.*, I, II, q. 93, art. 5, ad. 1.

Rights, therefore, are basically grounded in law, the law of human nature. That nature, as we have seen, is a social nature. Man is dependent on his fellowman for the perfection of his powers and thus for the realization of his destiny. Though he is equal to his fellowman in nature, he differs from him as an individual, and to that extent needs his help. Yet equality of nature does confer a certain independence, for those of the same nature having the same end, subordination of one to another in the attainment of that end is automatically ruled out. Perceiving that others like himself **are** tending to the same goal, man must not, because of essential equality, interfere with those activities whereby another pursues his goal. The law of charity, imposing the duty of love of neighbor, is thus tied up with equality. Yet because of individual inequality that duty does not end with negative interference. Men are complementary precisely because one has what another lacks. Because all have the same nature and therefore the same end, man understands that he should act toward others as toward himself, and procure for them, as for himself, what each needs for the pursuit of his final goal.

Men are social, and the law of their nature demands that they perform those acts necessary to help another attain his end, and avoid those which hinder that attainment. Since men are free, this law can be only moral in character. Its execution, therefore, demands a moral power, a claim upon another that he abstain from inhibiting his neighbor in the pursuit of a divinely appointed goal, and a further claim that he actively assist that neighbor in such pursuit. Hence right implies a relation to another. It is a moral power in one that puts a bond on the will of another, constraining him to refrain from acts obstructive to man's fulfillment of his duties, or to place those acts auxiliary thereto. That bond is inviolable.[118] To break it is to break the natural moral law, and thus to place one's own end in jeopardy.

Broadly speaking rights are of two kinds, natural and positive, according as they are grounded in natural or positive law. Natural right is an essential property of man's nature, bestowed on the

---

118. Cronin, *op. cit.*, I, pp. 660-662. Cf. Francis P. LeBuffe, *Jurisprudence* (New York: Fordham University Press, 1938), p. 141.

nature by the moral law as the necessary means by which that
nature attains the end to which it is obligated. As human nature
is the same in every individual in which it is found, it follows that
the specific equality of men, entails the equality of specific rights.
If all are equally bound to pursue their end, all stand in equal need
of the necessary means. All are equally entitled to what is necessary to perfect the nature. In their specific rights, therefore, rights
grounded in the nature, men are equal. Such rights, involving
duties which men cannot forego, are inalienable. They may neither
be renounced by the individual nor curtailed by the State. Since
human nature is beyond the reach of political power, rights
intrinsic to the nature admit of no political interference. The
nature, in so far as it is a personal nature, with an end beyond the
State, is vested with rights which are personal rights, that is,
rights which are the means whereby the human person performs
those duties incumbent on him for the realization of his end. It is
these natural personal rights, safeguarding those functions which
transcend the State, that the State is bound to respect. Since the
State is a means deputed by nature to provide the material environment best conducive to human perfection, it has no authority to
rescind the powers of the nature whose servant it is.

When, however, we review such rights in their concrete setting,
they immediately take on the aspect of inequality, and fall under
the jurisdiction of the State. Men as individual members of a
species are unequal, and as such are graded in relation to the State.
Though man in his specific nature has the same generic end as
each of his fellows, as an individual he participates in that end
differently. Consequently, although he has in the abstract, the
same specific right as every other man, in the concrete, such rights
vary. To illustrate: every man has the right to life, liberty,
marriage, and property.

> These rights belong to (him) as a human being because they
> are all necessary for his existence, for the development of his
> personality, for reasonable human living, and for the attain-
> ment of the end which God commands him to attain.[119]

119. John A. Ryan & M. F. X. Millar, *Church and State* (New York:
The Macmillan Co., 1924), p. 277.

Such rights, however, are abstract. They are equal in all men to the degree that abstract natures are equal. Nevertheless, as they exist in the individual man, they differ from the same right possessed by another man, precisely to the extent that one individual differs from another.

It is in the exercise of these concrete rights that the State may step in, for these fall under the province of the positive law to the extent that the general precepts of the natural law require concrete determination. As the nature to exist needs to be individuated, and in that individuation is differentiated from every other individual, and, therefore, differentiated in its individual end, so the rights vested in the nature, become in their concrete form different from the rights of every other man. Thus every man has the right to property in so far as he is a human person, and in that right all are equal. But as men differ in the concrete, so their rights to property in the concrete likewise differ. Hence positive law, while respecting the right in its essence, may legislate as to its concrete existence, and specify, as in the case of property, its extent or the manner of its use. While "things established by human law cannot derogate from those of the natural or divine law,"[120] yet "since the natural law makes no distinction of possessions," [121] positive law, in virtue of its power to apply the general precept of the natural law to the concrete set of circumstances, may determine how specific rights operate in particular instances. Thus the State, while recognizing every man's right to marry, may specify the conditions under which that right may operate, provided that such conditions redound to the common good, and in no way conflict with the natural law.

In other words, positive law may legislate regarding rights in the concrete, in so far as the exercise of those rights are connected with functions contributing to the common good, or inimical to it. It may also legislate to protect the specific right in a concrete set of circumstances, as when labor laws protect man's right

120. *Summa Theol.*, II, II, q. 66, art. 7: ". . . ea quae sunt iuris humani non possunt derogare iuri naturali vel iuri divino. . . ."
121. *Summa Theol.*, II, II, q. 66, art. 2, ad. 1: "sed quia secundum ius naturale non est distinctio possessionum. . . ." Cf. I, II, q. 94, art. 5, ad. 3.

to life. Thus man has the right to work, but since youth is unequal to the tasks of maturity, and woman not endowed with the physical strength of man, the State may determine the concrete conditions under which that right may be exercised, and enact woman and child labor laws. Such laws are either the protection in particular cases of man's specific rights, or the protection of the common good in the concrete exercise of those rights. In either case the State never touches the right in its specific nature, but only in its individual exercise. This is in accordance with the equality of men in their specific natures, but their inequality as individuals. It is the duty of the State to protect the former, and to regulate the latter.

When we speak of equality of rights, however, we do not mean all rights are of the same basic importance. Rights vary in proportion to their proximity to the human person. As one writer very well puts it:

> Every individual may be considered as having around him a series of concentric circles. The circle nearest him includes his right to life, and the subsidiary rights necessary to give it validity, namely, the right to self-defense, and the right to the means of a livelihood in return for useful labor. The second circle includes the right to marry, to found a home, and to be a free person. The third circle includes the right to own property, and to remain free and unmolested in its enjoyment. Obviously, the rights within the first zone are more indispensable to the person than those in the second, and those within the second more indispensable than those within the third.[122]

Some rights, therefore, touch the person more intimately than others, and to that degree are more sacred. The right of the millionaire to his second million is less sacred than the right of the laborer to his daily bread; and the right of the mine worker to healthful working conditions takes precedence over the increased profits of the owner. The right to life is more basic than the right to property, because existence is the first requisite for the duty of pursuing an end. Though all men are equal in their

122. Francis J. Haas, *Man and Society* (New York: The Century Co., 1930), p. 51.

rights to property, since it is a necessary means to the perfection of personality, in the concrete, the right to property becomes more sacred in proportion as it answers the basic needs of the human person.[123] That is why superfluities must give way to the need of a starving man. On this point St. Thomas writes:

> Wherefore the division and appropriation of things which are based on human law, do not preclude the fact that man's needs have to be remedied by means of these very things. Hence whatever certain people have in superabundance is due, by natural law, to the purpose of succouring the poor . . . if need be so manifest and urgent . . . that it is evident that the present need must be remedied by whatever means be at hand, then it is lawful for a man to succour his own need by means of another's property by taking it openly or secretly.[124]

Applying these distinctions to men in their relation to positive civil law, three things are to be noted. (1). Before the law all men are equal in their specific rights. Such rights, flowing from the nature, are equal to the degree that natures are equal and, therefore, equally immune to political interference, and equally entitled to political protection. Thus, all men have the right to life, liberty, happiness, and property. These rights are as sacred in the pauper as in the prince, because they issue from human nature. Hence they must be respected and safeguarded with equal vigilance by the State. (2). Since in their concrete rights men differ, the law must be applied accordingly. Thus all men have the right to marry, yet the common good may necessitate that the exercise of that right be suspended in some. (3). Rights are preëminent in

123. Fulton J. Sheen, *Freedom under God* (Milwaukee: The Bruce Publishing Co., 1930), p. 41.
124. *Summa Theol.*, II, II, q. 66, art. 7: "Et ideo per rerum divisionem et appropriationem, de jure humano procedentem, non impeditur quin hominis necessitati sit subveniendum ex huiusmodi rebus. Et ideo res quas aliqui superabundantur habent, ex naturali iure debentur pauperum sustentationi. . . . Si tamen adeo sit urgens et evidens necessitas ut manifestum sit instanti necessitati de rebus occurrentibus esse subveniendum, puta cum imminet personae periculum et aliter subvenire non potest; tunc livite potest aliquis ex rebus alienis suae necessitati subvenire, sive manifeste sive occulte sublatis."

accordance with their proximity to the human person. If one's right to life conflicts with another's right to property, the property right must give way.

11. EQUALITY OF OPPORTUNITY

The doctrine of the equality of all men in their specific natural rights, and their inequality as to those same rights in the concrete, has a direct bearing on the right every man has to an opportunity to develop the capacities which are the endowments of his person and thus fulfill the obligation he is under of attaining his end. Such opportunity is essential to all, and the equal natures and destiny of men prohibit that one be favored more than another in the attainment of their final goal. Duke and ditchdigger may be widely separated in initial gifts, as well as in condition. If the condition be the natural result of the gift, nature is in no way violated. There is place in the social hierarchy for brain and brawn, for nobility and those of humble mien. Life is for all, to be enjoyed each according to his measure. Since men in their essential natures are neither greater nor less, the opportunity of each to realize the goal of his person, must be the equal concern of social authority. That painter and plumber, shepherd and scholar attain final beatitude is the purpose of civil society. Since that beatitude is an obligation incumbent on all, all stand in equal need of the opportunity to use the resources of the community that are necessary for final welfare. Such equality of opportunity is essential. To deny it to anyone is to deny a basic right, and to warp the social purpose.

There is another equality of opportunity, however, that is not so basic. It touches man not so much in his essential nature as in his accidental endowments. It is the opportunity that frees ability from obscuring hindrances, that permits capacity to assert itself, and every individual to do the work and fill the place for which nature has best fitted him. Such equality of opportunity results in those natural castes that go to make up the social hierarchy, and permits that hierarchy to be flexible enough to allow ability to rise and incapacity to seek its own level. It is an equality that asks only that all be given a chance to perfect the powers that are nature's gift, and to find that place in the social organization best suited to native ability.   Individual inequality, on the other hand, forbids that all be patterned after the same mould.   Given different capacities and the same training, the results will indeed be different, and probably disastrous both for the individual and society.

Adaptation of social facilities to individual needs may not give the banker and the baker the same start, but it will make each happier, and society function more smoothly.   As the exercise of a power perfects the power and brings satisfaction in its wake, so when the parts are fitted each to its proper place, the whole will be adjusted for perfect function.   The closer this is approached the more wholesome will be society.   Its perfect realization will be attained only in Utopia, for it must be remembered that perfect social order is the end of the rainbow.   Man forfeited his opportunity to live in an earthly paradise when the parent of the human race used his gift of freedom to violate the law of his nature, and set the creature in the place of the Creator.   Misfits in the social hierarchy had in that act a beginning that will end only with time.   From then on, human society was warped because natures were too easily frustrated.   Had man remained in the state of original justice, he would not have been perfect, but *en route* thereto.   His freedom was not a freedom to violate laws, but to obey them, and through that obedience reach the perfect realization of his powers.   Man chose to use his freedom otherwise, and by original sin add to a nature potential to perfection, the handicap of a nature deformed at its very start.   Prone to evil from his birth, man has the difficult task, not only of developing his aptitudes but of rectifying an original deformation.   The task would be almost hopeless, were divine liberality withheld.   But God did not choose to abandon the product of His love, and in grace offers man the divine opportunity to overcome the obstacle of his own sin.

That opportunity is offered to all alike, each according to his needs.   It remains for man, individually or collectively, to deny such opportunity to none, but to build a social structure that will enable each to realize the perfection which is his due.   That man will ever, in this vale of tears, attain to a society where everyone will reach the fullest development of all his powers, is but the idle fancy of the dreamer of dreams.   "Some mute inglorious Miltons" there will always be, some unfulfillment in this earthly progress to perfection. But unrealized capacity need not mean gift without purpose. It may mean the sacrifice of non-essentials for the sake of greater perfection. Not every grain of wheat fructifies. Some will not realize their natural tendencies to bring forth new sheaves, but will minister to men in higher ways. Likewise, he who is the painter of barns who could have been the painter of barons, may have sacrificed the less in a lower order to achieve the greater in a higher.

Equality of opportunity, therefore, does not mean that every latent capacity must be allowed self-realization. Still less does it mean that all given the same start, all will end equal. It does mean, however, that every man, woman, and child, equally endowed with the dignity of personality and equally destined for the same glorious end be not frustrated in its attainment by an unfair chance. Nor should anyone be forced to be the square peg in the round hole of society, when by an opportunity proportionate to ability, rather than to the claims of birth or wealth, function can be matched to capacity.

12. Economic Equality

As in the case of opportunity, the equality of specific natural rights, when these are concreted in individual differences, has its repercussions in the economic field. Man has three essential relations radicated in his nature, relations so necessary that the loss of any one of them would immediately imperil human life. These relations link man to God, to his fellowman, and to the irrational world of material things which minister to his bodily needs. In regard to all three he is dependent; but whereas he bears to God the relation of subordination, and to his fellowmen the equality of personal nature individuated amid a host of inequalities, to things below him he stands as a superior whom the irrational world was created to serve. That service is the essential due of every man, that the potentialities of his nature be adequately achieved, and his end thereby attained. This is a basic human right in which all share alike. To deprive anyone of it is to perpetrate an injustice of the first magnitude. Concerning this Maritain writes:

. . . every human person by reason of his membership in the human species ought in one way or another to derive advantage from this common dedication of material things to the good of the human race.[125]

If the vocation of material things is to serve human nature, then man must possess over the irrational world a certain dominion, a dominion which in virtue of human equality, belongs to one no more than to another. Such dominion is not absolute. God alone has absolute control of creation or any part of it, and He alone rules over the natures of things.[126] Man's power is twofold, to *procure* and *dispense* external things, and to *use* them.[127] This is a dictate of the natural law, and such law recognizes no distinctions among men. It merely indicates that the earth belongs to the human species. Since everyone partakes equally of that species, the right to the goods of the earth admits of neither more nor less. But this common right of ownership, like specific nature, must be individuated if human possession of the material world is to satisfy the needs of mankind. That individuation has its basis in the natural right of every person to possess privately a portion of earth's bounty. Common ownership refers to that which has not been privately claimed.[128] Unexplored territory belongs to men in general, but unless such territory comes under private dominion, not only may its potential service to men remain largely unrealized, but it is apt to become the source of social discord. St. Thomas gives three reasons why the division of communal property becomes necessary for human life:

First, because every man is more careful to procure what is for himself alone than that which is common to many or to all: since each one would shirk the labour and leave to another that which concerns the community, as happens where there is a great number of servants. Secondly, because human affairs are conducted in more orderly fashion if each is charged with taking care of some particular thing himself, whereas

125. Jacques Maritain, *Freedom in the Modern World* (New York: Charles Scribner's Sons, 1936), p. 194.
126. *Summa Theol.*, II, II, q. 66, art. 1.
127. *Ibid.*
128. *Ibid.*, q. 57, art. 3.

there would be confusion if everyone had to look after any one thing indeterminately. Thirdly, because a more peaceful state is ensured if each one is contented with his own. Hence it is to be observed that quarrels arise more frequently where there is no division of the things possessed.[129]

Private possession, however, is based on something more fundamental than expediency. It is a natural right attached to the human person. As every person is his own master, having dominion over his nature and his acts, it is natural that such dominion extend to that on which man has left the impress of his personality.[130] If "the cause has dominion over the effect," then man has power over those things which have been transformed by his own energies from mere matter to matter rendered competent to man. Such transformation resulting in an extension of human personality results likewise in an extension of human dominion. Here is the metaphysical ground of personal appropriation, for proprietary right naturally belongs to him who, by the application of his reason, has stamped material goods with something of his very own, something which connects such goods to his person. But since man may not stamp what is not his, reason demands that he have full and exclusive control over whatever is to receive the mark of his personality. If a man fashion marble into a representation of his mental image or idea, he has unquestionably left on the marble the character of his own person. The statue resulting has necessarily a close connection with him. It is imperative, therefore, that the marble be his, for whatever is destined to receive the design of a man's reason belongs rightfully to him whose mark has been left upon it.

---

129. *Summa Theol.*, II, II, q. 66, art. 2: "Primo quidem, quis magis sollicitus est unusquisque ad procurandum aliquid quod sibi soli competit quam aliquid quod est commune omnium vel multorum: quia unusquisque, laborem fugiens, relinquit alteri id quod pertinet ad commune; sicut accidit in multitudine ministrorum. Alio modo, quia ordinatius res humanae tractantur si singulis immineat propria cura alicuius rei procurandae: esset autem confusio si quilibet indistincte quaelibet procuraret. Tertio, quia per hoc magis pacificus status hominum conservatur, dum unusquisque re sua contentus est. Unde videmus quod inter eos qui communiter et ex indiviso aliquid possident, frequentius iurgia oriuntur."

130. Maritain, *op. cit.*, pp. 196-204.

It is thus that man's self-mastery passes to mastery over things. Individual ownership is, therefore, a corollary of human freedom. Animals do not own, for lacking mastery over themselves, they cannot extend it to what is outside of them. Man, on the other hand, is able to rule the world because he is first given power to rule himself. Since all men possess this power equally, all equally have the right to exercise it over the works of their own creation. The right to own privately is thus a specific right. Like every other specific right when it is concreted in the individual man, it immediately takes on the character of inequality. As such, it becomes the subject of positive law, which limited to the accidentals of human nature, operates within the sphere of inequality.

This distinction of property as the subject of both natural and positive right is the clear teaching of St. Thomas. Specifically, it flows from the *Jus gentium*, "that which is derived from the natural law by way of inference,"[131] but concretely, as a particular determination of the natural law, it is the precept of positive law.[132] In other words, the right to own privately being the *equal right* of every man is grounded in natural law, but the right of an individual man to a particular portion of material wealth is the application of the natural law to the concrete case, which application is always the province of positive law. In confirmation of this distinction St. Thomas writes:

> Community of goods is ascribed to the natural law, not that the natural law dictates that all things should be possessed in common, and that nothing should be possessed as one's own: but because the division of possessions is not according to natural law, but rather arose from human agreement which belongs to positive law. Hence the ownership of possessions

---

131. *Summa Theol.*, I, II, q. 95, art. 4, ad. 1: "Ius gentium est quidem aliquo modo naturale homini secundum quod est rationalis, inquantum derivatur a lege naturali per modum conclusionis quae non est multum remota a principiis." Cf. W. J. McDonald, *The Social Value of Property* (Washington: Catholic University, 1939), pp. 81-96.

132. *Summa Theol.*, I, II, q. 95, art. 4: "Quae vero derivantur a lege naturae per modum particularis determinationis, pertinent ad ius civile, secundum quod quaelibet civitas aliquid sibi accommodum determinat." Cf. McDonald, *op. cit.*

is *not contrary to the natural law, but an addition thereto devised by human reason.*[133]

(Hence) if a particular piece of land be considered absolutely, it contains no reason why it should belong to one man more than another, but if it be considered in respect of its adaptability to cultivation, and the unmolested use of land, it has a certain commensuration to be the property of one and not of another man.[134]

This commensuration is nothing more than the potentiality of matter to receive the design of reason, the impress of the personality of a particular man, which when actuated in matter connects it by a natural bond to him whose mark has been placed upon it. But as individually men are not equal, those things which bear the mark of man's artistry, and, therefore, the stamp of his person, will be in proportion to individual capacity. Hence in the concrete the right to possess privately differs from man to man, and as such must be regulated by positive law.

Regardless of how unequal men may be as individuals of the human species, that inequality stops short of the human essence. Men are equally human and as such equally destined for the same end. Since material wealth is a means for the development of the human person and the attainment of the end, there is a certain minimum beyond which that wealth may not fall. Hence, the natural law provides that although man's *right* to possess privately admits of no limitation other than the limitation of his own personal ability, in the *use* of that property he is restricted by the needs of his fellowmen. This restriction follows from the fact that nature places earthly goods at the disposal of the human race as the means

133. *Summa Theol.*, II, II, q. 66, art. 2, ad. 1: "Communitas rerum attribuitur iuri naturali, non quia ius naturale dictet omnia esse possidenda communiter et nihil esse quasi proprium possidendum: sed quia secundum ius naturale non est distinctio possessionum, sed magis secundum humanum condictum, quod pertinet ad ius positivum. . . . Unde proprietas possessionum non est contra ius naturale; sed iuri naturali supperadditur per adinventionem rationis humanae."

134. *Summa Theol.*, II, II, q. 57, art. 3: "Si enim consideretur iste ager absolute, non habet magis sit huius quam illius: sed si consideretur quantum ad opportunitatem colendi et ad pacificium usum agri, secundum hoc habet quandem commensurationem ad hoc quod sit unius et non alterius. . . ."

whereby every man may develop his capabilities, and thereby attain
his end. But though such disposal may not preclude individual
appropriation as the most fruitful manner of administering the
irrational world, nevertheless, it does forbid that any human person
be lacking in that amount of material wealth necessary for final
achievement. Consequently, those whose superior personal endowments bring to them a larger portion of earth's wealth must obey
nature's command, and give of their superfluities to those whom
inferior powers leave in danger of being deprived of that sufficiency
of wealth necessary for the realization of life's purpose. The peerless mind of St. Thomas did not miss this precept of nature, and
he transmits it as follows:

> Things which are of human right cannot derogate from natural
> right or Divine right. Now according to the natural order
> established by Divine providence, inferior things are ordained
> for the purpose of succouring man's needs by their means.
> Wherefore, the division and appropriation of things which are
> based on human law, do not preclude the fact that man's needs
> have to be remedied by means of these very things. Hence
> whatever certain people have in superabundance is due, by
> natural law, to the purpose of succouring the poor.[135]

> (And so) the second thing that is competent to man with
> regard to external things is their use. In this respect man
> ought to possess external things, not as his own, but as com-
> mon, so that, to wit, he is ready to communicate them to others
> in their need.[136]

---

135. *Summa Theol.*, II, II, q. 66, art. 7: "Ea quae sunt iuris humani non
possunt derogare iuri naturali vel iuri divino. Secundum autem naturalem
ordinem ex divina providentia institutum res inferiores sunt ordinatae
ad hoc quod ex his subveniatur hominum necessitati. Et ideo per rerum
divisionem et appropriationem, de iure humano procedentem, non impeditur
quin hominis necessitati sit subveniendum ex huiusmodi rebus. Et ideo res
quas aliqui superabundanter habent, ex naturali iure debentur pauperum
sustentationi."

136. *Summa Theol.*, II, II, p. 66, art. 2: "Aliud vero quod competit
homini circa res exteriores est usus ipsarum. Et quantum ad hoc non
debet homo habere res exteriores ut proprias, sed ut communes: ut scilicet
de facile aliquis ea communicet in necessitates aliorum."

If such be nature's dictate does it not involve a contradiction? Why is man obliged to individual ownership on the one hand and communal use on the other? Does this not imply a mutual negation? No more than individual inequality negates the equality of specific personal nature. Repeatedly it has been pointed out that man bears to others of his race a twofold relation, and in that twofold relation lies the answer why man may own privately goods which he must use in common. ¶When man stands to his fellowman as one person to another he stands on the basis of strict equality, endowed with the same nature, obliged to the same end, and morally bound by the same law to use the wealth of the earth to develop his person and attain his goal. When on the other hand man stands to his fellowman as one individual of a species to another, he stands on the basis of inequality, possessed of capabilities which vary from individual to individual, and endowed with gifts which mark him off from others of his kind. ¶

As it is these individual gifts which make the earth productive, and stamp it with the character of the individual human person, man *as an individual must own.* Since, on the other hand, the earth is God's gift to the human species as the means for the development of the personal nature, its *use is for all alike.* Hence though man owns the earth as an individual, his use of it is social. Since as individuals, men are unequal, their private possessions will vary in proportion to their abilities; since in their natures men are not superior one to another, the use of those possessions must be common. Such use, however, does not mean equal distribution of goods individually produced. It does mean, however, that whatever is in excess of a man's need proportionate to his social position, and the number of his dependents, must be used to relieve those needs of another that impede the development necessary for final perfection. Thus one man's right to a collection of the great masters must give way to another's need for a ton of coal. As the accidental is always for the sake of the essential, inequality must always be sacrificed that the equality of personal nature be not marred. Man cannot live as befits a person if he lacks those bodily necessities that leave him free to seek the goal of his nature. When a man shivers and starves, when he is forced to spend all his energies in pursuit of his bodily needs, he is not only turned from things of the spirit, but too often impelled to acts prohibited by the moral law, and thus to a violation of his rational nature. To that extent he is less a free rational being, and, therefore, less a person. This is a violation of the equality of personal nature, and, therefore, such equality demands that the superabundance of one be used to maintain the personal integrity of another.

Human inequality was meant to be rectified by service, and superiority of gift to be compensated for by ministrations to the lowly. Hence, those who by the excellence of their endowments amass an abundance of earth's wealth, must come to the aid of their less favored brothers, and by sharing their excess possessions help to equalize human conditions. Economic inequality is a thing of nature. It is justified when it corresponds to human endowment. But natural though it is, there is a limit beyond which it may not go. That limit is human personality. When extremes of wealth strip man of the dignity of his person, when they leave him exposed to the loss of his final goal, they are unjustifiable because unnatural. Extremes are never nature's way. To counteract them she establishes checks and balances. As in the hierarchy of creation she tempers inequality with a beautifully arranged gradation, so in human economy she prevents opulence and misery, not by leveling all to the same condition, but by spanning the distance between rich and poor with the virtues of justice and charity.

PART III
Modern Equality: A Critique

CHAPTER V

INDIVIDUAL EQUALITY: THING VS. PERSON

Three views of human equality have been offered to explain the social relations of men—the political equality of the Liberal, the economic equality of the Communist, and the spiritual equality of the Christian. The first is a protest against the privilege of birth, the second is a protest against the privilege of wealth, and the third is a protest against the reduction of the human person to the status of a thing. The Liberal denies the inequality of citizens; the Communist denies the inequality of classes; the Christian denies the inequality of persons. For the Liberal, civil society must equally respect the rights of citizens; for the Communist, economic society must equally protect the rights of workers; for the Christian, society, whether domestic, civil or economic, must equally guarantee the rights of man, the human person.

While the Liberal is satisfied with the equality of citizens before the law, and the Communist with the equality of workers in the collectivity, the Christian, satisfied with nothing less than the equality of men before God, can offer the ultimate reason why men must be without subordination one to another in that which touches human nature and its end. While the Liberal condones any inequality that is not civic, and the Communist would liquidate inequality altogether, the Christian neither condones inequality nor strives to liquidate it. Viewing men as substantially equal, he can, nevertheless, give inequality a place in the accidentals of human life. So long as men suffer no differentiation in their persons, so long as no race or class of men is deprived of the means requisite for human destiny, the Christian can view in human inequality a magnificent panorama in which the individual of the species never exhausts the grandeur of the human person.

It is this third view of human equality that places man in his proper perspective, a being bearing in his nature a dignity unsurpassed by others of his kind, possessed of a destiny that is the common heritage of all, endowed with a worth undenied his fellows; yet, distinguished from every other man by a myriad of non-essential differences that serve but to express the limitless potentialities of the human type. In the light of the principles emanating from this twofold human character we would weigh the other equalitarian doctrines that have been advanced to explain human likeness and human difference. These principles, already elaborated, may be set down as follows:

1. Man is both a person and an individual.
2. In their specific personal natures men are equal; society is, therefore, equally a means for all. As individuals they are subordinated one to another; society, therefore, becomes a hierarchy.
3. The specific personal equality of men demands that superiority in the social hierarchy be compensated for by service.
4. In the social structure, because of individual inequality, men function as part to whole on the basis of legal and distributive justice; because of the equality of personal nature they function as part to part on the basis of commutative justice. The presence of all three types of justice produces social justice, hence peace which is the fruit of justice.
5. The equality of personal nature demands the ultimate divine origin of civil power; human freedom and human equality demand that such power be derived proximately from the people.
6. Before the law, men are equal in their specific personal natures; as individuals they are unequal. In their specific personal rights they are equal; in their concrete individual rights they differ.
7. Because of individual inequality men have the right to possess material goods privately; because they are specifically equal the *use* of such goods must be common.

That Liberalism and Communism advance a view of equality in direct contradiction to the principles just enumerated remains to be shown. Whether it be the political equality of the Liberal, or the economic equality of the Communist, it is an equality, not of specific nature but of individuals. As such its repercussions in the social order are of far-reaching significance.

The relation of this equality to the two democratic traditions has already been pointed out. It is a fundamental political concept of secular democracy, just as equality of personal nature is fundamental to Christian democracy. As between these two concepts there is a marked difference, so between the democratic theories rooted in them there is a wide divergence. Christian democracy prevailed in the Middle Ages and left the impress of its character on the fundamental political philosophy of England and America. Secular democracy had its roots in Stoic philosophy and in the pagan law concepts of ancient Rome. With the revival of Roman law during the period of the Renaissance, these concepts filtered into European political thought, engendering a tradition that captured the political mind of continental Europe, and culminated in that birth of liberal democracy which was the French Revolution. Political Liberalism however was not confined within the borders of the French nation. Its tenets found favor wherever parliamentary government displaced the old régime, and it has had a parasitic growth in England and America.

It is such democracy and the notion of equality fundamental to it that we would evaluate, for in judging its basic notion we judge the institution reared upon it. That notion found favor with the Humanist, the Rationalist, and the Liberal. In short, it found favor with the modern pagan, that product of eighteenth century Enlightenment whose *Weltanschauung* has formed the "mental outlook of the active governing class of Western Europe"[1] for the past four hundred years. Diametrically opposed to the Christian world outlook, this *Weltanschauung* has fathered a philosophy of equality that knows naught of the human person; and, as a consequence, has substituted for the equality of specific personal nature, the mathematical equality of individuals. Qualitative equality it has replaced with quantitative; nature it has reduced to number; person it has deposed for thing.

Inasmuch as Liberalism was reared in this pagan tradition of democratic thought, it failed to distinguish between an individual and a person, and as a consequence espoused an equality of quantity. Inasmuch as Communism, though claiming to be a reaction against Liberalism, is in truth the transposition of the Liberal's tenets from the field of politics to the realm of economics, its con-

1. Rosalind Murray, *The Good Pagan's Failure* (London: Longmans, Green & Co., 1939), p. 40.

cept of equality is likewise but an equation of numbers. That the
Liberal and the Communist, therefore, are committed to an individual or quantitative equality is the position here maintained, and
in justification of that position the following propositions are
offered:

1. Both deny the distinction between an individual and a person,
   thus reducing man to the status of a thing.
2. Both reduce natural law to a physical law of nature.
3. Both equate natural rights with physical powers.

To an examination of these propositions this study now turns.
Their proof will establish the thesis that modern political and
economic equality as advanced by the Liberal and the Communist
is an equality of individuals, an equation of things and not of
persons.

1. Denial of the Distinction between an Individual and a Person

That the Liberal and the Communist both deny the distinction
between an individual and a person, is evident from an examination of their philosophies. An individual is only an inferior of a
species, merely the concrete expression of a specific nature. Its
existence guarantees specific preservation. This is its *raison
d'être;* to this it dedicates all its activities. There is one individual, however, which, though it expresses the specific nature in
its concrete existence, has nevertheless a reality which the species
cannot wholly claim. That individual is the human person. It is
unique in its individuality, for it preserves the species in its existence without making specific preservation the goal of its being.
It plays a double functional rôle because it is rooted in two worlds,
the world of matter and the world of spirit, thereby spanning a
chasm between two opposed actualities. The Liberal and the Communist fail not only to make this distinction, but also fail to note
the double functional rôle of the human person. The rational individual John is the person; the non-rational stone is only a thing.
The former possesses a function that transcends the species; hence
can never be wholly subjected to others of its kind. The latter is

wholly subordinate. Liberalism and Communism, seeing man only as an individual, see him as wholly subject.

Liberalism Reduces the Human Person to the Status of a Thing

Though liberal democracy, and Christian democracy, both spring from the notion of men as equal, the former has its roots in a complexus of philosophies that can equate things, but never persons because being antispiritual they must as a consequence be antipersonal. Into the Liberal mould there has poured a blend of philosophic influence, so that, theoretically, Liberalism is compounded of pagan Stoicism, English Empiricism, and French Rationalism. From the first came the version of the pre-political state with the emergence of law as a creation of the will. From the second came the view that only the particular, the individual, is real; the universal is only a fiction. From the third came the doctrine of the autonomy of reason.

The Influence of Stoicism. Stoicism is above all else a materialistic philosophy frankly and openly committed to a denial of the spirit. Its universal law of reason according to which men shape their conduct is nothing but a pantheistic force, a cosmic Logos, or a physical urge to consistency.[2] Its concept of man, including as it does a repudiation of the spiritual, reduces man to the level of a material thing. As a consequence, its notion of human equality can be nothing else than a quantitative equality of individuals. This is clearly confirmed by Cicero who, though not a Stoic, was influenced by the Stoic thinking of his age.[3] He writes as follows:

> There is nothing that so resembles or equals another, as is the case of man to man. And if the depravity of custom and vanity of opinion did not bring on an imbecility of mind and turn one from the other, no man would more resemble himself than all men would resemble one another. And, therefore, whatever definition be given to man, it is fitting to one and all.[4]

2. M. F. X. Millar, "The Modern State and Catholic Principle," *Thought*, XII (1937), pp. 42-63.
3. A. J. Carlyle, *A History of Medieval Political Theory in the West* (New York: G. P. Putnam's Sons, 1916).
4. Cicero, *De Leg.*, i. 10. 28-12. 33.

In other words, human inequality is the work of environment. It flows not from anything intrinsic to man, but from the external circumstances in which he finds himself placed. Apart from environment man individually mirrors his fellowman.

Such equality forbids that one man assume dominion of any kind over another. Civil society can only arise from a voluntary contract; and God, man, and the universe, being merged in a pantheistic materialism, positive law can have no source beyond the fiat of the human will. But whenever man becomes wholly subject to the will of another, he loses the dignity of an autonomous being and is no longer a person, but a thing.

The Influence of Empiricism. Barring Rousseau, perhaps no one is more loudly hailed as the father of modern democracy than John Locke; but he is likewise the father of Empiricism. In his epistemology must be sought the key to his politics. Empiricism of its very nature is antispiritual. If all we can know are our immediate sense experiences, the phenomena that loom up in consciousness, we can only know the material, the extended, the particular—never the universal, never the essence, for they are beyond the apprehension of sense. They are amenable only to a spiritual being. An empiricist, therefore, can only know at best *that* a thing is, never *what* it is. Such philosophy makes the concrete material image, or subjective sense impression, the immediate object of knowledge. The human faculty of cognition must, therefore, be a material extended faculty.

Empiricists recognize these facts, for they either make spiritual concepts mere components of sense images, as does Locke;[5] or they deny their existence altogether, as does Hume;[6] or they make them

---

5. John Locke, *Essay on Human Understanding*, Bk. II, ch. 23, sec. 4: "Hence, when we talk or think of any particular corporeal substance, as horse, stone, etc., though the idea we have of either of them be but the complication or collection of those several simple ideas of sensible qualities which we used to find united in the thing called horse or stone; yet because we cannot conceive how they should subsist alone, nor one in another, we suppose them existing in and supported by some common subject."

6. Friedrich Ueberweg, *History of Philosophy* (trans. by George S. Morris; New York: Charles Scribner's Sons, 1894), p. 132: "The creative

mere creations of the mind to which correspond no known reality, as does Kant.[7]   But if the spiritual is reduced to the material, denied outright, or made but a barren idea of the mind, man is no longer a person, an individual substance of a rational nature; he is only a thing, an individual of a species, whose existence has no other purpose than specific preservation.

When, therefore, an empiricist endows man with freedom, he does not mean a spiritual freedom,[8] for to an empiricist there can be no spirit.   Freedom for him means the absence of constraint. It is the freedom of the bird uncaged, the freedom of water when the container is broken, the freedom of the river when it overflows its banks.

With this empirical philosophy as a background the political theory of its advocates is better understood.   Locke begins with the notion of men as free and equal in a primitive state of nature. This is a Stoic concept, but it fits in with Locke's habit of mind of viewing nature, not as essence but as primitive or unconventional. Men, as free and equal, are the constituents out of which to make political society, just as simple ideas or images are the constituents

power of thought extends no further than to the faculty of combining, transposing, augmenting, or diminishing the material furnished by the senses and by experience."

7. Kant, *Critique of Pure Reason—Transcendental Dialectic* Introd.: "One may say that the object of a purely transcendental idea is something of which we have no concept, although the idea is produced with necessity according to the original laws of reason.   Nor is it possible indeed to form of an object that should be adequate to the demands of reason, a concept of the understanding, that is, a concept which could be shown as any possible experience and rendered intuitive.   It would be better, however, and less liable to misunderstanding, to say that we can have no knowledge of an object corresponding to an idea, but a problematic concept only."

8. Only spiritual beings are intelligent, and only intellectual beings are free.   Intellectual acts are the products of an immaterial, spiritual faculty, the intellect.   By this faculty the universal nature, or essence is grasped. Since this nature is capable of an indefinite number of realizations any one of which satisfies the essential specific requirements, it is possible to choose which realization will prevail.   Here is the basis of choice, the initial freedom, which is the reason for external freedom, the freedom of movement.   When choice is exercised wisely it results in that perfection of freedom, which is autonomy and self-mastery.   Where the spiritual is lacking, intelligence is also lacking, and with intelligence, freedom.

out of which to make complex ideas or essences.[9] Equality is the mathematical equality of individuals, for man, in whom reason is synonymous with sense, lacking any spiritual component, is only a material entity, a quantity devoid of any claim to the dignity of a person.[10] It is an equality of power, "no one having more than another,"[11] an equality of freedom, for "in that state of perfect equality where naturally there is no superiority or jurisdiction of one over another,"[12] all are equally free. When we consider that freedom for Locke is the absence of any external constraint, the freedom to do what one wills to do,[13] we can understand how in a state of primitive nature, the "natural liberty of man is to be free from any superior power on earth, and not to be under the will or legislative authority of man."[14] Such freedom is an external freedom and flows from no internal principle,[15] but from the absence

9. John Locke, *Essay on Human Understanding*, Bk. III, ch. 6, sec. 21: "But since, as has been remarked, we have need of general words, though we know not the real essence of things: all we can do is to collect such a number of simple ideas, as by examination we find to be united together in things existing, and thereof to make one complex idea. Which though it be not the real essence of any substance that exists, is yet the specific essence to which our name belongs, and is convertible with it."

10. John Locke, *Essay on Human Understanding*, Bk. II, ch. 27, secs. 9-17: "We must consider what person stands for; which, I think, is a thinking intelligent being, that has reason and reflection, and can consider itself as itself. . . . That with which the consciousness of this present thinking thing can join itself, makes the same person . . . should this consciousness go along with the little finger, and leave the rest of the body, it is evident the little finger would be the person, the same person." Note: Conscionsness for Locke, it must be remembered, can only be sense consciousness.

11. John Locke, *Two Treatises on Government* (London: 1821), Bk. II, ch. 2, sec. 4, p. 189.

12. *Ibid.*, ch. 2, sec. 7.

13. Locke, *Essay on Human Understanding*, Bk. II, ch. 21, sec. 56: "Liberty, it is plain, consists in a power to do, or not to do; to do, or forbear doing, as we will."

14. Locke, *Two Treatises on Government*, Bk. II, ch. 4, sec. 21.

15. Locke, *Essay on Human Understanding*, Bk. II, ch. 21, secs. 14, 16: "It is as insignificant to ask whether man's will be free as to ask whether his sleep be swift, or his virtue square; liberty being as little applicable to the will, as swiftness of motion is to sleep, or squareness to virtue. . . . liberty, which is but a power, belongs only to agents, and cannot be an

of an external restraining force. It is a freedom that admits of no higher reality than freedom in the animal world where birds uncaged and beasts unchained are all equally free.

Such freedom, of course, vanishes unless those possessing it are equal in power, for it is a freedom that is ever at the mercy of the strong. Yet equality of power is all that Locke can mean, for knowing nothing of nature or essence in its true sense, the *natural* becomes for him what is left when the conventions of civilization have been stripped off. Human nature is primitive nature, and natural equality is the condition of power men possess to enforce the instinctive law of self-preservation.[16] But to make men equal in power is to make them equal as individuals, for man, in Locke's philosophy, possessing only a material nature, can possess only the physical powers of matter. This is the Stoic notion of equality, but it is consistent with the denial of the spiritual and the personal which Locke's philosophy necessarily entails.

Kant's notion of equality is based on his notion of freedom. He is free whose actions are self-determined. Now as every man is the author of the law of his own nature, where each is sovereign, no one can be subjected to the will of another. Where every man is his own legislator and the author of his own imperium,[17] subordination, to another is unthinkable. All men are, therefore, equal, and all are equally free. When one realizes however that in Kant's philosophy spiritual substances have only an ideal existence, and

attribute or modification of the will, which is also a power. . . . It is plain, then, that the will is nothing but one power or ability, and freedom another power or ability; so to ask whether the will has freedom, is to ask whether one power has another power, one ability another ability; a question at first sight too grossly absurd to make a dispute, or need an answer."

16. Locke, *Two Treatises on Government*, Bk. II, ch. 2, sec. 7: "And if anyone in the state of nature may punish another for any evil he has done, everyone may do so. For in that state of perfect equality, where naturally there is no superiority or jurisdiction of any one over another, what any may do in prosecution of that law every one must needs have a right to do."

17. R. Falkenberg, *History of Modern Philosophy* (New York: Henry Holt & Co., 1893), p. 388: "The practical reason (*i.e.*, will) receives the law neither from the will of God, nor from natural impulses, but draws it out of its own depths; it binds itself."

freedom is only an ideal freedom,[18] all that Kant can hold with
certainty is that man is a material being, and material beings are
not free. Kant's freedom is, therefore, the same as Locke's. It is
an external freedom, a freedom from all law but that of one's own
will. The dictate of reason which says that one may act in such a
way that his act may be universalized is in substance the same as
saying, "You may do whatever you are willing that everyone else
may do." This is a dangerous freedom. There is nothing to keep
it from generating license, but the creation of some force strong
enough to curtail it. Both Locke and Kant, endowing man with
a freedom that can only mean the absence of external constraint,
were soon forced to impose a law on creatures whose nature it
was to be free from all law but that of their own reason.

The Influence of Rationalism. Rationalism was the third philosophy that contributed to the shaping of the Liberal mind. It is
a philosophy that recognizes in reason alone the true and valid
source of knowledge. Born of a hatred of revealed religion, and
of a reverence for the method of physical science, Rationalism
espoused the natural as opposed to the supernatural. Locke had
taught that the human mind at birth was equipped with no innate
knowledge. Experience alone would reveal the secrets of the universe, and reason was the key that would unlock the vaults of
knowledge. Newton had shown the power of unaided reason to
extract from nature the laws that governed its physical empire.
Might not that same reason meet with equal success when its light
was turned on nature at the human level? So argued Voltaire and
Montesquieu, Diderot and Holbach, Helvetius, Quesnay and Con-
dorcet, and the whole Encyclopedic School.[19]

18. *Ibid.*, p. 392: "It is true that freedom is a mere idea, whose object
can never be given to me in an experience, and whose reality, consequently,
cannot be objectively known and proved, but nevertheless, is required with
satisfactory subjective necessity on the condition of the moral law and
of the possibility of its fulfillment. I may not say it is certain, but with
safety, I am certain that I am free. Freedom is not a dogmatic proposition
of theoretical reason, but a *postulate* of practical reason."

19. Kingsley Martin, *French Liberal Thought in the Eighteenth Century*
(Boston: Little, Brown & Co., 1929), pp. 117-132; 281-291.

French Rationalism was permeated with materialism and atheism.[20] It was characterized by a deification of nature in which God was nothing more than a first premise, a peg on which the human mind could hang the whole of reality. He was the great Engineer who ran the universe, the Supreme Reason which permeated a world that was rational. God as a heavenly Father, the ineffable Spirit, who imparted to man, the child of His love, a spark of His divine reality, and destined him for life for which earthly existence was but a disciplinary preparation, was beyond the ken of eighteenth century mentality.[21] Man was of the earth, earthly. His supreme dignity lay in his membership in the human race. Any claim to participation in the life of the spirit, if spirit there were, was of a nebulous kind. Associationist Psychology, born of Hobbes and Locke, could not validly perceive in man the spiritual. In the hands of Condillac and the Encyclopedists, of Helvetius and Holbach, it logically reduced man to a superior animal who "differs from other animals in the greater complexity of his social life and his greater self-consciousness."[22]

Rousseau repudiated all the cherished dreams of the Rationalists. At the level of pure nature man is not reasonable; he is the creature of his impulses. He lives his happy careless existence by passing from one sensual delight to another. Reason is the faculty of human bondage. It restrains the gratification of sense, and brings repression and limitation of freedom in its wake. It invents the artificialities of life and imposes on man the chains of convention.

Though Rousseau romanticized at the level of primitive man, he was more reasonable than the Rationalism he opposed. Reason is a spiritual faculty, not a power of sense. If human power can have no higher operation than the manipulation of sensuous phenomena —and that is all Associationist Psychology can admit—then Rousreau is right in hailing man at the level of feeling and emotion as the natural man. At such level men are equal, for no one would

20. F. J. C. Hearnshaw, *The Social and Political Ideas of Some Great French Thinkers of the Age of Reason* (London: George G. Harrap & Co., 1930), pp. 9-38. Cf. Martin, *op. cit.*, pp. 123-132.

21. Carl Becker, *The Heavenly City of the Eighteenth Century Philosophers* (New Haven: Yale University Press, 1935), pp. 49-51.

22. Hearnshaw, *op. cit.*, p. 215.

be so unfeeling as to impose his will upon another. Though Rousseau opposed Rationalism as he sketched the drama of primitive man, yet in the development of his political panacea he fell into the rationalistic mode of thought and conceived of man as regaining his paradise lost according to the social tenets of rational society. Not by the individual will shall man live, but by the *general will*, for man, abstract man, humanity, is the unerring guide. In the multitude individual differences cancel. The totality alone reveals the natural, the general harmony amid endless variety. In Rousseau, Romanticist and Rationalist met. Man was indeed an animal; but, somehow or other, the animal had learned to *reason*. He had learned to put two and two together and in the totality discovered truth.

Such philosophy could understand the spiritual only as some higher expression of the material. It could prate about the immortality of the human soul, only because the human mind revolts at a concept of life whose final destiny is to be merged with the lifeless. It could do lip service to the Author of the universe, the vague abstract First Cause, only because reason revolts at a never-ending series of things that begin. And because deistic minds conceive the divine Architect, the great cosmic Engineer, as too divorced from the mechanism He created to waste much thought on its human parts, pantheistic minds deified nature as the Supreme Reason, the harmonizing force whose immanence in the universe explained its order and its regularity.

Man in such philosophy is robbed of the dignity of personality because he is robbed of any real participation in a spiritual nature. Bound by a hedonistic principle to satisfy the cravings of his animal instincts, man is offered a morality that imposes a duty of assuaging the desires of sense.[23] In civil society, such principle and such morality become the utilitarian formula which prescribes the greatest happiness for the greatest number as the norm of positive law.[24] If man is only a super-animal, only the fairest flower of a material universe, it is right that his ruling principle be the principle of sensuous life. And since the animal is wholly encompassed within

---

23. Martin, *op. cit.*, pp. 177-183.
24. *Ibid.*, pp. 184-190.

the confines of matter, it is right that his social life be organized by a principle that directs the activities of the aggregate only because it is the totality of the principles that direct each member. Rationalism, in reducing man to a thing, a mere material unit, must follow the principle of reason and conceive of human society as a sum of human atoms, and this Rationalism did.

Communism Reduces the Human Person to the Status of a Thing

The denial of the distinction between an individual and a person is inherent in the philosophy of Communism. The core of that philosophy is its theory of Dialectical Materialism. In this theory, matter is the sole reality; but it is matter that is autodynamic in character, ever unfolding according to an intrinsic dialectical law into higher and higher forms of reality. The peak of material existence is reached in the human mind, and thought is the supreme activity in a universe that is material. Between mind and matter there is a distinction, but a distinction that is not essential, for mind is matter at a higher stage of organization, and thought is an activity of the brain.

> Matter is primary nature. Sensation, thought, consciousness are the highest products of matter organized in a certain way. This is the doctrine of materialism, in general, and Marx and Engels in particular.[25]

> The physical realm existed before the psychical, for the latter is the highest product of the most highly developed forms of organic matter.[26]

Spirit is for the Communist, therefore, only a superior form of material energy. It is glorified matter, an emanation from matter, never a reality of a different nature having a subsistence of its own.

When the Communist makes thought an activity of the brain, and brain but matter highly organized, he denies to man all capability of grasping the universal essence; hence all knowledge in

25. V. I. Lenin, *Materialism and Empirio-Criticism* in *Collected Works of V. I. Lenin* (New York: International Publishers, 1924), III.

26. *Ibid.,* p. 191.

the true sense of that term. Man, therefore, is not free because he knows, for the simple reason that he lacks the only kind of knowledge capable of bestowing freedom; and he lacks that knowledge precisely because he lacks the principle from which it proceeds. That principle is immaterial, that is, spiritual; and because it is immaterial, it is not subject to the necessity that stamps matter. It is free. Deny such principle to man, and you must, in consequence, deny him freedom. Take freedom away from man, and you must take away all autonomy and self-mastery. Personality is centered in the spirit, and the spirit alone is free. Communism, in declaring man to be wholly material, robs him of his crowning glory. Instead of being that which is most perfect in all nature, a person, man is leveled to a thing.

2. Reduction of the Natural Law to a Physical Law

An examination of the philosophies that underlie Liberalism and Communism has revealed their antispiritual character. With a knowledge of this antispiritual bias as a background, we shall look into their doctrine of natural law. By this law neither the Liberal nor the Communist can understand a moral law. Such law implies a free creature, and logically neither the Liberal nor the Communist can concede that men are free. However much they may insist that man enjoys freedom, the freedom bestowed is of a pseudo variety. It neither follows logically from their premises, nor is it genuine in kind.

Stoicism identifies freedom with self-movement, in which case bulls and boaconstrictors are free. Empiricism makes freedom not a positive perfection, but a negative attribute—the absence of external restraint. It is the freedom of the anthropoid in the primeval forest. Rationalism cannot make men free for Rationalism is anti-spiritual, and what is not spiritual is not free. Communism equates freedom with knowledge of necessity, as though knowing *what one must do,* is the same as doing *what one may.* Liberalism and Communism, therefore, espousing at best a pseudo-freedom are logically driven to understand natural law as physical and not moral.

3. Reduction of the Natural Right to a Physical Power

If you ask a Liberal what he means by a right, he will usually reply by telling you which rights men ought to have: Life, liberty and property;[27] the power of doing whatever does not injure another;[28] the freedom to do what one wills provided it does not infringe on the equal freedom of any other man.[29] And if you turn to a Communist, he will answer the right to the fruits of your labor. However all these replies merely enumerate men's rights; they do not define them.

Now if I ask a scientist what a seismograph is, and he replies by pointing out various seismographs, he is not answering my question. Unless I see a seismograph at work, and understand its operation and its purpose, showing me seismographs is not telling me what they are. Likewise, when I ask a Liberal what a right is, and he answers by pointing out various rights, he may give me some illumination, but on the whole is avoiding my question.

The inability to define a right is the logical consequence of the inability to understand law. We have shown that the natural law for the Communist is definitely a physical law of nature, and we have shown by implication that it cannot be anything different for the Liberal. Now a right is a power conferred by law. If the law is physical, the power must be likewise. If the law is moral, rights are moral powers. Since neither the Communist nor the Liberal can validly hold to moral laws, they cannot validly look upon rights as moral powers. Rights, then, can only be equivalent to physical powers. This is the position of Hobbes for whom might was right; and it is also the position of Communism, as a glance at its doctrine of equality will reveal.

Marx frankly equates rights with physical powers when, in his *Critique of the Gotha Program*, he scoffs at the notion of equal rights. Man has a right to the fruits of his labor, because he has put into it so much of his energy. He has a right to that which his

27. Locke, *Two Treatises on Civil Government*, Bk. II, ch. 7, sec. 87.

28. David G. Ritchie, *Natural Right* (New York: The Macmillan Co., 1924), *appendix*, p. 292.

29. W. A. Dunning, *A History of Political Theory* (*From Rousseau to Spencer*; New York: The Macmillan Co., 1926), p. 399.

labor has transformed from raw material to useful product. But since the labor expended varies in proportion to the powers men possess, instead of enjoying equal rights, men can only claim unequal rights for unequal labor.

> . . . equality consists in the fact that measurement is made with an *equal standard,* labour.
> But one man is superior to another physically or mentally and so supplies more labour in the same time, or can labour for a longer time; and labour, to serve as a measure, must be defined by its duration or intensity, otherwise it ceases to be a standard of measurement. This *equal* right is an unequal right for unequal labour. It recognizes no class differences, because everyone is only a worker like everyone else; but it tacitly recognizes unequal individual endowment and thus productive capacity as natural privileges. *It is therefore a right of inequality in its content, like every right.*[30]

This explains why during the Dictatorship of the Proletariat the ruling principle must read:

> From each according to his ability; to each according to his work.[31]

While men are unequal in their physical powers, rewards must be likewise unequal. To talk, therefore, says Marx, of equal rights is to speak the language of the bourgeoisie.

The equality of natural rights is a favorite doctrine of the Liberal; but press him to define his terms and he is in an embarrassing position. Locke, whose theories Laski regards as defining the "essential outlines of the Liberal doctrine for nearly two centuries,"[32] understands such equality as:

> being that equal right that every man hath to his natural freedom without being subjected to the will or authority of any other man.[33]

30. Karl Marx, *Critique of the Gotha Program* (New York: International Publishers, 1938), p. 9.
31. *New Soviet Constitution,* art. 12.
32. Harold J. Laski, *The Rise of Liberalism* (Harper & Brothers, 1936), p. 113.
33. Locke, *Two Treatises on Civil Government,* Bk. II, ch. 6, sec. 54.

This freedom is not freedom of the will. It is an external freedom which "consists in our being able to act or not to act according as we choose or will."[34] Freedom in this sense is one with power. He is free who is strongest, and best able to effect his purpose. Right for Locke is thus reduced to a physical power, and equality of rights to an equality of physical powers. The blankness of the human mind at birth is proof of this equality. Any subsequent inequality men bring on themselves. If we examine Locke's doctrine of the executive power of the law of nature, the concept of right, as synonymous with physical power, forces itself upon us with equal insistency. That law being merely the instinct of self-preservation, its proper function in the state of nature necessitates the use of physical power:

> . . . the execution of the law of Nature is . . . put into every-man's hands, whereby everyone has a *right* to punish the transgressors of that law to such a degree as may hinder its violation. For the law of Nature would, as all other laws that concern men in this world, be in vain if there were nobody that in the State of Nature had a power to execute that law, and thereby preserve the innocent and restrain offenders.[35]

The execution of the law of nature is then the power everyone has of preserving his life, liberty, and property from violation on the part of another. Since it is this power that man hands over to society when he covenants with other men to form the body politic, civil authority being nothing more than the sum of individual powers, the State is merely an instrument of force. This is borne out by Locke's own words when he writes:

> For in the state of Nature . . . a man has two powers. The first is to do whatever he thinks fit for the preservation of himself and others within the permission of the law of Nature. . . . The other power a man has in the state of Nature, is the power to punish crimes committed against that law. Both these he gives up when he joins in . . . political society. . . . The first power, viz., of doing whatsoever he thought for the preservation of himself and the rest of mankind, he gives up

34. Locke, *Essay on Human Understanding*, Bk. II, ch. 21, sec. 27.
35. Locke, *Two Treatises on Government*, Bk. II, ch. 2, sec. 7, p. 20.

> to be regulated by laws made by the society. . . . Secondly,
> the power of punishing he wholly gives up, and engages his
> *natural force* to assist the executive power of society.[36]

The conception of the State as a superforce to execute the law
of self-preservation is the logical outcome of a theory that confuses
natural law with the laws of the physical universe, and natural
rights with the powers regulated by those laws. Likewise, the
conception that equates men on the basis of natural rights is a
conception which regards equality as "the condition of power men
possess until they give up the auto-centrism in which they are
born."[37] This view is in line with the Stoic version of equality.
It is a version that connects rights with origin and not with destiny,
with physics rather than morality.

It was Locke's concept of right that lay at the bottom of the
theory of natural rights of the eighteenth century thinkers. Imbued
with a concept of natural law in the sense of causal sequences of
uniformities, these theorists "conceived themselves . . . as doing
for matters of social constitution what the great scientists of the
seventeenth century had done for the physical universe."[38] They
conceived themselves as ushering in a society in which men, permitted the full exercise of their liberties as expressed in their
natural rights, would no longer suffer the "unnatural" stratifications which kept them from realizing their possibilities. As the
atom of the physical world, following the law of its nature, joins
with other atoms to realize a higher perfection in the harmonious
action of atoms in the molecule, so man, the atom of the social
world, uniting with other men, should reach a like perfection and
enjoy a like harmony in society. As the atom gives of its power
to the molecule, so man gives of his power to society. Since, however, the molecule only takes from the atom those powers necessary
for its peculiar molecular function, so society takes from man only
those powers necessary for its social function. There is a sphere

36. Locke, *Two Treatises on Government*, Bk. II, ch. 9, secs. 128-129, 130.
37. George Bull, "The Two Traditions in Political Philosophy," *Thought*,
VII (1933), pp. 404-417.
38. Laski, *op. cit.*, p. 208.

of atomic activity which the molecule cannot touch, and there is a sphere of human activity which society may not touch. For the natural right philosophers of the eighteenth century, the analogy ended at this point. That it can be pushed further the subsequent history of liberal democracy clearly proves. But that is matter for later consideration. Right, for the eighteenth century devotee of nature, was synonymous with physical power:

> In a universe in which man seemed only a chance deposit on the surface of the world, and the social process no more than a resolution of blind force, the "right" and the fact were indeed indistinguishable; in such a universe the right which nature gave to man was easily thought of as measured by the power he could exert.[39]

If rights are physical powers, to speak of equality of rights is to speak of the equality of men in their mental and physical capacities. This is, of course, absurd. Common sense belies such an assertion. When, therefore, the principles of Liberalism put into practice effected, in conjunction with the Industrial Revolution, tremendous inequalities, men took stock of their theories. Natural rights were relegated to the limbo of outmoded views, with the result that what was true in the theory was discarded along with what was false.

Natural rights are moral powers, not physical. They are grounded in a natural moral law which directs the *free* actions of men. Free actions are human actions, and the natural moral law is the law of human nature. It tells man what he *ought* to do to attain his natural perfection, and the Creator of the nature, Who imposes the law on the nature, gives also the means whereby it may be observed. Those means are rights, moral powers. They do indeed place a restraint on another, but that restraint is not physical. It is a bond placed on a free faculty, the will, through the instrumentality of knowledge. That bond may not be broken without the violation of the natural moral law. When it is broken,

39. Carl Becker, *The Declaration of Independence* (New York: Peter Smith, 1933), p. 276.

man is less a man. He acts contrary to his nature. The result is
not only the loss of his own perfection, the failure to realize the
possibilities of which his nature is capable, but it entails the same
chaos in the human world as would follow in the sub-human were
calcium to act like carbon, pythons like panthers, and birds like
baboons.

The failure on the part of Liberalism and Communism to distinguish between the individual and the person, between natural
law as physical and natural law as moral, between right as a
physical power and right as a moral power, forces a triple conclusion:

1. If man is a thing and not a person, human equality becomes
   an equality of mere number.
2. If natural law is physical and not moral, rights are grounded
   in force.
3. If natural rights are physical powers, men are mentally and
   physically equal.

To none of these propositions will the Liberal or the Communist
submit, though all three follow with necessity from the fundamental
premises of both philosophies. Nevertheless, the quantitative character of equality is evident in both systems. It reveals itself in the
atomic nature of the Liberal State where "everyone counts for one
and no one for more than one;" and it reveals itself likewise in the
classless society of Communism where any of the social functions
can be performed by any of the social units. If men are not mentally and physically equal, if quality and not quantity equates them,
then the liberal State and the classless society will have to abandon
some of their most cherished practices, practices which, as will be
shown later, have a meaning only on the supposition that men are
numerically equal.

The absurdity to which the false concept of man and the false
theory of natural rights reduced equality has resulted, in some
circles, in a sneering attitude toward a valuable and fundamental
human relation. It has become, in other cases, one of the "glittering generalities" that sends man out to seek the pot of gold at the

end of the rainbow; and when he finds it, he discovers it to be a worthless bauble. Others, convinced that equality is but a fiction, have adopted a pragmatic attitude. Unwilling to give up the "shibboleth that has been effective in action," and "regardless of its factual accuracy," they know "that emblazoned on democratic banners it has been one of those electric words that have challenged the indifferent, awakened the neutral, and inflamed the zealous." Loathe "to sacrifice this effective stimulus," which "has been used more to challenge action than to state a fact," they would reinterpret the "slogan that has been meaningful in the past." "Unquestionably" they say, "the primary connotation of the term equality is quantitative." Such a connotation does not fit the change that has come to pass in contemporary society. Individuals today are unimportant, for that reason they are not equal in the old sense. Hence, the reason "for desiring to treat equality as a fiction rather than a falsehood consists in the fact that the concept is functionally useful without being statically true. It is useful because we are still in need of a type of action which the concept has historically motivated."[40]

Such is the confusion to which modern thought has been reduced in its attempts to explain an important human relation, a relation which it has consistently misunderstood for the past four hundred years. Starting with a false premise that necessitated the denial of the spiritual, it has been unable to distinguish between a person and an individual, unable to distinguish between moral and physical laws, and as a consequence, between moral and physical powers. The personality of man having been lowered to the individuality of a thing, men were equated in terms of quantity. When the equation would not work, modern thinkers, instead of retracing their steps and reconsidering their premises, either abandoned a notion that has kept man from being a tool of his fellowman, or deluded themselves with the hope that an empty formula might still contain dynamic value.

---

40. T. V. Smith, *The American Philosophy of Equality* (Chicago: University of Chicago Press, 1927), pp. 255-270.

Only the Communist has maintained faith in equality, but his equality will not work unless he destroys freedom. These two, freedom and equality, are correlative. Take them out of their proper setting and give them a meaning and a function they were never meant to have, and you inflict on man such a distortion of nature that the heart-rending groans of humanity make the whole of creation shudder.

CHAPTER VI

INDIVIDUAL EQUALITY: ANARCHY VS. HIERARCHY

The collapse of democratic institutions which now threaten the world can hardly be attributed to any one factor. Nevertheless, sober minds will do well to submit to a critical analysis some of the fundamental concepts upon which the current neo-democracies have been erected. Not the least important of these concepts is equality. An examination of the fundamental philosophies of Liberalism and Communism has yielded its numerical and quantitative character in those systems. An examination of Christian philosophy has yielded its spiritual character. We have seen the relation of spiritual equality to man's social life. We have seen it preserve human dignity despite menial function and humble station. The effect of the application of quantitative equality to society remains to be shown. We propose to discuss that application under the following headings:

1. Individual equality and the social structure.
2. Individual equality and social justice.
3. Individual equality and civil power.
4. Individual equality and law.
5. Individual equality and economic life.

1. Individual Equality and the Social Structure

A. *Principles*

The conception of men as individually equal has repercussions in the whole of social life. So profound is the influence of this notion that we do not hesitate to say that it has shaken to its very foundations the whole structure of the State. Indeed, any permanent and durable structure is impossible in the presence of a principle which, emphasizing the absolute character of the individual to the neglect of his social nature, destroys the basis of fraternity and extinguishes any true liberty. That individual equality jeopardizes the other two principles of the democratic

217

trilogy, thus undermining the whole social structure we now propose to show.

Human society, whatever else its character, has an intrinsic urge to achieve an ordered and unified whole. It is possessed of something more than a herd instinct, something nobler than mere arithmetical union, something more rational than blank uniformity. It demands organization, and whatever involves organization, involves in turn a structural or hierarchical order, a subordination of the less to the greater, of means to end; and wherever there is subordination there is bound to be inequality. It is thus that intelligence leaves its stamp on the material universe. But if man, when he fashions matter into organized wholes, acts rationally, will he be less wise in his attempts to organize his fellows into social wholes? To the degree that equality forms the basis of the social ordering, society will be irrational. Equality cannot be structured. It is opposed to subordination as to its contradictory. When, therefore, men group themselves together, they must forego individual equality and consent to rank themselves in the social structure according as nature has endowed them with the capacity to function with greater or less importance in the attainment of the social purpose, the common good. To insist that equality form the warp and woof of social life is to reduce that life to the aggregate level of the irrational world.

Equality and organization are antithetical. The one demands uniformity, the other diversity. The one repels subordination, the other cannot exist without it. The one necessitates identity of function, the other requires that parts contribute by their diverse acts to the attainment of a common purpose. Hence things that are individually equal are incapable of effecting any true unity. Lacking any real ordination to oneness, they cannot, as a consequence, operate to a common end. Whatever unity they achieve is external. The parts are in reality not parts, but complete entities functioning in the same way, because their function is not for the whole, but for their own independent being. Hence, such individuals can be massed together; but they form no wholes, no structures, only aggregates of unrelated and independent units. Any function in the aggregate can be performed by any of the atomic parts; and whatever distinctive function issues from the totality is mere mass action, the uniform repetition of one and the same operation. Such "wholes," devoid of any finality, are devoid of a principle of order; and what is not ordered, is not the work of intelligence.

B. *Application of the Principles*

To the Liberal State. When the Liberal and the Communist seek to order man's political and social life on the basis of equality, it is but natural that the society achieved be governed by the principles that operate in a numerical aggregation. If men are individually equal, their social life is bound to be atomic. It will be characterized by the same superficial union that is apparent when equal individuals are banded into "wholes." Its unity will be imperiled to the degree that its members, lacking any social purpose, pursue their own independent interests. It will be irrational in proportion as it lacks order and finality.

The atomic liberal State with its emphasis on the individual equality of its members is characterized by just such disintegrating and irrational factors. A moment's reflection will clearly indicate this. The theory of the liberal democrat begins with the absolute sovereignty of the individual, a sovereignty that is equal in all men. When such independent sovereigns agree to form a political union, the resultant State is a collection of equal individuals whose sole bond is an artificial contract, whereby the contracting parties agree to hand over to some central authority such pieces of their self-government as will best protect their individual interests. The individuals thus become prior to the State, and true to the principles that govern the grouping of equal atomic units, act from motives of self-interest, rather than contribute by some determined function to the realization of any social purpose. Tawney, in observing this characteristic of the liberal State, remarks:

> The currents of social activity did not converge upon common ends, but were dispersed through a multitude of channels, created by the private interests of the individuals who composed society.[1]

1. R. H. Tawney, *The Acquisitive Society* (New York: Harcourt, Brace & Co., 1920), pp. 13-14.

Such dispersion acts as a centrifugal force in society, tearing asunder the tenuous bond that marks the aggregate whole. In the contractual society of the liberal democrat, the emphasis on individual rights rather than on social duties and the demand that civil authority be limited to the safeguarding of those rights, is consistent with the principles that operate in any aggregate of equals. The unhampered exercise of contractual freedom is the necessary correlate of individual equality, but it is also the nemesis of social union.

This emphasis on the priority of the individual, as opposed to the common good, is consistent with the empirical or nominalist philosophy which formed the liberal mind. As the Empiricist in his epistemology is bound to the individual and the concrete, and knows the common nature only as a compound of particulars, so the Liberal in his politics, true to his nominalist training, exalts the individual above the social. He sees the State as the sum of the men who compose it; the common good as the compound of individual self-interest, and the sovereignty of the people as the totality of the absolute sovereignty of individuals, men who are the supreme arbiters of their own volitions.

Nothing more truly illustrates the destructive character of the inorganic freedom of the modern democratic State than its operation in the economic world. *Laissez-faire* may not be the pivot of contractual society, but it is the logical outcome of rights which are. In a society where rights are primary and functions of nebulous importance, economic rights far outweigh social responsibilities. And when it is believed that such rights are equal in all men, government has no other obligation than to maintain a neutral attitude, as equal contestants for economic gain exercise their natural freedom to engage in competitive struggle to capture the most alluring markets or strike the most favorable bargains. In the liberal theory, such struggles are but the natural expression of self-interest; and the statistical concept of society which it sponsors, involving the Benthamite formula of the greatest good of the greatest number, sees economic egoism as the best guarantee of social prosperity. That it is also the best guarantee of social chaos, the history of the liberal State too well attests.*

The freedom of the parts to seek their own interests is inherent in a union of equals. Such is their proper function for they bear no intrinsic relation to the whole. Furthermore, being equal there is nothing to differentiate one function from another; and any function in the whole can be performed by any of the parts. Hence such functions are interchangeable. Where there is structural unity, on the other hand, each part has its own peculiar function. Its operation in the whole is distinctively its own, its unique contribution to the general well-being. It is that operation which gives it significant status. These same principles hold good in society. It is the function a man plays in society that locates him in the social structure and gives him social status. But the atomic liberal State, founded on the quantitative and accidental equality of men, must of necessity equate social function. No man is, therefore, unique in the State because of his peculiar contribution to its well-being. Hence there is nothing to give him status. There is only contract, a bargain struck between the parts to trade just that amount of freedom which will permit any man to do whatever he considers every other man has the same right to do.

> The exercise of the natural rights of every man has no other limits than those which are necessary to concede to every other man the free exercise of the same rights.[2]

There is no function in the liberal State, therefore, which cannot be the equal prerogative of any other member. That is why fitness for public office has no other determinant than the difference between 10,000,000 votes and 9,000,000. This is consistent practice if men are quantitatively equal. Citizenship is not the reward of function, but a right grounded on the absolute sovereignty of the individual. Since the contracting parties to the liberal State are all equally sovereign, citizenship is equally the right of each. This bestowal of citizenship, contingent on the mere fact of birth, obviates any distinction between the inhabitant and the citizen. Universal suffrage and equality of voting power are man's by natural right. As a consequence, ballots are "counted and not

2. David Ritchie, *Natural Rights* (New York: The Macmillan Co., 1924), *appendix,* pp. 290-294.

weighed."[3]　Competence has no other gauge than quantity, and no function in the liberal State is denied the aspiration of any man who can claim it by the "divine right of 51%." Rotation in public office is but the expression of nature's logic, and no question of public policy is too delicate or too intricate to baffle the powers of whatever agent of the people's will universal suffrage has endowed with political authority.

Nor is the mass mind less able to solve complicated matters of State. Initiative, referendum and the popular election of high-ranking judges, legislators and executives are samples of mass action in government, while the shower of telegrams that fall upon the heads of our lawmakers whenever significant issues arise, not only relieves them of the responsibility of rational choice in determining the course of public affairs, but indicates the evolution of direct legislation into a form of mail-order government. As a consequence the representative does not lead; he is merely the instrument for voicing the popular will in legislative chambers. He looks not to the well-being of the body politic or the establishment of the common good, but to the particular interests of his constituents.[4]　And rightly so. Where society is regarded as the aggregate of equal atomic units and the general good as the summation of individual self-interest, a representative could hardly function otherwise. He does not lead the mass because it has no place to go.[5] A union of equals has no finality. His function is not unique because there is no characteristic function of the social whole to which he may contribute in a special way. He is but the mouthpiece of his constituents, any of whom can replace him if the majority so decides. Universal suffrage, rotation in office, initiative, referendum and recall, the popular election of public officials, and the various methods of direct legislation—all these are

3. P. H. Odegard, "Majorities, Minorities, and Legislation," *The Annals of Am. Acad. Pol. and Soc. Sc.*, Vol. 169 (1933), pp. 69-70.

4. Ray Tucker, "The Men Who Make Our Laws," *The Annals*, vol. 169 (1933), pp. 47-54.

5. T. V. Smith, *The Democratic Way of Life* (Chicago: University of Chicago Press, 1939), p. 174: "We are not on a journey, and if we are, no one knows where we are going." Cf. Tawney, *op. cit.*, p. 12.

democratic devices which attest the fact that the liberal State is regarded as a society of men individually and politically equal. Regardless of how vehemently the Liberal may deny individual equality, there is present in the liberal State all the characteristics of atomic unity, characteristics which are at the same time factors of disintegration.

The fallacy of attempting to form any durable social structure in the presence of factors intrinsically destructive of sound unity, is aptly illustrated when we examine the mechanical structures of men. A typewriter constructed entirely of keys equal in size and shape would not be a typewriter, but a heap of unrelated objects. To be a typewriter there must be bolts, and springs, and space-bars, whose function it is not to type, but to provide the conditions necessary for the keys which do. Were the bolt to claim equality with the key and insist upon doing what the key does, and were the spring to insist that it had a right to be a space-bar, the typewriter would soon be a worthless mechanism, for bolts would do a bad job of typing, and springs an equally bad job of spacing. Only when bolts are made to do the kind of work bolts are fitted to do, and springs are made to contract and expand, which is the only thing a spring can do, will a typewriter be able to turn out an attractive and readable paper, which is the ultimate purpose of the typewriters. The same is true of society. To function it must be a hierarchy, an ordered whole, and not an atomic mass. It must have a purpose to the attainment of which the parts contribute by their function with greater or less immediacy. The modern Liberal, however, has forgotten this principle of common sense. In his passion for equality he has made men so equal that a sound social structure is impossible.

Individual equality destroys the social structure because it destroys the bond of fraternity. Things individually and quantitatively equal are independent one of the other. Incapable of being subordinated as parts, each seeks its own good rather than the good of the whole. There is no common bond, for there is no need of union; no mutual helpfulness because no variation of ability; no compensatory service because there is no high privilege. In the modern liberal democracy, with its emphasis on the arithmetical equality of men, these same features are clearly manifest. Men are independent atomic units, each seeking the good of self and cognizant of the State only when their own interests are in jeopardy. There is no compensation because there is no exalted privilege; no humble station because there exists no high dignity from which anyone is excluded. There are no leaders, for where each is considered capable of performing any public function or deciding on any public issue, there is no one to be led. Representatives merely express the people's wish; they do not indicate a sound course of action. But where there is no mutual dependence, no reciprocity, no spirit of service, there is no bond that knits a nation together.

When a nation has come to such a pass it can avoid disintegration only at the cost of liberty. Unity can be achieved not by some internal principle from within, but by the application of external force. Mass-men must be herded together under the whip of the leader; and freedom, which tore the State asunder, must give way to complete subjection. Liberal democracy was guilty of the fallacy of making men too equal. As a consequence it has been faced with three alternatives: social chaos, the abandonment of a false equality, or totalitarianism. Unfortunately it has chosen the last; but the choice was not necessary. Had the Liberal been willing to abandon his principle of individual equality and construct a social order based on the dignity of personality, he would not only have established a well-ordered State, but he would have gained a truer and more exalted equality, which would be proud enough to honor those individually superior, and humble enough to serve those individually inferior. Thence is begotten brotherhood, and of brotherhood unity. When men are ordered as one there is strength and solidity, and as a result a durable social structure.

To Communism. What has been said of the atomic liberal State holds equally true of the classless one, with this exception. Communism is more consistent than Liberalism. Having endowed individuals with equality, it knows it has made the State impossible. Hence, when the classless society will have come into being the State will "wither away." This is consistent teaching for organized equality is an anomaly indeed. Yet despite the consistency, the passing of political organization does not remove the anomaly. Society remains, a unified whole to which each individual is completely subordinated, having no independence of his own, and functioning only for the well-being of the whole.[6] If the principle of this unity be intrinsic, then society is an organism, yet an organism functioning on the basis of equality, a patent contradiction.

Communism repudiates individualism and substitutes in its place the social collectivity, wherein each individual so exactly duplicates the other that publisher and plumber could easily interchange without any discernible difference.[7] Yet the functions of these various individuals are directed to a common end.[8] Now such direction must be either according to an internal principle, and then you have organism, or according to an external principle, in which case there is not only loss of freedom, but a contradiction in the communistic theory.

If the direction of individual activities to a common end be according to an internal principle, there is the anomaly of organized equality. If it be according to an external principle, there is the anomaly of coerced equality, which, with the disappearance of the State, is effected in the absence of any coercive power.[9] That the classless society operates according to an internal principle of unity, and therefore according to a principle of organization, follows from the theory of Dialectical Materialism. This basic philosophy of Communism holds that the factors shaping society are inherently

6. F. J. Sheed, *Communism and Man* (New York: Sheed and Ward, 1938), ch. 7.

7. Bukharin and Preobraschensky, *The A B C of Communism* (trans. by E. C. Paul; Great Britain, 1922), pp. 79-80. Cf. V. I. Lenin, *State and Revolution* (New York: International Publishers, 1932), pp. 78-85.

8. *Ibid.*

9. Lenin, *op. cit.*, p. 74: ". . . people will gradually *become accustomed* to the observance of the elementary rules of social life . . . they will become accustomed to observing them without force, without compulsion. . . ."

controlled by the physical laws of nature.[10]   Then under the supposition that men are by nature individually equal, any natural law
that directs them to a common end violates their equality.   Hence
the classless society, in presenting the phenomenon of organized
equality, presents the amazing spectacle of nature in contradiction.
Nowhere has experience revealed the laws of nature directing
natural unity on the basis of equality.   If contradiction in nature is
possible then the classless society is unpredictable.

Granted that equality consists only in the absence of classes,
such absence is either the natural result of individual equality, or
it is an enforced leveling.   If it is the result of natural equality,
then nature cannot impose unity but only uniformity.   To insist
that it impose unity, and Communism makes such insistence,[11] is
to insist that nature is self-contradictory.   On the other hand, if
the absence of classes results from enforced leveling, this can only
mean that men are by nature unequal.   Such inequality is indeed
the candid admission of Communism.[12]   Leaving aside for a
moment the legitimacy of the candor, if men are not inherently
equal, if equality is placed in something external to man, as in
property, which is precisely where Communism places it,[13] then

10. F. Engels, *Anti-Dühring* (New York: International Publishers, 1935),
p. 79: "A purpose which is not imparted into Nature by some third party
acting purposively, such as the wisdom of a providence, but lies in the
necessity of the thing itself, constantly leads . . . to the unthinking inter-
polation of conscious and purposive activity." Dr. McFadden in comment-
ing on this inner necessity writes: "The Marxist contends that the development of a being towards a specific end is to be accounted for by the
material organization of the being itself." *Philosophy of Communism* (New
York: Benziger Bros., 1939), p. 128.

11. Communism not only admits the existence of finality in nature, but
a finality in the very constitution of things. In the dialectic process there
is the unity of opposites, and in the classless society all human activity
has a social purpose. Such social purpose, however, is not the result of
free choice. Rather it is the goal of nature's laws, and man's freedom
consists merely in the fact that he has become aware of *how* and *why*
natural forces operate. Cf. Engels, *"Socialism, Utopian and Scientific,"* in
Karl Marx, *Selected Works* (New York: International Publishers, 1933),
I, p. 186.

12. Karl Marx, *Critique of the Gotha Program* (New York: International Publishers, 1938), p. 9.

13. Since in the communist theory equality consists essentially in the
absense of classes, only the socialization of the means of production can

under the assumption that all this takes place according to an intrinsic principle, nature is doubly contradictory. It makes men unequal internally, but equal externally; unequal individually, but equal socially. Now if men are unequal by nature and social by nature, they must fall into a social hierarchy or find themselves in a society ill-suited to their nature. Hence an internal principle of unity presents the amazing phenomenon of an organized equality, or the equally amazing phenomenon of a leveled inequality.

An external principle of unity confronts the Communist with a like dilemma. He must either admit a coercion which is not coerced, or claim that men contribute freely to a common end, which in his own definition of freedom means not choice, but *knowledge of necessity*. Now with the advent of the classless society, the State will "wither away." Where, then, is the power to enforce unity? There is no internal principle for that involves contradiction; there is no external principle for the State has disappeared. Hence we are left with a society wherein equality is coerced and unity enforced in the absence of any coercive or enforcing power. While it is true that the Communist seeks to escape the absurdity of a coercion that is not coerced with the claim that men will freely direct their actions to a common end,[14] such escape impales him on the other horn of the dilemma. Freedom for the Communist consists in this—that man knows why he *must* act.[15] Not only is this another absurdity, for freedom consists in the absence of necessity, not in its presence; but since the Communist can explain the necessity neither by an internal principle nor by an external one, he does not *know* why he *must* act. Hence under the terms of his own definition, he cannot be free.

destroy classes and therefore affect equality. Hence, equality does not flow from anything intrinsic to man, but from the conditions external to him, *viz.*, common ownership of the means of production.

14. Lenin teaches that men will *voluntarily* work according to their ability, and each will take freely according to his needs. Cf. Lenin, *op. cit.*, p. 80.

15. Engels, *op. cit.*, pp. 130-131: "Freedom therefore consists in the control over ourselves and over external nature which is founded on the knowledge of natural necessity."

But aside from the pseudo-freedom, which knowledge of necessity confers, the materialistic basis of Communism must deny that freedom is any natural endowment of man. Hence for the Communist to assert that men will *voluntarily* contribute by their functions to the common welfare is to speak the language of deception.

Even granted the presence of an external force, coerced equality, like organized equality, is an anomaly. Coerced equality can mean two things. It can mean either that men are individually equal, and coercion is needed for the direction of their activities to a common end, or it can mean that men are individually unequal, and then social leveling must be coerced. If men as individuals are really equal—and Communism implies it in spite of explicit denials—then there is no real unity at all, but only uniformity, that is, mass action. This is not action directed to a common end, but to individual ends, which, though alike, are numerically different. Such ends do not require coercion for they are attainable naturally. The use of external coercion, therefore, would be futile. If the common end is but the sum of the individual ends, then the Communist is merely boot-legging the Liberal's principle which he has already repudiated. Furthermore, being equal, men are independent atomic units. They cannot be put under the domination of other men without the violation of their natures. Nor can they be formed into a social whole, that is a society, for that involves subordination of individual ends to a common end which involves, in turn, order and order hierarchy. Hence an equality that is coerced is either coercion without purpose or it is an organized equality which is a contradiction.

If men are individually unequal, as the Communist frankly contends, then coercion can only be directed to a leveled inequality, another contradiction. As unequal, men naturally fall into a social hierarchy, particularly where social grouping is effected by the laws of nature. Whether direction to a common end be the work of an internal or an external principle, where such direction is on the basis of inequality, it must result in a hierarchical and not a classless society. Hence the Communist must either give up his concept of equality, or abandon his dream of a society which is classless.

An external principle of unity, therefore, presents the Communist with a series of dilemmas. First, he must either admit a coercion which is not coerced or abandon his definition of freedom. Secondly, if an external force is conceded him, two untenable positions follow. If he admits individual equality, he is confronted with the further dilemma of denying unity or accepting hierarchy. If he admits individual inequality, he is faced with the absurdity of a leveled inequality or the abandonment of a classless society.

Not only does the communistic concept of equality end in absurdity, but, like its liberal forerunner, it is destructive of liberty and fraternity. Numerical equality is either natural or enforced. If the former, then unity must be artificially imposed from without; if the latter, uniformity. In either case liberty is destroyed. Such destruction, however, is no violation of Communism since, as has already been pointed out, its freedom consists not in the absence of restraint, but in the presence of necessity. Men are free to do not what they *ought* but what they *must,* which of course is no freedom at all.

If freedom has lost its meaning in Communism, fraternity has been equally emptied of any brotherly content. Love dies when hatred is born; and when men are taught to hate one another, and to envy an endowment other than their own, brotherly love is absurd. That is why a Communist must call another *comrade,* joint occupant of the prison of slavery. Shorn of love, he is no longer free to call another *brother.*

2. Individual Equality and Social Justice

Liberalism and Communism, in conceiving men as individually equal, have leveled society to mass unity, which is not unity at all but uniformity. As a consequence, justice is distorted in the one and destroyed in the other. The liberal State distorts social justice by reducing all justice to commutative. Its principle of individual equality has resulted in a society leveled to mass unity. Such unity admits only of the relation of part to part. The individual lacking any distinctive function ordered to the unique function of the whole, has no proper relation to the whole.

The substitution of part to part relationship for part to whole relationship is characteristic of the liberal State. Its mass unity requires that men function on the horizontal plane of human relations. Now horizontally men are equal. Their commutations, therefore, must be on the basis of strict arithmetical equality—that given must be the exact equivalent of that received. This is commutative justice or the equality of thing with thing. It is the justice which operates when men contract with one another. When the contract between the whole and the part is no different from the contract between the parts themselves, that is, when men contract with the State in the same manner as they contract with one another, social justice or "the common welfare taken distributively as well as collectively"[16] is reduced to commutative justice. The social whole being the summation of the individual parts, the common welfare is taken collectively when each part renders to every other part its just due. In the liberal State man was thought to have no other obligation than that of respecting the rights of his fellowman.[17] It was consistent, therefore, that emphasis be placed upon individual rights rather than social duties. The consequence of such emphasis was the reduction of social justice to the level of commutative, a reduction consistent with the Liberal's equation of men as things rather than persons.

Now if the liberal State can account for no other relationship than that of man to man, if it can recognize no other justice than the interchange of individual just dues, then it must regard all social function as horizontal rather than vertical. This eliminates all need for legal and distributive justice, both of which operate on the vertical plane of human relations. It is the former which regulates the duty of the individual to the State, obligating him to obey just laws and to contribute to the general welfare in proportion to his ability.[18] It is the second which regulates the relation between the State and the individual, causing such distribution of the common good that each individual receives all that is needed for the

16. J. A. Ryan and F. J. Boland, *Catholic Principles of Politics* (New York: The Macmillan Co., 1940), p. 145.

17. Tawney, *op. cit.*, pp. 8-19.

18. Ryan and Boland, *op. cit.*, p. 143. Cf. F. J. Haas, *Man and Society* (New York: The Century Co., 1930), p. 74.

performance of his social function.[19]　But a State which cannot adequately account for the relation of the individual to the social whole, which equates vertical functions with horizontal because it believes that it best maintains the common welfare when it balances individual rights, must of necessity distort social justice. Despite the liberal theory, men are not equal as individuals; hence any attempt to fit them into a political structure ill-suited to their natural differences will automatically result in a distortion.　One cannot fit squares to triangles without pulling the one or the other out of shape.　Neither can men, distinguished by differences, be patterned into uniformity without the accompaniment of human pain.

The theory of the liberal State taught that human equality required political leveling.　As a consequence, it bestowed on men, differing in the concrete realization of the same specific nature, functions politically the same.[20]　This misplaced equality resulted in forcing men who were not the same into the same political mould.　It thus required from each individual what was not in proportion to his ability, a requirement essentially unjust.　If men contribute to the common welfare equally, they must share in its benefits in like manner.　Yet to bestow on men whose needs are not the same, the same social benefits, is to give to man what is not his due, a distribution essentially unjust.　Hence the liberal State in equating men as individuals violated both legal and distributive justice.　It threw public office open to any individual irrespective of qualifications.[21]　In its passion for equalizing indi-

19. *Ibid.*, p. 141.　Haas, *op. cit.*, p. 76.
20. Senero Mallet-Prevost, "United States—Democracy or Oligarchy," *The Annals*, Vol. 168 (1933), p. 160: "Ordinarily, if the laws of a country declare men to be equal, if they announce that all shall equally have the right of suffrage and that all shall be equally eligible to office, men conclude that such equality exists.　This is untrue.　The basis of deception lies in the mistaken assumption that men are in fact equal; that they are equally capable of exercising rights, and that the enactment of that doctrine into law suffices to insure such equality in the political sphere."
21. S. de Madariaga, *op. cit.*, pp. 34-35: "The levelling attitude . . . accounts for one of the most fallacious aspects of the current conception of equality—that which takes for granted that men are interchangeable, at any rate in public life. . . . In our liberal democracies every Tom, Dick or Harry is assumed to be apt to perform any public function which may be in the giving of his party, and we take pride in the open-mindedness wherewith we admit to the most delicate functions of government the roughest diamonds—or pebbles—which universal suffrage may throw up."

vidual rights, it refused in a conflict of rights to judge those attaching to the human person of more importance than those centering in superfluous wealth. As a consequence, it tried to balance personality with property, an equation without justice, and then sought to deaden the pain of injustice with the opium of charity. It substituted for the honor of a just due, the humiliation of a dole. It exchanged justice for philanthropy, and respectability for beggary, an exchange in keeping with the Liberal's degradation of the person to the status of a thing.

Against this iniquitous substitution, this compensation for the equation of person with property, men reacted with the repudiation of property, and the repudiation was Communism. But Communism cannot rectify the Liberal's mistake. It can only replace one distortion of justice with a distortion in another direction, and then replace this new distortion with no justice at all. The Liberal reduced all justice to commutative. He emphasized the horizontal plane of human relations to the neglect of the vertical. The Communist would but reverse the order. Man has no business on the horizontal plane at all. His transactions are entirely with society. Men are not isolated units embarking on a social career in virtue of a compact. They are parts of a social organism and as such are completely subordinated to the whole. Property, therefore, is no longer individual but communal. Hence all man's relations are vertical. Social justice rather than being leveled to commutative as in the liberal State, is elongated as legal and distributive, in the Dictatorship of the Proletariat. With the advent of the classless society the *bourgeois* virtue disappears and there is no justice at all.

Communism distorts justice in the Dictatorship of the Proletariat by the commission of two fallacies. First, by making social justice the sum of legal and distributive justice; secondly, by making distributive justice the equivalent of commutative. Now to make social justice the sum of legal and distributive justice is to assume that the parts of the social whole have only a vertical function, a thing which Communism definitely assumes. This obviates the need of commutative justice, for if the individuals exchange no services among themselves, there is no relation of justice between them. Not only does this obviate the principle of a healthy organism, but it contradicts the principle of individual equality which lies at the basis of the communistic theory.

In every organism besides the vertical there are horizontal functions, some organs contributing to the good of the whole by the interchange of functions among themselves. Disturb this interchange and the good of the whole organism is disturbed. The blood furnishes iodine to the thyroid and the thyroid supplies thyroxin to the blood, a substance which it needs for oxidation. Eliminate this interchange of iodine for thyroxin and the well-being of the whole is seriously affected. In like manner, the well-being of the social organism suffers and social justice is violated when individuals are denied an interchange of services, and forced to contribute directly to and receive directly from the whole. If Communism insists on the organic nature of society which it does, then to violate a fundamental principle of that nature is to throw the whole out of balance.

Such distortion, however, is the necessary correlate of the communistic attempt to organize equality. Organized equality is a hybrid, a cross between organism and mass, between unity and uniformity. The one demands that the parts contribute according to their ability to the common good, the other demands the equal distribution of that good. Organic equality, however, will characterize only the higher phase of communistic society. It will emerge only after a long process of formation during the first or lower phase of Communism, the Dictatorship of the Proletariat. During this period, distribution, instead of being according to need as in an organism will be according to contribution or work. This is the bourgeois notion of justice. Labor, being a commodity, can be exchanged only for its exact equivalent. Hence man has a right only to that which is the exact measure of his labor. But an exchange of equal values constitutes commutative justice. The Communist, therefore, has taken commutative justice from the horizontal plane of human relations where it naturally operates in regulating the exchange of functions between the parts, and has transferred it to the vertical plane where it regulates the relation between the whole and the part. The result is distortion and disorder. However since an organism made up of equal parts is bound to violate right order, it follows that it is bound to violate justice which is the fruit of order.

In his *Critique of the Gotha Program* Marx verifies this appraisal of justice characteristic of the Dictatorship of the Proletariat.

> Within the coöperative society based on the common ownership of the means of production, the producers do not exchange their products. . . . Accordingly the individual producer receives back from society . . . exactly what he gives to it. What he has given to it is his individual amount of labor. . . . He receives a certificate from society that he has furnished such an amount of labor and with this certificate he draws from the social stock of means of consumption as much as the same amount of labor costs. . . . Here obviously the same principle prevails as that which regulates the exchange of commodities, as far as this is exchange of equal values. . . . As far as the distribution of the (means of production) among the individual producers is concerned, the same principle prevails as in the exchange of commodity-equivalents, so much labor in one form is exchanged for an equal amount of labor in another form.[22]

That this is a distortion of justice, Marx frankly admits, but he excuses it with the remark that *"equal right* is still stigmatized by a bourgeois limitation,"[23] a stigma which Lenin explains as an "injustice consisting in the distribution of the articles of consumption 'according to the work performed'."[24]

Bourgeois right suffered from an enlargement of the commutative principle. Marx dispenses with the principle altogether, once the classless society renders individual exchange impossible.

> In a higher phase of Communist society . . . only then can the narrow horizon of bourgeois right be fully left behind and society inscribe on its banners: *from each according to his ability, to each according to his need.*[25]

This communistic slogan is meant to epitomize the reign of justice in the classless society. Lenin gives a deeper insight into its meaning when he defines it as that condition of society wherein

22. Karl Marx, *Critique of the Gotha Program* (New York: International Publishers, 1938), pp. 8-9.
23. *Ibid.*, p. 9.
24. Lenin, *op. cit.*, p. 77.
25. Marx, *Critique of the Gotha Program*, p. 10.

. . . people have become so accustomed to observe the fundamental rules of social life, and their labour is so productive,
that they voluntarily work *according to their ability.* The
'narrow horizon of bourgeois rights,' which compels one to
calculate with the hard-heartedness of a Shylock, whether he
has not worked half an hour more than another, whether he
is not getting less pay than another, this narrow horizon will
then be left behind. Then will there be no need for any exact
calculation by society of the quality of products to be distributed to each of its members, each will take freely "according
to his needs."[26]

If this be justice, then indeed it "involves the most radical
rupture with traditional ideas."[27] The Communist, however, has
confused the traditional ideas with the Liberal's distortion of them,
and in uprooting the cockle has uprooted also the wheat. Justice
does not consist in the absence of envy, nor in the lack of a standard for measuring one's just due. On the contrary, it is the habitual
will to render to another what is rightfully his. But to determine
what is one's just due, there is needed an objective measurement.
It is this objective standard the Communist has repudiated, and
substituted in its place a subjective one. Now nothing is more
inadequate for measuring one's just due than a subjective standard.
Man is notoriously prejudiced in his own favor, which makes him
incompetent to act as judge of his own case. Yet in the absence
of any objective standard, what is to determine whether an individual has put forth the maximum of effort and taken only minimum
of need? There are only two possible answers—men are either
completely equal or completely unselfish. If the former, then they
are mere automata, giving equally and receiving equally in return.
The least deviation would thus be immediately detected.[28] Abso-

26. Lenin, *op. cit.,* pp. 79-80.

27. Karl Marx and F. Engels, *The Communist Manifesto* (New York:
League for Industrial Democracy, 1933), p. 80.

28. H. J. Laski, *Communism* (New York: Henry Holt & Co., 1927),
p. 178: "For we cannot measure powers, especially in the realm of intellectual effort; and the only criterion of needs that is possible is one that
assumes a rough identity between men and the insistence that the claim
of this identity upon the social product is the first charge we must recognize."

lute equality is implicit in communistic doctrine, otherwise directors and ditch-diggers could never replace each other.[29]   Absolute unselfishness, however, is explicit for "the great Socialists . . . presupposed . . . a person not like the present man in the street capable of spoiling without reflection . . . the stores of social wealth and demanding the impossible."[30]   Nevertheless, since "it has never entered the head of any Socialist to 'promise' that the highest phase of Communism will arrive"[31] one need not take too seriously the maxim: *From each according to his ability, to each according to his need.*

Individual inequality as the concrete expression of the equality of personal nature begets not only fraternity and freedom, but begets as well social justice. Because men are individually unequal, they are ranked in the social hierarchy according as ability has fitted them to contribute more or less immediately to the attainment of the social purpose, the common good. And since that good cannot be attained unless "each individual man in the dignity of his human personality is supplied with all that is necessary for the exercise of his social functions,"[32] social justice is described as the common good taken distributively as well as collectively. Now the common good taken collectively is the good of the whole community; taken distributively, it is the good of the individual parts. The former is a function of legal justice, the latter of distributive. Social justice, however, cannot be limited merely to the functioning of these two types of justice. Commutative justice also is bound up intimately with the common good, and in so far as there is any interference with its proper operation, to that degree will the common good be impaired. Social justice, therefore, is the harmonious operation of this threefold order of justice. Thus commutative justice regulates the contract between the employer and the employed, requiring the one to give to the other the exact value of the work performed. Now should one demand more or the other less than this value, commutative justice is violated. As a consequence the economic

29. Bukharin and Proebraschencky, *op. cit.*
30. Lenin, *op. cit.*, p. 80.
31. *Ibid.*
32. Pius XI, "Atheistic Communism," *The Catholic Mind*, XXXV (1937), p. 163.

structure is thrown out of balance and the common good impaired. As this is a function of legal and distributive justice, then these are likewise disrupted and social justice violated.

Legal and distributive justice spring from individual inequality, commutative justice from specific equality. Since men are individually unequal, they do not function the same way in the social hierarchy. As a consequence legal justice requires that they contribute to the common good according to ability, while distributive justice requires that reward be proportionate to function. Should any condition exist which disturbs this proper balance, the common good suffers. Now the weaker members of society are not always able to meet their social obligations. Distributive justice, therefore, requires that such be the recipients of greater aid from the State. In contracts between wealth and poverty, between corporations and individuals, equalization is brought about by legislation protecting the weak against exploitation by the strong. Distributive justice, therefore, requires that commutative justice be observed. It throws the weight of the State to the side of the weak, not from any impulse of charity, but because financier and factory-hand being equal in their personal natures are equally in need of whatever share in the common good is necessary for the development of their persons and the attainment of their ends. Commutative justice, on the other hand, demands that since men are substantially equal, they must treat with one another on the basis of strict equality. Thus the banker and the baker, in the exchange of commodities, stand on a par in the dignity of man to man.

Intimately bound up, therefore, with the proper functioning of legal and distributive justice, and hence with a society characterized by social justice, is the concept of human equality. A distorted notion of this important human relation begets a distorted social order, the malfunctioning of justice and the disappearance of peace. Inequality begets order and of order is born justice; from the union of these two, there issues peace, for peace is the fruit of justice and the tranquillity of order.

3. INDIVIDUAL EQUALITY AND CIVIL POWER: *Liberalism*

In the framework of the liberal democratic State, the individual and quantitative interpretation of equality has three important political effects:

1. It makes civil society an artificial rather than a natural institution.
2. It makes the end of the State the protection of property rather than the perfection of personality.
3. It involves a totalitarian principle.

A. *Civil Society an Artificial rather than a Natural Institution*

In their *specific natures* men are free and equal, but because man has no dominion over natures his freedom does not contradict his equality; it complements it. To the Liberal all this is changed. Nature is not something intrinsic to man, but something external to him. He is free in so far as there is no restraining force in his environment to curtail his action. He is equal to his fellowman in that such restraint is absent to the same degree in all men. Human equality is, therefore, placed in the externals of nature rather than in nature itself. That is why it is brought under the jurisdiction of men and thus becomes antinomic to freedom. Man is free to exercise his powers over the accidentals of a nature, but never over the nature itself.[33] When, therefore, the Liberal's pre-political man seeks to exercise his freedom, it immediately comes into conflict with his equality. To preserve equality man becomes political, but he does it at the expense of freedom. Hence civil society, far from bringing man's nature to perfection, puts a limitation upon it. It is consistent, therefore, that between man and the State there should be an antinomy. But things antinomous to nature never issue from it.[34] The liberal democratic State, with its antithesis between

33. Man discovers a nature, he does not invent it. Having discovered the nature he may actualize it, but he is bound by the laws which govern it. The reason for this lies in the fact that only God is the source of being. Man merely discovers the beings God sees as possible, and in actualizing them is limited by their laws.

34. R. M. MacIver, "The Meaning of Liberty and Its Perversions," *Freedom Its Meaning* (Ed. by R. N. Anschen; Harcourt, Brace & Co., 1940), p. 281.

liberty and equality on the one hand, and liberty and authority on
the other, took its rise not in nature but in contract. Its concept
of equality could hardly permit it to do otherwise. Where men are
equally free no man can assume political jurisdiction over another.
Where that freedom refers to the external placement of acts, its
equality must forever forbid that man place himself under the yoke
of an authority exercised by another man. No man can rule his
equals. In the Liberal's theory there is no law beyond that of
atoms and molecules to which man must bow, hence there is nothing to urge him into political union but his own free choice. The
right of man to rule men, therefore, can arise only by the alienation
on the part of equal individuals of equal portions of their self-rule.
Such alienation curtails freedom, but it preserves equality, for if
political authority has its source equally in all men, then before it
all men stand on a par. Yet to the Liberal, it must be remembered,
equality touches men in their accidental rather than in their essential nature. Hence any institution erected for the preservation of
an accidental character answers no primary need of man. It is,
therefore, of passing and not of permanent value, thus its dissolution is bound to ensue. The passing of the liberal democratic State
is the natural result of its transitory character. Having fulfilled no
distinctly human need its termination will be no human catastrophe.

B. *The End of the State is the Protection of Property, not Perfection of Personality*

Not only does the quantitative nature of equality stamp the
liberal State with an accidental character, but it makes the end of
the State the protection of property rather than the perfection of
personality. In the liberal theory the only reason why men enter
political union is to preserve their equal right to property. Primitive equality was lost and discord ensued through a violation of
that right. To insure a return of peace and to balance men's right
to own the State came into being. Its end and purpose is to act
as an impartial arbiter in a conflict of rights, and to throw the
weight of its authority to the side of the contestant, the seizure of
whose just due unbalanced the scales of natural right. Now men
have an equal right to property precisely because they have an

equal obligation to perfect their persons. It is the perfection of personality, however, and not the possession of property into which the State should issue. Property is the extension of personality. It is one of the means whereby the capabilities of the person are realized. A necessary means no doubt, and, therefore, one which the State should make available for all men. Nevertheless, the possession of property is subordinate to the perfection of persons, as the means is subordinate to the end. Generically all men have the same end, and all being under the same obligation of attaining it have need of the same means. But men realize their ends in diverse ways because their natures are concretized in diverse ways. Consequently, diversity enters the means not qualitatively but quantitatively. In equating the right to property the liberal State is equating not abstract rights but concrete ones; not specific rights, which are qualitative, but individual rights which are quantitative. Thus one man's right to excess wealth is judged as basic and as inalienable as another man's right to bare sustenance. Such balancing overlooks the fact that property is a means and not an end. It is not property that is sacred but person. Yet a State that will balance a banker's right to a palatial yacht with a baker's right to his pastry shop is not only placing property above personality, and the accidental above the substantial, but is in reality violating the very equality it so scrupulously seeks to maintain. All men are equally obligated to the perfection of their persons, and regardless of how accidentally those persons may differ, they have an equal right to the things necessary for such perfection. But if rights to property in the concrete are equally sacred, then the State which insists that a banker's right to his palatial yacht is as sacred as the baker's right to his pastry shop, must also insist that the baker in paying interest to the banker give up his right to a child, that the banker may not have to give up his right to a cruise.

Now obviously these rights are not of equal value. One man's right to a family is of greater value than another's right to a luxurious craft. Yet a State which declares that a man's right to superfluous wealth cannot be denied because another man lacks the means necessary to raise a family in decent comfort, is definitely committed to the protection of property rather than the perfection of personality.

The refusal of the liberal State to interfere with an economic state of affairs where human life is sacrificed to higher profits, values the accidental above the substantial, the means above the end, and property above person. In its zeal for equalizing the non-essentials, the liberal State not only makes one man subordinate to another in that which touches his humanity, but makes the subordination so great that the subhuman becomes preferable to the human. The spectacle of nations today blasting human lives to pave the way for economic empires had its precedent in a Liberalism that made total régimes possible by first subjecting man to man, and then man to things.

C. *It Invokes a Totalitarian Principle*

The divine origin of civil power is beyond the comprehension of the Liberal. Unconscious of any law outside the body politic, save the physical law of nature, he is unconscious of any obligation on the part of man to perfect his person, hence, unconscious of the true function of the State. Now rightly the Liberal knows that the equality of men forbid that one man assume jurisdiction over another. Whence then the origin of civil power? Not from outside humanity for outside humanity there is only the physical universe or at best a Deity whose works evoke no divine concern. The power of man to rule men, therefore, can have its source only in the contract of free and equal men, which means ultimately, only in human will. Even those Liberals who deny the doctrines of natural law and natural right, and their consequent notion of social contract, can derive political authority only from some human source.[35] When human will becomes the source of law there is nothing to prevent law from becoming arbitrary or deteriorating into caprice, and nothing to prevent man from falling totally under the power of other men. Make human will the source of law and the way is open for man to become a victim to what other men want. Place man under the domination of another man's will and you violate not only his equality but his liberty as well.

Now individually man has only the power to rule himself, which

35. Lerner, *op. cit.*, pp. 22-24.

is essentially different from the power to rule the multitude. Self-rule means self-mastery, the control and direction of man's animal nature by his rational. The power to rule the multitude is meant to issue into something quite different. Its end is to effect the common good requisite for human beatitude. Unless this latter power has its source in some power outside and above humanity, it becomes nothing but the collection of human wills, each of which, released from obligation to any law higher than itself, is without limitation and, therefore, absolutely sovereign. But if individually man has only the power of self-rule, the exercise of power over any other man is but the exercise of brute force. Such exercise is without justification unless it be the only way to fulfill an obligation imposed on man by divine authority.

The recognition of a higher law emanating from a divine source not only serves as an objective standard for testing the validity of human law, but it serves as the very foundation of civil power, and saves man from the humiliation of submitting to his equals or to the arbitrariness of his fellows. When human law is valid, it is but the concrete application of Divine Law. Hence, in obeying it, man is not violating his equality in submitting to the will of another man. He is only bowing to that in another which is divine. This is a preservation both of his equality and his dignity. The Creator of human nature accorded it a unique honor when He asked of it only obeisance to Divinity. Though all below man is subject to his rule, man himself is ruled directly from the throne of the Most High, without submitting to the angelic orders far above him in the hierarchy of creation. That is why positions of human authority are rightfully surrounded with external splendor, and public officials accorded the deference proportionate to the power they wield. They are the executors of divine commands and in honoring them, man honors, not his equals, but his Creator. The human executor of divine power may be an infamous rogue, but in obeying him man condones neither his infamy nor submits to his villainy. He honors that in him which is of God.

In his repudiation of a higher law emanating from a divine source, the Liberal would undo all this. He not only robs man of his dignity, but robs him likewise of his equality and his freedom by placing him under the will of other men, and thus exposing him to the possibility of falling a victim to the arbitrariness of his fellows. It is the refusal of Liberalism to take cognizance of a higher law, which gives divine origin to civil power, that is the seed bed of modern totalitarianism and arbitrary rule. No one sees this more clearly than Walter Lippmann when he writes:

> Among a people which does not try to obey this higher law, no constitution is worth the paper it is written on: though they have all the forms of liberty, they will not enjoy its substance.[36]

Not only does Lippmann, who defends Liberalism, see the need for a higher law, but he finds Liberalism guilty of its repudiation because it is guilty of its falsification:

> Now obviously if the higher law of the state is simply the traditional law as it has evolved in the course of history, to insist upon its supremacy is to put the living under the dominion of the dead, and to deny to them the power to remedy injustice and improve their condition. . . .

> That, as we have already seen, was the reason why the progressive thinkers of the nineteenth century rejected the supremacy of law and poured contempt and ridicule upon the conception of a higher law. They had found that in practice the higher law meant either the traditional law, with all its historic injustices, or the vague, subjective, and irresponsible fantasies of doctrinaires agitating the crowd. The traditional law was in many vital respects intolerably unsuited to the modern world. The doctrinaires, when they appealed to the supposedly universal law, were observed to be violently unable to agree on what it was. Thus the whole conception was lost, and by the twentieth century political thinking had ceased to have any criteria beyond those of immediate expediency, self-assertiveness, and momentary success. . . .

> The pioneer liberals vindicated the supremacy of law over the arbitrary power of men. That is the abiding truth which we inherit from them. But the law which they vindicated was in many respects the mere defense of ancient privileges and immunities. Thus they made it easy to invoke the supremacy

36. Lippmann, *op. cit.*, p. 346.

of the law in order to prohibit the improvement of human affairs. In the decadence of liberalism the conception of a higher law was used to defend vested interests and obstruct reform. That was its fatal defect and the cause of its downfall. But in the debacle there was swept away not only the mistaken insistence upon the supremacy of the traditional law, but the nobler intuition that liberty and human dignity depend upon the supremacy of the spirit of the law.[37]

Yet Lippmann himself can be found guilty of ignoring or not understanding the divine nature of this higher law. In seeking its substance and source he writes:

> The denial that men may be arbitrary in human transactions *is* the higher law. . . . To those who ask where this higher law is to be found, the answer is that it is a progressive discovery of men striving to realize themselves, and that its scope and implications are a gradual revelation that is by no means completed. In the beginning of law men could aim no higher than to keep the peace. They had made a great advance when the injured man agreed to take in vengeance no more than an eye for an eye. They advanced further when the dominion of the strong over the weak was legalized as caste, and bounds were put on their superior strength. They advanced still further when the masters had duties as well as rights over their subjects. The advance continued as the rights of the masters were progressively checked and liquidated as having no intrinsic justification.[38]

This higher law of Mr. Lippmann will not do. Analysis reveals it as some vague evolving code progressively formed by men in their struggle against arbitrary power. There is nothing to indicate that it has anything other than a human origin, and nothing to indicate why arbitrary power is wrong. Man may not deal arbitrarily with his fellows for the simple reason he has no power of any kind over them unless it be given him from above. The reason why he has no power is because other men have a nature like his own. No man may rule his equals, for generically every

37. *Ibid.*, pp. 344-345. Cf. E. S. Corwin, "Liberty and Juridical Restraint," in *Freedom Its Meaning* (ed. by R. N. Anschen; New York: Harcourt, Brace & Co., 1940), pp. 84-103.
  38. *Ibid.*, pp. 346-347.

man has the same end, and law is nothing more than direction to an end. Only the creator of a nature can direct it to its end, for only the creator of a nature can formulate the law that governs it. All that man can do is to administer that law in concrete cases, and the power to administer is not his own. It originates only in the power that enacts, and that power is divine. God shares this power with men only because, having made the individuals of human nature unequal, they stand in need of mutual aid, hence, in need of social union. The purpose of this union is to bring about that sufficiency of well-being in which each individual can best fulfill the obligation he is under of attaining his end. Since both the obligation and the end are determined for him by his Creator, society is only a means by which he obeys a divinely imposed obligation. Its laws, therefore, have but one purpose, the creation of those conditions wherein man individually can best observe the law of his nature directing him to the perfection of his person and the attainment of his end. Such laws, subordinated to a higher law originating in a power outside humanity, can never become arbitrary. Being at the service of man, they can never subject him. Rather they direct and can even coerce if man elects to go the wrong way.[39]

If it was out of respect for human equality that God would not subject man to the will of his fellows, it was out of respect for human freedom that He gave to man the power to rule himself, not only individually, but collectively. Nevertheless, the power to rule the multitude was not bestowed unmindful of human equality. God does not select the wielder of power nor does He decree the manner of its exercise. All that is left to man's free choice. Because men are equal, God will not permit that one man fall under the power of another man unless that power be divinely bestowed and its executor humanly chosen. Because men are free, God grants them the power to rule themselves in whatever manner they decide best suited to their cultural development.

The Liberal, on the other hand, by endowing man with an exaggerated freedom that would absolve him from obligation to any will

39. M. F. X. Millar, "Burke and the Moral Basis of Liberty," *Thought*, XVI (1931), pp. 79-101.

but his own, destroyed equality while severing the roots of liberty. The destruction of one has always repercussions on the other, because both are rooted in human nature. Man has no power over natures, not even his own. While under no physical compulsion to obey their laws, he must either obey them or take the consequences. He is free to jump from the roof of a towering skyscraper, but when he does, he must submit to the law of falling bodies and not look forward to a brisk stride down the avenue when he hits the concrete below. Likewise, man may elect to live on the rational or animal level, but when he makes the latter his choice, he cannot expect to escape the law of the jungle. To take liberty and equality out of their intrinsic setting in human nature and make them accidental thereto, is bound to bring dynamic results to man's individual and social life. If human freedom means obedience to no law but that of man, submission to the strong will always be the fate of the mass of men. And if human equality means no more than a balance struck between quantitative entities, human rule will always be iniquitous.

Add to the denial of a higher law the quantitative equality of men, and you have concocted the explosive mixture that will dynamite social life. It makes no difference whether dictators or majorities be the wielders of power, the principles are the same. Human will is *not* the source of law, and whether it be the will of the dictator or the will of the majority, it destroys human freedom and makes a mockery of human equality. Totalitarianism may be the madness of modern dictators, but it is not their unique disease. They inherited the malady from their liberal ancestors by the simple process of replacing the will of many by the will of one.

3. Individual Equality and Civil Power: *Communism*

The conception of the State as a conventional institution, brought into being to protect private property and maintain order, was the Liberal's premise. Communism has accepted that premise as fundamental, using it as the underlying theme of a political theory, advanced with certain variations in keeping with the philosophy of Dialectical Materialism. Instead of the State springing from the alienated powers of equal individuals, through the medium of free contract, the Communist sees it as the seizure of power on the part of the class which has gained control of the means of production.[40] It is thus an organ of class domination necessary for keeping down class conflict and maintaining order, when society becomes divided into antagonistic classes having irreconcilable economic interests.[41] These conflicting economic interests, having issued from a method of production consequent upon the advent of private property, would rend society asunder did not the exploiting class organize itself as a power equipped for the oppression of the class it wishes to use for its own benefit.

In the communistic theory, therefore, as in the liberal, political power is a thing of force. It is wielded in both cases as a coercive measure necessary to maintain peace when property is threatened and equality violated. But whereas in the liberal theory the State is supposed to preserve equality, in the communistic one its function is to induce inequality. In either case it involves an alienation of power and, therefore, not only a curtailment of the "natural" man, but the subjection of one man to the will of the other. Hence, in the communistic theory, as well as in the liberal, the concept of the State involves the notion of totalitarianism. Furthermore, in both theories, political power, being synonymous with coercion, is looked upon as a necessary evil springing from the iniquity of men.

While the State in the liberal theory is an organization of the good for the punishment of the wicked, it is for the Communist just the reverse. Nevertheless, both theories, postulating the progressive goodness of men, involve the diminution of political power inversely proportional to man's advance in virtue. Only the Communist, however, admits the transitory character of the State. To the Liberal the growth of human virtue culminates in a wider dissemination of political power, thereby giving to the State a broader popular base. Political equality is for him the surest guarantee of economic equality. The Communist is more logical. Though the Dictatorship of the Proletariat is indeed a wider dissemination of political power, it is still the rule of man over man, and, therefore,

40. F. Engels, *The Origin of the Family* (Chicago: Charles H. Kerr & Co., 1902), pp. 205-212.
41. *Ibid.*

still an instrument of inequality. Only when the proletariat becomes synonymous with the whole people will the Dictatorship disappear, and the rule of man over man cease.[42]

Hence for the Communist complete equality means the dissolution of the State, whereas for the Liberal it means a State with a broader foundation, and, therefore, a State more strongly entrenched. For the one, men become politically equal only when their economic conditions become nicely balanced; for the other, economic equality will prevail only when political power is equally the right of all. Both are wrong. Equality consists neither in the power men wield nor in the property they own, nor does inequality consist in the unequal distribution of either. Both of these things are accidental to man and therefore of a transitory character. Yet since the Communist and the Liberal are committed to an equality centered in the accidentals of life, it is consistent that the State they postulate, as the organ regulating that equality, should rest on the external, the fleeting and the imperfect.

The State is not an instrument in the hands of either the virtuous or the wicked to coerce those who will not conform to its rule. Nor does its purpose consist in the balancing or unbalancing of the scales of equality. Coercion is the least of its functions, and the protection of property but a means to its proper end. That the Liberal and the Communist confuse the essential functions of the State with those of its activities subordinate to its proper end is consistent with a conception of man which exalts the individual above the species, the material above the spiritual, the accidental above the substantial, means above end, and thing above person.

The purpose of political authority is to create that sufficiency of well-being wherein the pursuit of human perfection becomes possible. Since it is associated with man's end, it is associated with his nature. Man has no jurisdiction over natures, therefore, he cannot enact their laws. Human nature being the same in every man, no one man can fall under the will of another, for whatever is subject to human will exists primarily for human benefit. Polit-

42. Engels, "Socialism: Utopian and Scientific," *op. cit.*, pp. 181-182. Cf. Lenin, *op. cit.*, pp. 69-85. S. H. M. Chang, *The Marxian Theory of the State* (Philadelphia: University of Pennsylvania, 1931), pp. 125-139. Lerner, *op. cit.*, pp. 98-99.

ical authority, therefore, cannot arise from human will, nor from any combination of human wills. Its source ultimately must be in the mind of Him who brought human nature into existence for His own divine purpose.

The equality of human nature, therefore, demands that political authority issue from divine source. Since that is so, the concrete exercise of it can never be at variance with the purpose of the nature whose end it serves to achieve. The following parable will suffice to illustrate these principles. A man finds in his garden two seeds. One he knows clearly to be the seed of an apple tree, the other he is unable to classify. Knowing the nature of the apple seed, he knows the conditions under which it will best develop into a tree. He does not determine those conditions, he discovers them and takes steps to actualize them. He plants the seed in good soil and in proper climate. He waters the earth and keeps it fertile, and sees that nothing harmful to the development of that little seed has a chance to hinder its growth. After that, he sits back and waits until the seed, by the activities inherent in it takes root, shoots up through the soil, and grows into a fruit-bearing tree. The second seed is of a strange unknown variety. Having only a confused knowledge of its nature, the man is uncertain of the conditions necessary for its development. He, therefore, determines what those conditions shall be, and plants the seed accordingly. In due time, there springs up a stunted and deficient growth that mars the beauty of the man's garden, and is productive of neither flower nor fruit.

Translating the parable in terms of human life, let it be noted that in regard to the first seed the man neither determined how the seed should act, nor the conditions best suited for its development. All he did was to use the power given to him with his own being to actualize those conditions which he discovered to be necessary for the seed's growth. The same is true of political authority. It is a power given by God to man to actualize the conditions necessary for the individual man to act in a manner leading to his personal development. Beyond that political authority may not go. That is why it differs from the power man has over things. While the owner of the seed was free to bring about the conditions suitable for the production of a new tree, or use the seed for an entirely different purpose, the same is not true of the use of political power. The ultimate reason of the seed's existence is the service of man. Hence that service can be rendered in whatever way man wills. The ultimate reason of any man's existence, on the other hand, is not the service of another man. Therefore, he cannot fall under another man's will. His end being the glorification of God by his own intrinsic perfection, only Divine Will can become paramount in human affairs. This causes no dishonor for, in recognizing the excellence of God, man merely extols the Infinite Source of every good he cherishes.

The second seed exemplifies the fate of man in the hands of the Liberal and the Communist. Their insufficient knowledge of human nature and their misunderstanding of its purpose leaves them with an inadequate knowledge of the conditions necessary for human development. Seeing man as only the highest expression of the material universe, they are interested only in his material well-being. His spiritual and personal development are therefore ignored; and man, turned from his true end, becomes an anomalous creature gracing neither the animal nor the rational kingdom.

It is this deficient knowledge of man and his destiny that is reflected in the fictitious concept of the State, and in the nature of political authority advanced by Liberalism and Communism. Neither can understand the source and purpose of political authority because neither can grasp the true nature of human equality. Having placed that equality in the individual and in the externals of human nature, they can keep humanity balanced only by force. Hence their conception of political authority is necessarily coercive. It is the instrument used by the Liberal to compel equality, or that seen by the Communist to enforce inequality. Since in either case the balancing or the unbalancing is the work of iniquitous men, coercion recedes as men progress in virtue, which means as they become more social-minded.

But though in Communism the State disappears when all men have reached that stage of perfection where the good of self is wholly submerged in the good of the collectivity, in Liberalism there is no such withering away of the State. Progress in human virtue but strengthens political power. For the classical Liberal, clothed with the mantle of natural rights and the sacredness of nature's laws, that State is more secure which gives the whole people an equal voice in public affairs. For his more progressive descendant, who has shed such "sacrosanct absurdities" and substituted the *political* for the natural, the State takes on an ever-wider sphere of activity.[43] But whatever the brand of Liberalism he professes, the Liberal holds in common with the Marxist a purely human source of civil power. For both, this civil power is derived by alienating a part of human activity; for both it necessarily issues from some deficiency in man; and for both it is identical with coercion. This is consistent with their view of human nature. The Communist and the Liberal, however, misread that nature, thereby replacing the eternal with the temporal, the permanent with the transitory, the equal with the unequal. It was but logical, therefore, that the essential function of the State give way to its auxiliary task.

The equality of specific personal nature and the inequality of the individuals who concrete it are concepts which not only make the State a natural institution whose end is the perfection of personality, but those which endow the State with the function of preserving human freedom rather than becoming inimical thereto. It has already been pointed out that any nature is concretized in diverse ways, thus making the individuals of that nature unequal. Men are essentially the same wherever men are found, but though the *manness* of a Stalin differs not one whit from the *manness* of a Washington, who would be so rash as to predicate their equality in other respects? Their differences are manifest, and while external influences may play important rôles in determining what those differences shall be, their initial seat is within the individual rather than without. Nevertheless, the source of inequality is not that inner core of man's being which makes him what he is, a *man*, but that which while interior to man is yet outside his essential nature. Inequality flows from a nature individuated in settings which are never the same, not from identical twins made different by the play of external forces. Hence sameness of environment will never produce sameness in men. Though they are reared alike, they will

43. Thurman Arnold, *The Folklore of Capitalism* (New Haven: Yale University Press). Cf. Lerner, *op. cit.*, pp. 13-19; 159-166.

be everlastingly different. Those differences, however, are in degree rather than in kind. They are quantitative not qualitative. Indeed men are more alike than different. They possess the same kind of powers though in varying degrees. While all are rational, all possess sensitivity, all are endowed with memory, imagination, instinct and voluntary control, some are more richly endowed than others. Such differences involve human interdependence, a give and take between man and his fellows. It is this dependence of man on man, incident on one's having what another lacks, that makes man social by nature. He must live in the community of his kind if he is not to be a warped individual, stunted in growth and undeveloped in powers. Since no man was created in the perfection of his being, but rather *en route* thereto, he not only needs the help of other men to realize his perfection, but he is under a positive obligation to his Creator to achieve the purpose for which he was brought into being, namely, such development of his personality that will forever give honor to Him who designed his nature and gave it existence.

It was not mere rhetoric that made St. Thomas describe the person as that which is noblest in all nature. No one realized more than he that the fullness of personality bespeaks a creature of such marvelous beauty, that not only does it necessarily glorify Him Who conceived it, as the sculptured work of art gives glory to the artist, but its beauty so enraptures its Creator, in its reflection of His divine perfections that He is moved to dignify it with the gift of His own divine life. Michelangelo, carried away with the human perfections reflected by his Moses, yearned to bestow upon his masterpiece real humanity. Had his creation remained an imperfect or distorted realization of a great biblical character, Michelangelo's purpose would never have been achieved, nor his heart touched, nor would his handiwork have done credit to his masterly skill. So it is with men. Their temporal life is given to them to sculpture on the rough clay of humanity, the image of the Divine. That is their *raison d'être,* and when they have accomplished it, God so loves in them His own Divine Image, that He vivifies it with a life that is Divine; and there proceeds once again, as in the ineffable mystery of the Trinity, another divine person. But since no one man can ever fully reflect Divinity, it is given to each of the adopted sons to portray some divine phase so that human nature, indefinitely multiplied, sketches in dimly the infinite perfections of Him Whose Unity is Triune.

As no single feature of a portrait will convey a likeness without the complementary features which bring out its perfection, so the individual man, engaged in his divine artistry, will never realize in himself that divine perfection he was meant to reflect unless his fellowmen supply what he himself lacks. This can be done only by each performing a social function that will bring about the common good, that sufficiency of life under which man can best perfect his person and thus play his part in manifesting the divine. And just as there must be a unifying principle where diverse parts are contributing to a common end, so when men in their diverse social functions are seeking to achieve the same goal, the common good, there must be some authority whose essential function it is to unify the actions of the multitude by directing them to a common end. Hence political authority, far from being an artificial contrivance whereby men keep or lose their equality, becomes an essential requirement of a nature whose individual existence, realized in diverse ways, has ever the same goal—the glorification of its Creator through the beauty of its own perfection. Yet since this perfection to which all men are equally obligated can never be achieved unless the conditions necessary for human development be present, there is need for some power to actualize these conditions by directing the actions of the multitude to their realization. This is the essential function of political authority. And though it must be endowed with coercive power sufficient to punish those who would injure the common good or compel those who fail to contribute to its formation, such is not its chief task.

Political authority, therefore, is not necessitated by some deficiency in men as the Liberal and the Communist hold. Its presence would be necessary, not indeed where men are perfect, but where their imperfections, far from being any positive deficiency or any malicious abnormality, are rather unripened capacities. The closed bud of human life needs for human flowering the warmth of human charity, the moisture of human sympathy, and the light of human understanding. Earth, sun, and rain contribute by their diverse functions, under the guidance of nature's laws, to a common good

wherein little buds can develop into flowers of such enchanting
beauty that man plucks them to keep their fragrance ever near. In
like manner, men, directed by political authority, contribute by
their diverse social functions to a common good wherein each little
bud of human life can flower into a manhood of such surpassing
beauty that Divinity is moved to pluck it in order that it may waft
its perfume close to the Triune God.

Though the Liberal and the Communist err in identifying political authority with coercion, the Communist at least is not wholly
wrong when he sees the diminution of political power coincident
with man's advance in virtue. Men, habituated to choosing the
good, do not need to be coerced, but will freely embrace any law
whose good they apprehend. As Yves Simon so aptly put it, "The
virtuous man is no longer subject to the law, since the law has
become interior to him and rules him from within."[44]

This virtue, however, does not dispense with political power in
its essential function of direction. That is why its presence still
would have been necessary had man remained in the garden of paradise, endowed with all the perfection of his original innocence.
The Communist, in leading man back to another earthly paradise,
rightly dispenses with a coercive power and, though he claims that
by so doing he has rid man of the State, since he does not claim
that society needs no power to direct its several members to unity
of action,[45] the State has not withered away nor has man achieved
the equality which the body politic was presumed to have destroyed.

If the natural inequality of men calls for political union and the
exercise of civil power, their equality of personal nature and oneness of generic end, forbid that such power ever issue from purely
human source. Its roots are embedded in the eternal law of Him
Who, being the Creator of every nature, is the source of nature's
law. Here is the surest guarantee of human equality and the
strongest defense of human freedom. So long as man recognizes
God as the source of law, he will never wear the chains of human
slavery. Let him refuse to bear the sweetness of the divine yoke,

44. Yves R. Simon, *The Nature and Functions of Authority* (Milwaukee:
Marquette University Press, 1940), p. 42.
45. Lenin, *op. cit.*, pp. 83-85.

and his back will bend beneath the burden of human cruelty and
the whip of human tyranny. Freedom was slain in modern culture
long before modern dictators devised, with satanic ingenuity, the
latest chambers of horror. It was slain the day human equality
was slain, the day man was made subject to the will of another
man. It will rise again when there is brought forth on this continent or any continent a nation conceived in *spiritual* liberty and
dedicated to the proposition that all men are created equal in the
depths of their essential natures and in the sacredness of their
human persons.

4. Individual Equality and Law

It has already been pointed out that if men are individually
equal, law can only be the expression of the popular will. Biologic
equality is a denial of the social nature of man. Therefore any
social institution erected on it must be conventional. Sociality and
individual equality contradict each other. Espouse one and the
other must go by the board, for the one involves dependence, the
other independence. That being the case, biologic equals can enter
into social relations only through a pact of some kind. Hence the
laws controlling those relations, having nothing to do with the
directions of a nature to its final perfection, must originate in the
will of those who have freely agreed to associate. This, however,
is a denial of inalienable rights and entails the subjection of the
minority to the will of the majority.

No more fruitful source of discord is needed to rend national
unity or disrupt social life than the denial of minority rights. Yet
what meaning can a right have other than a concession granted by
the State, where majority rule is thought to be the basic democratic
principle?[46] And if rights are State-conferred, can there be any
possible objection to their rescission by the State? Grant the principle of majority rule—it must be granted if men are individually
equal—and the minority has lost not only freedom, but equality
as well.

46. Max Lerner, *It Is Later Than You Think*, pp. 107-112.

Here is a paradox indeed. Liberal democracy started as the political institution guaranteed to preserve human liberty and human equality. It has had its day, and has made an ardent campaign in behalf of the twin principles. Yet it approaches its end through an inherent violation of both. The paradox is not difficult to explain. When a good thing has been pushed too far it becomes more than absurd; it becomes a thing of evil. The equality and freedom espoused by the liberal democracy were extreme. What that democracy gave man was neither true liberty nor genuine equality, but a caricature of both. As a consequence we are served today with the spectacle of the State becoming the victim of the liberty and the equality it labored so hard to beget.

Under the tenets of Liberalism equality of opportunity may indeed have intended a *career open to talent,* but it also intended that government could only umpire in the contest between the weak and the strong. If the former crumpled under the mighty blows of the latter there could be no injustice, for individual talent had won the day. Only a view of man that regards him as a quantitative entity could justify such a neutral rôle. But if men lack any higher dignity than matter at its highest stage of development why should not life's race be to the swift and life's battle to the strong? If the survival of the fittest is the law of life, it is consistent that it be applied to the human level. But when it is applied, need we stand aghast if "nature red in tooth and claw" be written large on the face of humanity?

Exclude from men all vestige of the spirit and the only equality that makes sense is biologic. The Liberal cannot evade the charge that he has made man mere matter. Neither can he evade the charge that when he speaks of the equality of matter he can only mean an equality that is quantitative. On the basis of such equality the principle of a "fair field and no favor" takes on a semblance of reason. If the effect of the principle be a society of plutocrats and paupers, there is no more need to be horrified at the human anguish incident than to bewail the mongrel starving while the blue-ribbon feasts.

5. Individual Equality and Economic Life

Quantitative equality implies, not only equal ability and equal need, but it necessitates the equal distribution of material wealth. Now if this equality is to be maintained several necessary prerequisites have to be realized. There must be a universality of plenty, the unselfishness of men, and an authority, not only to apportion work, but to distribute equally the products and conserve surplus wealth. In short, it means the abolition of private property, and only in a society characterized by individual equality is such abolition justified.

The appropriation by society of the means of production and the articles produced is to be followed, in the communistic theory, by the extermination of classes.[47] Now it is the essence of communistic equality that society be purged of classes.[48] But since the division of society into classes has its roots in the division of labor,[49] only when such division is abolished will society be classless. In other words when man is no longer imprisoned "for his whole life to a given function and to a given tool,"[50] when he can be shifted from one occupation to another, when there will be, to quote Engels, "a mobility of labor, a fluidity of functions, and a complete adaptability on the part of laborers,"[51] then all distinctions between social functions will cease. Manufacture will no longer be separated from agriculture nor town from country,[52] and in the administrative work of the bureau "there will be one set of workers to-day and another to-morrow."[53] Indeed even the difference between intellectual and manual labor will cease for as Marx observes:

47. Karl Marx and F. Engels, *The Communist Manifesto*, p. 82.

48. Joseph Stalin, "Report at the Seventeenth Congress of the Communist Party," in E. Burns, *Handbook of Marxism*, p. 938.

49. F. Engels, "Socialism, Utopian and Scientific," *op. cit.*, p. 183: "It is therefore the law of the division of labor which lies at the root of the division into classes."

50. F. Engels, *Anti-Dühring*, p. 238.

51. *Ibid.*, p. 242.

52. *Ibid.*, p. 242.

53. Bukharin and Preobraschensky, *op. cit.*, pp. 59-60.

> In principle a porter differs less from a philosopher than a
> mastiff from a greyhound. It is the division of labor that has
> placed an abyss between the two.[54]

But if man can perform one social function equally as well as
another, if differences of ability are due merely to differences of
training, there is only one conclusion to be drawn—the inequality
of men claimed by the Communist is due to no inherent difference,
but to environment. Make environment equal and men will be
identical. And when men are identical any social order which
allows them to be different permits injustice and should be over-
thrown. Hence the classless society to exist will require men who
are biologically equal.

To maintain this equality, however, the Communist sees the need
of three prerequisites: a universality of plenty,[55] a new type of
man,[56] and an authority vested in the community as a whole.[57] In
other words he conditions his classless society with the same
factors which keep men individually equal. He makes provision
for a universality of plenty in his theory, on the supposition that
every member of society be a producer of wealth, and a producer
to the utmost of his ability. Such supposition, however, leaves no
opportunity for cultural development. It is thus a hindrance to
human perfection, so that "an opportunity to everyone to develop
his full powers in every direction,"[58] becomes impossible. Indeed
to provide for cultural development means to curtail material productivity for culture grows out of leisure. It is the work of a
leisure class whose members freed from manual labor have time to
pursue the arts and the sciences. To the Communist, however,
a leisure class is anathema. Hence if abundance is to be so universal
that men will be free from temptations to selfishness, and, therefore,
society from the dangers of class division, men will have to forego
cultural development.

54. K. Marx, *The Poverty of Philosophy* (London: Martin Laurence,
1936), pp. 59-50.

55. V. Lenin, *State and Revolution*, pp. 78-85.

56. *Ibid.*, p. 80.

57. *Ibid.*, pp. 78-85.

58. F. Engels, *Anti-Dühring*, p. 241.

Should the Communist argue that a universality of plenty is possible even if the individual worker gives less time to material production than he does today, and more time to cultural development, he must be reminded that in the absence of empirical evidence such argument is in the realm of mere conjecture. There will always be the old, the sick, and the young, as well as some who take care of these, and unless we are asked to envision a society from which the aged, the ailing, and the infant have somehow or other been excluded, there will always be a goodly portion of society that will remain unproductive. In addition it is difficult to see how men in the space of a lifetime can acquire all the various skills and intellectual acumen an interchange of functions will require, and still have time to increase production, and progress culturally. Furthermore, will earthquakes, typhoons, and other violent eruptions of nature never destroy the stores of social wealth in the classless society? To assure this is to make a rather gratuitous assumption. To concede it is to concede that a universality of plenty may sometimes be lacking. And when it is lacking are we to believe that man will be so virtuous that no one will take more than his just share?

The possibility of the classless society rests on just such a gratuitous assumption, the assumption that the man of the future will be purged of all self-seeking inclinations. He will not be like the "present man in the street capable of spoiling without reflection the stores of social wealth and of demanding the impossible."[59] He always will give according to his ability and only take according to need. But though the Communist offers no guarantee that such a future race will actually materialize, he does admit "the possibility and inevitability of excesses on the part of individual persons (and) the need to suppress such excesses."[60] But in the absence of the State who will have the power to punish the occasional malefactor, and who will be the infallible judge to accurately weigh his effort and accurately estimate his need? Only the community as a whole may assume such jurisdiction, an assumption it may be recalled that rests on a society of equals. Nor need the

59. V. Lenin, *State and Revolution*, p. 80.
60. *Ibid.*, p. 75.

accuracy of the weighing and the accounting be anything phenomenal.

> For when *all* have learned to manage, and independently are
> actually managing by themselves social production, keeping
> accounts, controlling idlers, the gentlefolk, the swindlers and
> similar "guardians of capitalist traditions," then the escape
> from this national accounting and control will inevitably be-
> come so increasingly difficult, such a rare exception, and will
> probably be accompanied by such swift and severe punish-
> ment . . . that very soon the *necessity* of observing the
> simple, fundamental rules of every-day social life in common
> will have become a *habit*.[61]

In other words biologic equality will make the violation of the social rule, "from each according to his ability to each according to his need," so clearly evident, that no one will be able to escape detection. Life will have become so standardized that anyone who knows the "first four rules of arithmetic"[62] will quickly discover who has given less or taken more than the norm. He will merely have to compare his neighbor to himself to discover if his neighbor has cheated.

That the economic equality of the Communist, or more precisely, the absence of classes, puts a severe strain on human credulity is evident. That it involves the arithmetical equality of men is like-wise evident. The Communist, however, explicitly denies such equality. That his denial logically implies the necessity of private property we propose to show. Presently, however, the principle of the classless society can stand a little probing. "From each according to his ability to each according to his need," seems to offer a just distribution of both social duties and consumptive property. If men are individually equal the measure of ability and the estimation of need is a simple task. *The Communist admits that it is very simple.* But if men are unequal, who is to determine whether one has not shirked his duty or another exceeded his need? And according to what norm will the individual be measured? If one gives less and another takes more is it by mis-

---

61. *Ibid.,* pp. 84-85.
62. *Ibid.,* p. 84.

take or through deliberate intent? Here are problems which offer no easy solution; yet a solution will have to be found, an accurate one, if injustice is not to be incurred. The Communist reaches a solution in this simple assumption of Lenin:

> "The narrow horizon of bourgeois rights" which compels one to calculate, with the hard-heartedness of a Shylock, whether he has not worked half an hour more than another, whether he is not getting less pay than another, this narrow horizon will then be left behind. There will then be no need for any exact calculation by society of the quantity of products to be distributed to each of its members; each will take freely according to his needs."[63]

A society of perfect men may indeed be devoid of envy and discord, but justice does not consist in the absence of either. It consists in rendering to each his due. Nor will a society of perfect men ever be realized in the temporal span of human life. It is not meant to be, for perfection is the end of the human journey. Man gathers it as he goes. But since the Communist understands neither whence man came nor whither he goes, his understanding of human perfection is bound to be a little unrealistic. Nor will his understanding of human need contain more of realism. Need is measured by end. A nature *needs* that which brings its powers to fruition. In Communism such fruition is sought in the abundance of material wealth. But since material wealth will never satisfy human desire, because the distinctively human craving is for a happiness which the perishable things of time are impotent to assuage, man's need will be measured not by his end but by his wants. Man thus becomes a slave to his individual passions, which released from service to the whole man in ministering to his end, have become insatiable in their demands. Make want the determinant of need and the classless society will be characterized, not by human altruism but by greed. There will not be Communism but individualism run riot.

The economic equality of the Communist, like the political equality of the Liberal, can never realize for man a just social

63. *Ibid.,* p. 80.

order. Exalting the social above the individual, and collective ownership above private, it presents the strange paradox of denying an equality in keeping with man's social nature, and emphasizing one which renders him antisocial. Indeed, Communism presents several strange paradoxes. It repudiates private property with the very argument which supports it; it renders society classless by espousing the every equality upon which classes are built; and it seeks human perfection in the very thing that keeps man forever imperfect. And yet Communism is not wholly wrong. Pernicious doctrines never are. It is always the truth in them that persuades.

Communism is not wrong in claiming men are unequal; it is wrong in denying equality of men altogether. For what equality can men have when it is not in themselves but in the things they possess? Communism is not wrong in recognizing the social value of labor; it is wrong in denying that there is any individual value. Communism is not wrong in emphasizing man's social duties; it is wrong only when it emphasizes nothing else. Lastly, Communism is not wrong in claiming the need for a new type of man; it is wrong in thinking that new social institutions will beget him.

The doctrine of the essential equality of men who differ in their individual endowments offers a sounder solution of economic inequality. Recognizing man's right to possess material goods privately, it recognizes also his duty to use them socially. Now the right to private property, as already pointed out, is rooted in the specific nature. Concretely, however, such right is connected with the individual. Because men are equal in their specific natures they have an equal right to own; because in their individual natures they are unequal, one man's right to property need never quantitatively balance that of another. All that is necessary is that every man be permitted whatever material wealth is needed to free him from such slavery to bodily needs, as would imperil the pursuit of his final end. Communism would do otherwise. Believing the goal of human life to consist in material well-being, it would tie man to the pursuit of the very thing which is the principle of this imperfection and limitation. It would tie him to the pursuit of finite good when he is consumed with thirst for the Infinite.

The essential equality of men and their accidental inequality, in providing for man's right to own, forbids that such right ever become inordinate. It agrees with the Communist that when man expends his labor on a material thing he stamps that thing with something of his very own. It is not mere physical energy, however, that renders matter competent to man. His physical labor was merely the means whereby matter received the impress of his personality. It is the rational in it that gives it value. Nevertheless, when something of the human has gone into the thing, it does belong in some way to those who have left their mark upon it. That is why the Communist's argument for the abolition of private property is the very one which gives it metaphysical foundation. The Communist, however, can see in labor the only title to property, but it must be remembered it belongs to him as well whose idea has been incorporated in it. Furthermore, where production is not merely for individual use, but to meet the needs of the social group, man has not only expended energy to meet his own needs, but to meet the needs of his neighbor as well. Hence his return should compensate him not only for his individual labor, but his social labor also. Now the Liberal compensated man merely for his individual labor; the Communist compensates him only for his social. The Christian would compensate him for both.

Human equality insists that man love his neighbor as himself, since both are possessed of the same nature, and both are destined for the same glorious end. Human inequality likewise insists that superiority was meant for service, and greater endowment to compensate for lesser gift. Because of inequality men cannot attain their end without mutual aid; because of equality one cannot attain his end at the expense of another. Hence in rendering matter competent to man the individual is not only shaping the means necessary for the attainment of his own perfection, but he must likewise shape those through which his neighbor can attain to his. That is why in his economic life man has not only the right to own, but the duty to assist his neighbor in the possession of the same right. Man is both an individual and a member of a species. His equality flows from the latter, his inequality from the former. But it is the supreme dignity of the human person that makes men equally sacred, thus imposing on their inequality the duty of service. Thence is begotten not only individual worth but social nature. In the one is rooted the right to own privately, in the other the duty to use socially.

From this dual aspect of man springs the individual and social character of labor as well as the individual and social value of property, concerning which the late Holy Father wrote:

> First, let it be made clear beyond all doubt that . . . those . . .
> who have taught under the guidance and direction of the
> Church, have (never) denied or called into question the two-
> fold aspect of ownership, which is individual or social accord-
> ing as it regards individuals or concerns the common good.
> (Likewise) in labor . . . as in ownership, there is a social
> as well as a personal or individual aspect to be con-
> sidered. . . . Hence if the social and individual character in
> labor be overlooked, it can be neither equitably appraised nor
> properly recompensed according to strict justice.[64]

Liberalism violated the social character of labor and property; Communism would violate their individual character. Both are wrong. Having valued the human, not as a person but a thing, the one so exaggerated his equality that man became antisocial, that is, supremely selfish. The other likewise reducing man to matter, makes his equality so quantitative that his individual value is lost in mere bulk—the collectivity. Man thus becomes supremely unselfish. Both go to such opposite extremes from the human norm that they meet. The Liberal stressed equality so much he broke it. The Communist does the same thing but in a different way. Political equality ended for the Liberal in economic inequality while for the Communist economic equality ends in organic inequality.

Only in the Christian concept of man is equality preserved without destroying society, and man's social nature maintained without compromising the equal sacredness of the individual. Yet the Christian, like the Communist, knows that his new social order will bring peace to the ranks of men only when man himself is

64. Pius XI, *Quadragesimo Anno* (Catholic Truth Society, London, 1931), pp. 20, 32.

radically changed. He knows he can effect a revolution in society only when he effects a revolution within the individual man. The Christian revolution, however, involves not only the rectification of human life, but its divinization as well, for the Christian understands what the Liberal and Communist failed to grasp—that human nature though good, suffers from an original deformation which requires for its correction superhuman means. Nevertheless, it is the task of the philosopher to indicate that reordering of individual human life which will flower into social harmony. The conclusion of this study will indicate the relation of that reordering to the principles of equality and inequality.

CONCLUSION

It has been the burden of this study to point out that those social philosophies which misconceived an important human relation basic to all social ordering, necessarily induced a society that violated the social nature of man. Truly then does society need to be reformed. The relation of this reformation to a sound principle of equality has already been indicated. The essential equality of men demands that the common good, the end of the social ordering, benefit one no more than another. Society exists neither for the aristocrat nor the plutocrat and certainly not for the proletariat. Neither does it exist for the governing clique. Its end is to bring about that sufficiency of well-being wherein each individual can best develop his person and achieve that self-mastery in which true freedom consists. Yet because men are individually unequal, society must be formed along hierarchical lines. Men take their place in society according to their social function, and that function must be determined neither by birth nor wealth, but individual capacity.

Nevertheless, a social order, even though it pays due regard to human equality and inequality by ranking men according to individual differences while respecting the equal sacredness of human person, will be impotent to effect social tranquillity unless that tranquillity be the reflection of a peace that is resident in the hearts of men. Since a tranquil society is but the outward expression of that inner tranquillity which reigns within the individual member, to the degree that each man restores order within himself will society be rightly ordered. It is this inner and deeper restoration the Christian revolution seeks to effect. Seeing man as a hierarchy of lower powers subordinated to higher, with the chemical ordered to the biological, the biological to the sense, and the sense to rational, the Christian insists that the rule of reason within the individual man be the foundation upon which to build a rational society. Only when reason rules will the individual be rightly ordered, and only from this right order can tranquillity ensue. Corresponding to the relation of these individual faculties within

267

man there must be a like relation of men to one another, with this exception: that whereas reason being essentially superior to all the other human faculties keeps them wholly subject, men of superior wisdom, differing from their fellows in degree but not in kind, may direct but never subject those who are less wise. Society, therefore, cannot be truly organic, its unity must be that of order, never of organism.

Love is the natural bond that effects social unity, and the natural roots of love are two, equality and inequality. Equality of nature demands that one man love another as himself. Inequality of individuals demands that one supply what another lacks, thus making one man good for another, that is, lovable. Human failings, however, tend to corrode these natural bonds. Sublimated by the supernatural, they are able to resist the corroding influences of human selfishness, because man, seeing his neighbor as the beloved of God, sees not his faults, but the dim image of the Divine. As it was the divorce of reason from revelation which broke this supernatural bond, and the failure to understand aright human equality that broke the natural one, so it was human selfishness which, seeing no reason why man should love his brother, betrayed him and tore society asunder.

Only a proper understanding of human equality can provide man with a natural reason for loving his neighbor, for only when one man sees another as his equal and his good, will he see him as lovable. And only when that love is sublimated by the further insight that the beloved of man has ravished the heart of God, will it stand the wear and tear of human failings. In those aflame with love for God the bonds of human brotherhood shall never weaken. Here is the key to human happiness both individual and social. To the degree that it unlocks the door of each human heart will it flood social life with peace.

The Christian revolution offers man no future Utopia. Its aim is to effect the gradual formation of each human person according to the divine type. This is a lifelong task to achieve, yet to the degree that it is achieved will society be just and, therefore, peaceful. Since the destruction of man's social life had its roots in the moral order, its reconstruction must begin in the same order. And since disorder in society was begotten of disorder in the individual, a just social order can only be built on reordered men. This reordering however must be something more than the mere rule of reason. It must be the rule of reason subordinated to revelation, which in the individual means sculpturing on the rough clay of humanity the image of the divine. The more men are dedicated to this, life's prime task, the more will society know the blessings of peace. As this reforming must be the work of man's free choice, the reformation of society must be likewise. Though a just society can be effected only through just men, the realization of the latter does not automatically beget the former. There is a well ordered society corresponding to human nature but its establishment must be freely undertaken by men. Just as men freely accomplish their own perfection, so they must freely accomplish the perfection of society. The relation between the two though natural is not necessary. The achievement of the one is the life history of the individual; the achievement of the other is the life history of the race.

It is not our present task to lay down concrete plans for the new society. Such plans must be localized by time and place. There are, however, broad general principles to which any just society must conform. This study has been concerned with two of them, the equality of essential nature and the inequality of individuals. These must form the warp and woof of the social fabric. From the one is spun a society which affords human nature with the essentials for proper development; from the other is woven an order fitting to individual function. As at the social loom all are employed, but not in the same way, so the social fabric, woven to protect human nature, must be worn by all though each may wear it differently. This concept gives rise to a hierarchical organization of society of which the corporate State is the best expression.

Here is an organic arrangement of society in which the individual interests of locality and vocation become the basis upon which to build autonomous corporations, working in harmony for the establishment of the common good. In such a structure the individuality of men is recognized in the representation of local and vocational interests; their freedom is recognized, not only in the autonomous character of the corporations, but in the fact that such corporations, far from being arbitrarily imposed from above are encouraged to develop naturally and spontaneously from below. Finally, equality is recognized in the goal of corporate union, the realization of the common good, wherein each individual, regardless of his social rank, is permitted all that is necessary for the perfection of his person.

Such organization of society parallels the organization of human nature, for just as the various powers of man are subordinated to reason and by it directed to the good of the whole man, so the various corporations of society are subordinate to the State and directed by it to promote the common good. But as in the individual there is subordination of reason to revelation without the destruction of freedom, so in society there is subordination of individual to group, and group to nation, without the loss of autonomy.

If reason can leave to the vegetative and sense powers of man functions they are better adapted to perform, thus leaving itself free to care for the welfare of the whole man, society can likewise leave to local and vocational groups the determination of their own affairs, and concern itself with those larger issues which directly influence the common good. Finally, if the individual man in establishing within himself true human order attains not only self-mastery which is the nobility of personality, but attains as well interior peace and tranquillity, so society paralleling the order of human nature achieves not only social autonomy, without denying freedom to men, but achieves as well that tranquillity of order which is the "Peace of Christ in the reign of Christ."

BIBLIOGRAPHY

PRIMARY SOURCES

Aquinas, St. Thomas, *Opera Omnia*. Vives ed. Paris: 1872-1880.
    Summa Theologica.
    Summa Contra Gentiles.
    Commentarium in IV Libros Sententiarum Magistri Petri Lombardi.
    Commentaria in Aristotelis Libros.
        In Libros Metaphysicorum.
        In Libros Ethicorum.
        In Libros Politicorum.
        In Perihermeneias.
    De Regimine Principum.
    Quaestiones Disputatae.
        De Veritate.
        De Potentia.
        De Malo.
        De Spiritualibus Creaturis.
    Opuscula.
        De Principis Individuationes.
        De Natura Materiae.
        De Ente et Essentia.
        De Divinis Nominibus.
    Summa Theologica Commentarium Cajetani. Leonine ed., Rome: 1888-1906.
    Summa Theologica. English Dominican trans. London: Burns, Oates and Washbourne, 1912-1925.
    Summa Contra Gentiles. English Dominican trans. London: Burns, Oates and Washbourne, 1923-1929.
    Summa Contra Gentiles—Commentarium, Francisci de Sylvestus Ferrariensis. Leonine ed. Rome: 1918-1930.
    De Regimine Principum. Trans. by Gerald B. Phelan. Toronto, Canada: St. Michael's College, 1935.
    De Ente et Essentia. Trans. by Clare C. Riedl. Toronto, Canada: St. Michael's College, 1934.
Aristotle, *The Works of Aristotle*. English Translation. Ed. by W. D. Ross. Oxford: 1912-1930. Clarendon Press.
    The Ethics, Vol. 9, 1925.
    The Politics. (Trans. by B. Jowett), Vol. 10, 1921.
Augustine, St., *De Civitate Dei*. Trans. by M. Dod. Edinburgh: T. & T. Clark, 1888.

Bellarmine, Robert, *De Laicis*. Trans. by Kathleen E. Murphy. New York: Fordham Univ. Press, 1928.
—— *Opera Omnia*. Vives ed. Paris: 1870.
—— "De Laicis," *Opera Omnia*. Vol. III.

271

——— "De Officis Principis Christiani," *Opera Omnia.* Vol. III.
——— "De Summo Pontifice," *Opera Omnia.* Vol. III.
Burns, Emile, *Handbook of Marxism.* London: Victor Gollancz, 1935.

Cicero, *De Legibus.*

Davis, J. C. Bancroft, *United States Reports.* New York: Banks Law
    Publishing Co., 1920.

Engels, F., and Marx, K., *The Communist Manifesto.* New York: League
    for Industrial Democracy, 1933.
Engels, Frederick, *Ludwig Feuerbach.* London: Martin Lawrence, n.d.
——— *Origin of the Family, Private Property and the State.* Chicago,
    Ill.: Charles H. Kerr, 1902.
——— *Herr Eugene Dühring's Revolution in Science.* (Anti-Dühring.)
    London: Lawrence and Wishart, n.d.
——— *Landmarks of Scientific Socialism.* (Anti-Dühring.) Chicago:
    Charles Kerr Co., 1907.

Filmore, Robert, *Patriarcha* in Locke, John. *Two Treatises on Civil Gov-
    ernment.* London: 1884.

Hamilton, Alexander, *Works of Alexander Hamilton.* Ed. by C. C. Francis.
    New York: 1851.
Hegel, G. W. F., *Philosophy of History.* Trans. by J. Sibree. London:
    1900.
Hobbes, Thomas, *Leviathan.* London: 1651.

James I, *Political Works of James I.* Cambridge: Harvard Univ. Press,
    1918.
Jefferson, Thomas, *Writings of Thomas Jefferson.* Ed. by P. L. Ford.
    New York: G. P. Putnam's Sons, 1904.
——— *Works of Thomas Jefferson.* 2nd Randolph edition.

Kant, Immanuel, *Critique of Pure Reason.* Trans. by F. M. Miller. New
    York: Macmillan, 1922.

Lenin, V. I., *Collected Works.* New York: International Publishers.
    Materialism and Empirico-Criticism, vol. 8 of *Collected Works.* Trans.
    by David Kvitko. New York: International Publishers, 1927.
——— *Selected Works.* New York: International Publishers. 1914-1917.
    Imperialism and Imperialist, vol. 5 of *Selected Works.* Trans. by
    Marx-Engels-Lenin, *Institute.* New York: International Publishers.
    n.d.
——— *On Deceiving the People with Slogans about Liberty and Equality.*
    London: Martin Lawrence, 1919.
——— *The State and Revolution.* New York: International Publishers,
    1932.

Bibliography 273

Locke, John, *Essay on Human Understanding.* 10th edition, *Works of John Locke.* London: Bye and Law, 1801.
——— *Of Civil Government.* Everyman's Library Edition. New York: E. P. Dutton & Co., 1936.

Marx, Karl, *Gesamtausgabe.* Berlin: 1932.
——— *The Poverty of Philosophy.* London: Martin Lawrence, 1936.
——— *Capital.* Trans. by S. Moore and E. Aveling. Chicago: Charles H. Kerr and Co., 1906.
——— *Letters to Dr. Kugelmann.* New York: International Publishing Co., 1934.
——— *Critique of the Gotha Program.* New York: International Publishing Co., 1938.
——— *Selected Works.* New York: International Publishing Co., 1936. 2 vols.
——— *Contribution to Critique of Political Economy.* Trans. by N. I. Stone. Chicago: Chas. Kerr Co., 1911.
Marx, Karl, and Engels, F., *Communist Manifesto.* New York: League for Industrial Democracy. 1933.
——— *German Ideology.* New York: International Publishers, 1939.
Montesquieu, Charles-Louis, *The Spirit of the Laws.* Trans. by Thomas Nugent. New York: Colonial Press, 1900.

Poole, R. L., *Illustrations of the History of Medieval Thought.* London: Williams and Hargate, 1884.
Pufendorf, Samuel, *De Jure Naturae et Gentium.* Oxford: Clarendon Press, 1934.

Rousseau, J. J., *Emile,* Paris, n.d.
——— *Political Writings of J. J. Rousseau.* ed. C. E. Vaughan. Cambridge: Cambridge Univ. Press, 1915.

Sidney, Algernon, *Discourses in Government.* New York: Deare and Andrews, 1805.
Stalin, Joseph, *Leninism.* London, George Allen and Unwin, 1933.
——— *Problems of Leninism.* Trans. by Eden and Cedar Paul. New York: International Publishers, 1934.
——— *Foundations of Leninism.* New York: International Publishers. 1932.
——— *Theory and Practice of Leninism.* London: Communist Party of Great Britain.
Suarez, Francis, S.J., *Opera Omnia,* Vives ed. Paris: 1856.
——— "Tractatus De Legibus," *Opera Omnia.* Vol. III.
——— "Defensio Fidei Catholicae," *Opera Omnia.* Vol. XXIV.

Voltaire, *Dictionnaire Philosophique.* Paris: 1764.

Wilson, James, *The Works of James Wilson*. Ed. by James DeWitt An-
drews. Chicago: Callahan and Company, 1896.
—— *Selected Political Essays of James Wilson*. Ed. by R. G. Adams.
New York: 1930.
Wright, B. F., *Source Book in American Political Theory*. New York:
Macmillan Company, 1929.

SECONDARY SOURCES

Acton, J. E. Dalberg, Lord, *Lectures on the French Revolution*. London:
Macmillan Co., 1910.
—— *History of Freedom and Other Essays*. London: Macmillan Co.,
1909.
Adams, R. G., *Political Ideas of the American Revolution*. Durham, N. C.:
Trinity College Press, 1922.
Adoratsky, V., *Dialectical Materialism*. London: Martin Lawrence, n.d.
Allen, J. W., *History of Political Thought in the 16th Century*. New
York: Dial Press, 1928.
Anschen, R. N., *Freedom Its Meaning*. New York: Harcourt, Brace &
Co., 1940.
Arnold, E. V., *Roman Stoicism*. Cambridge: Cambridge Univ. Press, 1911.
Arnold, Thurman, *The Folklore of Capitalism*. New Haven, Conn.: Yale
Univ, Press, 1937.

Bakewell, Chas. M., *Source Book in Ancient Philosophy*. Revised ed.
New York: Chas, Scribner's Sons, 1939.
Bandas, Rudolph G., *Contemporary Philosophy and Thomistic Principles*.
Milwaukee, Wis.: Bruce Publishing Co., 1932.
Becker, Carl, *Our Great Experiment in Democracy*. New York: Harper
Bros., 1938.
—— *Declaration of Independence*. New York: Peter Smith, 1933.
—— *Heavenly City of the Eighteenth Century Philosophers*. New
Haven, Conn.: Yale Univ. Press, 1935.
Belloc, Hilaire, *Restoration of Property*. New York: Sheed and Ward,
1936.
—— *French Revolution*. New York: Henry Holt Co., 1911.
—— *Servile State*. 3rd ed. London: Constable and Co., 1927.
—— *The Crisis of Civilisation*. New York: Fordham Univ. Press, 1937.
Benson, Christopher A., "Essay on Equality," *Essays at Large*. New York:
G. P. Putnam's Sons, 1908.
Berdyaev, Nicholas, *The End of Our Time*. New York: Sheed and Ward,
1933.
—— *The Fate of Man in the Modern World*. New York and Milwau-
kee: Morehouse Publishing Co., 1935.
—— *The Bourgeois Mind and Other Essays*. New York: Sheed and
Ward, 1934.
—— *Christianity and Class War*. Trans. by D. Attwater. London:
Sheed & Ward, 1933.

Bober, M. M., *Karl Marx's Interpretation of History*. Cambridge: Cambridge Univ. Press, 1927.

Bohm-Bawerk, E., *Karl Marx and the Close of His System*. Trans. by A. N. McDonald. London: F. Fisher Unwin, 1898.

Brameld, Theo., *A Philosophic Approach to Communism*. Chicago, Ill.: University of Chicago Press, 1933.

Browder, Earl, *What Is Communism*. New York: Workers' Library Publishers, 1936.

Bukharin, Nikolai, *Historical Materialism*. New York: International Publishers, 1925.

Bukharin, N., and Proebrazhensky, E., *The A B C of Communism*. Trans. by Eden and Cedar Paul. Great Britain: 1922.

Carlyle, R. W., and A. J., *A History of Medieval Political Theory in the West*. New York: G. P. Putnam's Sons, 1903-1906. 6 vols.

———— *Christian Church and Liberty*. London: James Clark & Co., 1924.

Chang, S. H. M., *The Marxian Theory of the State*. Philadelphia, Pa.: University of Pennsylvania Press, 1931.

Channing, E., *Students' History of the United States*. New York: Macmillan Co., 1926.

Coffey, P., *Ontology*. New York: Longmans, Green & Co., 1926.

Coker, F. W., *Recent Political Thought*. New York: D. Appleton Century Co., 1934.

Cole, C. D. H., *What Marx Really Meant*. London: Victor Gollancz, 1934.

Coleman, John, *Concept of Equality as Held by Thomas Jefferson*. Pittsburgh: University of Pittsburgh, 1934.

Combes, Gustave, *La Doctrine Politique de Saint Augustine*. Paris: 1927.

Cook, Thos. I., *History of Political Philosophy from Plato to Burke*. New York: Prentice-Hall Inc., 1936.

Coudenhove-Kalergi, Count Richard N., *The Totalitarian State Against Man*. Trans. by Sir Andrew McFadyean. Clarus, Switzerland: Paneurope Editions, 1939.

Crahay, Edouard, *La Politique de Saint Thomas d'Aquin*. Louvain: 1896.

Cram, R. A., *End of Democracy*. Boston: Marshall Jones Co., 1937.

Cronin, Michael, *The Science of Ethics*. Dublin: M. H. Gill and Son, 1929.

Davis, Jerome, *Capitalism and Its Culture*. New York: Farrar and Rinehart, 1935.

Dawson, Christopher, *Progress and Religion*. London: Sheed and Ward, 1933.

———— *Beyond Politics*. New York: Sheed and Ward, 1939.

———— *Christianity and the New Age*. London: Sheed and Ward, 1931.

———— *Religion and the Modern State*. New York: Sheed and Ward, 1936.

Delaye, E., S.J., *La Personne Humaine en Péril*. Paris: 1937.

———— *What is Communism*. Trans. by F. Schumacker. St. Louis, Mo.: B. Herder Co., 1938.

DeMan, Henri, *Au Dela du Marxisme*. Paris: Libraire Felix Alçon, 1929.

Deploige, Simon, *The Conflict Between Ethics and Sociology*. St. Louis, Mo.: B. Herder Co., 1938.

Dewey, John, *Individualism Old and New*. New York: Minton Bolch and Co., 1930.
—— *Liberalism and Social Action*. New York: G. P. Putnam's Sons, 1935.
Dickinson, E. DeWitt, *The Equality of States in International Law*. Cambridge: Harvard University Press, 1920.

Eustace, Cecil John, *Catholicism, Communism and Dictatorship*. New York: Benziger Bros., 1938.

Faguet, Emile, *Cult of Incompetence*. New York: E. P. Dutton, 1911.
Falkenburg, R., *History of Modern Philosophy*. New York: Henry Holt and Co., 1893.
Fanfani, Amintore, *Catholicism, Protestantism and Capitalism*. New York: Sheed and Ward, 1935.
Figgis, J. M., *The Divine Right of Kings*. Cambridge: Cambridge Univ. Press, 1914.
Fitzgerald, Desmond, *Preface to Statecraft*. New York: Sheed and Ward, 1939.
Fritts, Frank, *The Concept of Equality in Relation to a Principle of Political Obligation*. Princeton, N. J.: Princeton Univ. Press, 1915.

Gettell, Raymond H., *History of American Political Theory*. New York: Century Company, 1928.
Gierke, Otto, *Political Theories of the Middle Ages*. Trans. by F. W. Maitland. Cambridge: Cambridge Univ. Press, 1922.
—— *The Natural Law and the Theory of Society 1500-1800*. Cambridge: Cambridge Univ. Press, 1934. 2 vols.
Gilson, Etienne, *Philosophy of St. Thomas*. St. Louis, Mo.: B. Herder, 1924.
Gredt, Joseph, *Elementa Philosophiae Aristotelica-Thomisticae*. Friburg: 1932.
Gregory, Raymond, *A Study of Locke's Theory of Knowledge*. Wilmington, Ohio: 1919.
Grabmann, Martin, *Thomas Aquinas, His Personality and Thought*. Trans. by Virgil Michel, O.S.B. New York: Longmans, Green and Co., 1928.
Gurian, Waldemar, *The Rise and Decline of Marxism*. Trans. by E. F. Peeler. London: Burns, Oates and Washbourne, 1938.
—— *Bolshevism in Theory and Practice*. New York: Macmillan Company, 1932.
—— *The Future of Bolshevism*. New York: Sheed and Ward, 1936.

Haas, Francis J., *Man and Society*. New York: The Century Company, 1930.
Hadley, Arthur Twining, *The Conflict between Liberty and Equality*. New York: Houghton, Mifflin Company, 1925.
Haines, Chas. Grove, *The Revival of Natural Law Concepts*. Cambridge, Mass.: Harvard Univ. Press, 1930.

Harris, George, *Inequality and Progress.* Boston: Houghton, Mifflin Co., 1897.

Hart, Charles A., *Aspects of the New Scholastic Philosophy.* New York: Benziger Bros., 1932.

Hayes, Carlton J. H., *Political and Social History of Modern Europe.* New York: Macmillan Co., 1924. 2 vols.

Hearnshaw, F. J. C., *The Social and Political Ideas of Some Great Thinkers of the Renaissance and the Reformation.* London: George G. Harrap and Co., 1925.

—— *Social and Political Ideas of Some Great Thinkers of the Age of Reason.* London: George G. Harrap and Co., 1930.

—— *A Survey of Socialism.* London: Macmillan Co., 1929.

—— *Social and Political Ideas of Some Representative Thinkers of the Revolutionary Era.* London: George G. Harrap and Co., 1931.

—— *The Social and Political Ideas of Some Great Medieval Thinkers.* London: George Harrap and Co., 1923.

Hefelbower, S. G., *The Relation of John Locke to English Deism.* Chicago: Univ. of Chicago Press, 1918.

Heimann, Edouard, *Communism, Fascism and Democracy.* New York: W. W. Norton & Company, 1938.

Hoban, James H., *The Philosophy of Personality in the Thomistic Synthesis and Contemporary Thought.* Washington, D. C.: Catholic University Press, 1939.

Hobhouse, L. T., *Liberalism.* New York: Henry Holt & Co., n.d.

—— *Metaphysical Theory of State.* London: George, Allen & Unwin, 1918.

Höffding, Harold, *History of Modern Philosophy.* Trans. by B. E. Meyer. London: Macmillan Co., 1900.

Hoffman, Ross, *Restoration.* New York: Sheed and Ward, 1934.

—— *The Will to Freedom.* New York: Sheed and Ward, 1935.

—— *The Organic State.* New York: Sheed and Ward, 1939.

—— *Tradition and Progress.* Milwaukee, Wis.: Bruce Publishing Co., 1938.

Hofstadter, Albert, *Locke and Scepticism.* New York: Columbia Univ. Press, 1935.

Hook, Sidney, *From Hegel to Marx.* London: Victor Gollancz, 1936.

—— *John Dewey, America's Philosopher.* New York: John Day Company, 1939.

Husslein, J., S.J., *Social Wellsprings.* Milwaukee, Wis.: The Bruce Publishing Co., 1940.

—— *The Christian Social Manifesto.* Milwaukee, Wis.: The Bruce Publishing Co., 1931.

Iswolsky, Helen, *Soviet Man—Now.* New York: Sheed and Ward, 1936.

Jackson, T. O., *Dialectics.* London: Lawrence & Wishart, 1936.

Jellinik, George, *Declaration of Rights of Man and of Citizens.* New York: Henry Holt and Co., 1901.

Jarrett, Bede, *Social Theories of Middle Ages.* Boston: Little, Brown & Co., 1926.

—— *Medieval Socialism.* London: Burns, Oates and Washbourne, 1935.

Jerrold, Douglas, *Future of Freedom.* New York: Sheed and Ward Co., 1938.

Joad, Cyril E. M., *Guide to Philosophy.* New York: Random House, 1938.

Keynes, John Maynard, *Laissez-faire and Communism.* New York: New Republic Inc., 1926.

Lagarde, Geo. de, *Recherches sur l'esprit politique de la Reforme.* Paris: August Picard, 1926.

Laski, H. J., *Political Thought in England.* New York: H. Holt & Co., 1920.

—— *Communism.* New York: Henry Holt and Co., 1927.

—— Ed. *A Defense of Liberty Against Tyrants.* London: G. Bell and Sons, 1924.

—— *Foundations of Sovereignty.* New York: Harcourt, Brace & Co., 1921.

—— *Dangers of Obedience and Other Essays.* New York: Harper Bros., 1930.

—— *Rise of Liberalism.* New York: Harper Bros., 1936.

—— *Democracy in Crisis.* University of North Carolina Press, 1933.

—— *Liberty in the Modern State.* New York: Harper Bros., 1936.

LeBuffe, Francis P., *Jurisprudence.* New York: Fordham Univ. Press, 1938.

Leo XIII, *The Great Encyclical Letters.* New York: Benziger Bros., 1903.

—— *Quod Apostolici Muneris.* 1878.

—— *Humanum Genus.* 1884.

—— *Immortale Dei.* 1885.

—— *Libertas Praestantissimum.* 1888.

—— *Rerum Novarum.* 1891.

—— *Arcanum Divinae.*

—— *Sapientiae.* 1880.

—— *Diuturnum.* 1881.

Lerner, Max, *It Is Later Than You Think.* New York: Viking Press, 1938.

—— *Ideas Are Weapons.* New York: Viking Press, 1939.

Lippmann, Walter, *The Good Society.* Boston: Little, Brown & Co., 1938.

Littlejohn, J. M., *The Political Theory of the Schoolmen and Grotius.* New York: Columbia Univ. Press, 1895.

Lowell, Edward J., *Eve of the French Revolution.* Boston: Houghton Mifflin and Co., 1926.

Lugan, Alphonse, *Social Principles of the Gospel.* Trans. by T. L. Riggs. New York: Macmillan Co., 1928.

—— *La grande loi sociale de la justice.* Paris: 1924.

MacLeane, Douglas, *Equality and Fraternity.* London: George, Allen and Unwin, 1924.

Madariaga, S. de, *Anarchy or Hierarchy.* New York: Macmillan Co., 1937.

Maitland, F. W., *Historical Sketch of Liberty and Equality in Collected Papers,* ed. by H. A. L. Fischer. Cambridge Univ. Press, 1911. Vol. I.

Mallock, William H. *Social Equality.* New York: G. P. Putnam's Sons, 1882.

Manion, Clarence, *Lessons in Liberty.* South Bend, Ind.: Univ. of Notre Dame Press, 1939.

Maritain, Jacques, *Freedom in the Modern World.* New York: Charles Scribner's Sons, 1936.

–––––– *The Three Reformers.* rev. ed. London: Sheed and Ward, 1929.

–––––– *True Humanism.* New York: Charles Scribner's Sons, 1938.

–––––– *Scholasticism and Politics.* New York: Macmillan Co., n.d.

–––––– *The Things That Are Not—Caesar's.* New York: Sheed and Ward, 1932.

Martin, Kingsley, *French Liberal Thought in the Eighteenth Century.* Boston: Little, Brown & Co., 1929.

Matthews, Shailer, *Jesus on the Social Institutions.* New York: Macmillan Co., 1928.

Maxey, Chester C., *Political Philosophies.* New York: Macmillan Co., 1938.

May, Sir Thomas Erskine, *Democracy in Europe.* London: Longmans, Green & Company, 1877.

McDonald, W. J., *The Social Value of Property.* Washington, D. C.: Catholic University Press, 1939.

McFadden, C. J., *The Metaphysical Foundations of Dialectical Materialism.* Washington, D. C.: Catholic Univ. Press, 1938.

–––––– *The Philosophy of Communism.* New York: Benziger Bros. Inc., 1939.

McIlwain, C. H., *The American Revolution.* New York: Macmillan Co., 1923.

–––––– *The Growth of Political Thought in the West.* New York: Macmillan Co., 1932.

McNamara, S. J., *American Democracy and Catholic Doctrine.* New York; International Catholic Truth Society, n.d.

Mercier, Cardinal, *Manual of Modern Scholastic Philosophy.* St. Louis: B. Herder, 1919. 2 vols.

Merriam, C. E., *History of American Political Theories.* New York: Macmillan Co., 1920.

Miller, Rene Fülöp, *The Mind and Face of Bolshevism.* New York: Alfred N. Knopf, 1928.

Morley, John, *Rousseau.* New York: Macmillan Co., 1915.

Murphy, C. F., *St. Thomas' Political Doctrine and Democracy.* Washington, D. C.: Catholic Univ. Press, 1921.

Murray, Rosalind, *The Good Pagan's Failure.* London: Longmans, Green & Co., 1939.

Nell-Breuning, Oswald Von, S.J., *Reorganization of Social Economy.* Milwaukee, Wis.: *The Bruce Publishing Co.,* 1936.

Obering, W. F., S.J., *The Philosophy of Law of James Wilson.* Washington, D. C.: n.d.

Parsons, Wilfrid, *Which Way Democracy.* New York: Macmillan Co., 1939.

Penty, A. J., *Tradition and Modernism in Politics.* London: Sheed and Ward, 1937.

—— *Communism and the Alternative.* London: Student Christian Movement Press, 1933.

Phillips, R. P., *Modern Thomistic Philosophy.* London: Burns, Oates and Washbourne, 1935. 2 vols.

Philosophy of State: Proceedings of the American Catholic Philosophical Association. Washington, D. C.: Catholic Univ. of America, 1939.

Pius XI, *Sixteen Encyclical Letters.* Washington, D. C.: National Catholic Welfare Conference. 1926-1937.

  Quadragesimo Anno. 1931.
  Non Abbiamo Bisogno. 1931.
  Casti-Connubi. 1930.
  Divine Redemptoris. 1937.

Pius XII, *Summi Pontificatus.* Washington, D. C.: National Catholic Welfare Conference, 1939.

Problems of Liberty: Proceedings of American Catholic Philosophical Association. Washington, D. C.: Catholic Univ. of America, 1940.

Rager, J. C., *Democracy and Bellarmine.* Washington, D. C.: Catholic Univ. Press, 1926.

Rickaby, Jos., S.J., *Free Will and Four English Philosophers.* New York: Benziger Bros., 1906.

Ritchie, David, *Natural Rights.* New York: Macmillan Co., 1924.

Robertson, H. M., *Economic Effects of the Reformation.* Cambridge, England: 1933.

Roland, Gosselin B., *La doctrine politique de saint Thomas d'Aquin.* Paris: Marcel Rivière, 1928.

Roosevelt, Nicholas, *A New Birth of Freedom.* New York: Charles Scribner's Sons, 1938.

Rousselot, Pierre, *The Intellectualism of St. Thomas.* London: Sheed and Ward, 1935.

Rouston, M., *Pioneers of the French Revolution.* Boston: Little, Brown & Co., 1926.

Ruhl, Otto, *Karl Marx.* Trans. by Eden and Cedar Paul. London: George, Allen & Unwin, 1929.

Ruggiero, Guido de, *History of European Liberalism.* London: Oxford Univ. Press, 1927.

Russell, W. F., *Liberty vs. Equality.* New York: Macmillan Company, 1936.

Ryan, J. A., *Questions of the Day.* Boston: Stratford Co., 1931.

Ryan, J. A., and Millar, M. F., *Church and State.* New York: Macmillan Co., 1922.

Ryan, J. A., and Boland, F. J., *Catholic Principles of Politics.* New York: Macmillan Co., 1940.

Sabine, G. H., *A History of Political Theory.* New York: Henry Holt & Co., 1937.

Sotou, Roger, *Franch Political Thought of 19th Century.* London: E. Benn, Ltd., 1931.

Schaff, D. S., *The Bellarmine-Jefferson Legends and the Declaration of Independence.* New York: G. P. Putnam's Sons, 1927.

Schwalm, R. P., *Leçons de philosophie sociale.* Paris: Bloud et Cie, 1911.

Seligman, E. R. A., *The Economic Interpretation of History.* New York: Columbia Univ. Press, 1934.

Sheed, F. J., *Communism and Man.* New York: Sheed and Ward, 1938.

Sheen, Fulton J., *Liberty, Equality and Fraternity.* New York: Macmillan Co., 1938.

———— *Freedom Under God.* Milwaukee: Bruce Publishing Co., 1940.

———— *God and Intelligence.* New York: Longmans, Green & Co., 1925.

———— *A Declaration of Dependence.* Milwaukee: Bruce Publishing Co., 1941.

———— *Philosophy of Science.* Milwaukee: Bruce Publishing Co., 1934.

———— *Whence Come Wars.* New York: Sheed and Ward, 1940.

Simon, Yves R., *The Nature and Functions of Authority.* Milwaukee: Marquette Univ. Press, 1940.

Slavin, R. J., *The Philosophical Basis for Individual Differences.* Washington, D. C.: Catholic Univ. Press, 1936.

Smith, T. V., *The American Philosophy of Equality.* Chicago: Univ. of Chicago Press, 1927.

———— *The Democratic Way of Life.* Chicago: Univ. of Chicago Press, 1939.

Stephen, James F., *Liberty, Equality, Fraternity.* New York: H. Holt and Williams Co., 1873.

Strong, Anna Louise, *The New Soviet Constitution.* New York: Henry Holt and Co., 1937.

Sturzo, Luigi, *Church and State.* New York: Longmans, Green & Co., 1939.

Thalheimer, August, *Introduction to Dialectical Materialism.* Trans. by Simpson and Weltner. New York: Covici-Friede, 1936.

Thilly, F., *History of Philosophy.* New York: Henry Holt & Co., 1929.

Tocqueville, Alexis de, *L'Ancien Regime.* Paris: 1887.

———— *Democracy in America.* Trans. by Henry Reeve. rev. ed. New York: Colonial Press, 1900.

Taparelli, D'Azeglio, R.P., *Le droit naturel.* Paris: 1857.

Tawney, R. H., *Equality.* 2nd rev. ed. London: Allen and Unwin, Ltd., 1931.

———— *The Acquisitive Society.* New York: Harcourt, Brace & Co., 1920.

———— *Religion and the Rise of Modern Capitalism.* New York: Harcourt, Brace & Co., 1926.

Trunk, Joseph V., *A Thomistic Interpretation of Civic Right.* Dayton, Ohio: Univ. of Dayton Press, 1937.

Turner, W. H., *History of Philosophy.* New York: Ginn & Company, 1903.

Ueberweg, Friedrich, *History of Philosophy.* Trans. by George S. Morris.
    New York: Chas. Scribner's Sons, 1894.

Vann, Gerald, O.P., *Morals Makyth Man.* London: Longmans, Green &
    Co., 1937.
Vaughan, C. R., *Studies in the History of Political Philosophy.* New
    York: Longmans, Green & Co., 1925. 2 vols.

Walsh, J. J., *Education of the Founding Fathers of the Republic.* New
    York: Fordham Univ. Press, 1935.
Weber, Max, *The Protestant Ethic.* London: George, Allen & Unwin,
    1930.
Welty, Eberhard, O.P., *Gemeinschaft und Einzelmensch.* Salsburg-Leipzig:
    Anton Pustet, 1935.
Wenley, Robert Mark, *Stoicism and Its Influence.* Boston: Marshall Jones
    Co., 1924.
Williams, A. T., *The Concept of Equality in the Writings of Rousseau, of
    Bentham, and Kant.* New York: Columbia Univ. Press, 1907.
Wulf, Maurice de, *History of Medieval Philosophy.* Trans. by E. C.
    Messenger. New York: Longmans, Green & Co., 1926.

Zeller, Edward, *Stoics, Epicureans, and Sceptics.* Trans. by O. J. Reichel.
    New York: Longmans, Green & Co., 1892.
——— *Outlines of History of Greek Philosophy.* 13th ed., revised by Dr.
    Wilhelm Nestle. New York: Harcourt, Brace & Co., 1931.
Zimmern, Sir Alfred, *Prospects of Democracy.* London: Chatto & Windus,
    1929.
——— *Spiritual Values and World Affairs.* Oxford: Oxford Univ. Press,
    1939.
——— *Modern Political Doctrines.* Oxford: Oxford Univ. Press, 1939.
Zybura, John S., *Present Day Thinkers and The New Scholasticism.*
    St. Louis: B. Herder & Co., 1926.

GENERAL REFERENCES

Baldwin, John Mark, *Dictionary of Philosophy and Psychology.* New
    York: Peter Smith, 1940.
Bergamo, Peter, *Tabula Aurea.* Vives ed. Paris: 1940.

Carlen, Sr. M. Claudia, I.H.M., *A Guide to the Encyclicals of the Roman
    Pontiffs.* New York: H. W. Wilson Company, 1939.
Cambridge Modern History. Ed. by A. W. Ward, G. W. Prothero, and
    Stanley Leathes. New York: Macmillan Company, 1907-1911. 13 vols.
Catholic Encyclopedia. Ed. by John J. Wynne, S.J., *et al.* New York:
    Robert Appleton Company, 1907-1912. 15 vols.

Encyclopedia of Social Sciences. Ed. by E. R. A. Seligman and Alvin Johnson. New York: Macmillan Company, 1937. 15 vols.

Dictionary of Philosophy. Ed. by Dagobert D. Reeves. New York: Philosophical Library, 1942.

PAMPHLETS

Adler, Mortimer J., *Hierarchy.* Notre Dame, Indiana: St. Mary's College, 1940.
Anderson, Francis, *Liberty, Equality and Fraternity.* Sidney, Australia: Australian Association of Psychology and Philosophy, 1922.

Eliot, Charles W., *The Contemporary American Conception of Equality Among Men as a Social and Political Ideal.* Univ. of Missouri, 1909.

Feely, Raymond T., S.J., *Just What Is Communism?* New York: The Paulist Press, 1935.
―――― *Fascism—Communism—The U. S. A.* New York: The Paulist Press, 1937.

LaFarge, John, S.J., *Communism's Threat to Democracy.* New York: The American Press, 1937.

MacDonnell, Joseph F., S.J., *An Approach to Social Justice.* New York: American Press, 1937.

Parsons, Rev. Wilfred, S.J., *God and Government.* Washington, D. C.: National Catholic Welfare Conference, 1939.

Ryan, Rt. Rev. Msgr. John A., *Relations of Catholicism to Fascism, Communism and Democracy.* Washington, D. C.: National Catholic Welfare Conference, 1938.

Sheen, Rt. Rev. Msgr. Fulton J., *Liberty Under Communism.* New York: The Paulist Press, 1938.

The Church and the Social Order. Washington, D. C.: National Catholic Welfare Conference, 1940.

A Code of Social Principles. Oxford: The Catholic Social Guild. Reprinted by National Catholic Welfare Conference, Washington, D. C.

PERIODICALS

Adler, Mortimer J., "Theory of Democracy," *The Thomist*, III, 1941.
Arnold, Matthew, "Equality," *Atlantic Monthly*, XLV, 1880.

Becker, Carl, "After Thoughts on the Constitution," *Yale Review*, 1938.
Benn, Wm. J., "Democracy in America Needs a More Secure Basis," *America*, XXXI, 1939.
Bennett, John, "The Myth of Equal Opportunity," *Christian Century*, XLVII, 1930.
Berdyaev, N., "Marxism and the Conception of Personality," *Christendom*, V, 1935-1936.
Bull, George, S.J., "What Did Lock Borrow from Hooker?," *Thought*, VII, 1932.
——— "Two Traditions in Political Philosophy," *Thought*, XII, 1933.

Carver, Thos. N., "The Coming Revolution in America," *The Outlook*, CXXXIX, 1925.
——— "The Meaning of Economic Equality," *Quarterly Journal of Economics*, XXXIX, 1925.
Corbin, John, "Liberty Above Equality," *The North American Review*, CCXII, 1920.

Delaney, Selden P., "Equality and Authority," *Commonweal*, X, 1929.
Dunning, W. A., "Liberty and Equality in International Relations," *American Political Science Review*, XIX, 1923.

Fischer, Louis, "Inequality in Soviet Russia," *Current History*, XLI, 1934-1935.
Fox, S. F., Darwin, "Equality and Order," *The Month*, CLVII, 1931.
——— "False Fruits of Modern Democracy," *Blackfriars*, XII, 1931.
——— "Equality of Opportunity," *Hibbert Journal*, XXXI, 1932-1933.
Fraser, A. C., "John Locke as a Factor in Modern Thought," *British Academy*, 1903-1904.
Frazier, E. F., "What Is Social Equality," *World Tomorrow*, VIII-IX, 1925-1926.
Furuseth, Andrew, "The Deadly Parallels," *The American Federationist*, XLI, 1934.

Garrigou-Lagrange, R., "Humility According to St. Thomas," *Thomist*, I, 1939.
——— "La Personalité," *Revue Thomiste*, XXXVIII, 1933.

Haldone, J. B. S., "The Inequality of Man," *Century Magazine*, CXVIII, 1929.
Hankins, F. H., "Individual Differences and Democratic Theory," *Political Science Quarterly*, XXXVIII, 1923.

Heinburg, John G., "History of the Majority Principle," *American Political Science Review*, XX, 1926.

Hoover, H. H., "Kings Mountain Speech," *Christian Century*, XLVII, 1930.

Howerth, Ira Woods, "The Natural Law of Inequality," *Scientific Monthly*, XIX, 1924.

Hudson, Adelbert L., "Equality Before the Law," *Atlantic Monthly*, CXII, 1913.

Hugon, Edward, O.P., "La notion de hierarchie," *Revue Thomiste*, VII, 1899.

Hunt, Gaillard, "The Virginia Declaration of Rights and Cardinal Bellarmine," *American Catholic Historical Review*, III, 1917.

Husslein, Joseph, S.J., "Equality, True and False," *America*, VIII, 1912-1913.

Ives, J. Moss, "St. Thomas and The Constitution," *Thought*, XII, 1937.

Lincoln, C. H., "Rousseau and the French Revolution," *Annals of the American Academy of Political and Social Science*, X, 1897.

Mahoney, Michael J., "Intimations of Kant in the Philosophy of Locke," *Thought*, II, 1927-1928.

MacLean, Donald, "Equality of Opportunity," *The Nineteenth Century*, X, 1921.

Mathieu, Robert, "Hierarchie necéssaire des fonctions economiques d'après Saint Thomas D'Aquin," *Revue Thomiste*, XXI, 1913.

Maumus, R. P., "Les Doctrines Politique de St. Thomas," *Revue Thomiste*, I, 1893.

McCadden, H. R., "Bewildered America," *Thought*, VI, 1932.

—— "Elusive Equality," *Thought*, VIII, 1932.

McGann, J. A. C., "The Political Philosophy of Edmund Burke," *Thought*, V, 1930.

McMahon, Francis E., "A Thomistic Analysis of Peace," *Thomist*, I, 1939.

McSorley, Joseph, "Christian Ideas of Justice and Equality," *Catholic University Bulletin*, IV, 1898.

Michel, Virgil, "Ownership and the Human Person," *Review of Politics*, I, 1939.

—— "Liberalism Yesterday, and Tomorrow," *Ethics*, XLIX, 1939.

Millar, M. F. X., "Aquinas and Missing Link in the Philosophy of History," *Thought*, VIII, 1933-1934.

—— "Does the Majority Rule," *America*, XXXII, 1925.

—— "Origin of Sound Democratic Principles in Catholic Tradition," *Thought*, II, 1927-1928.

—— "St. Augustine and Political Theory," *Thought*, V, 1930-1931.

—— "Stoicism in Modern Thought," *Thought*, III, 1928.

—— "Do Politics Make Sense?," *Commonweal*, XXI, 1934-1935.

—— "St. Augustine's and Cicero's Definition of the State," *Thought*, IV, 1929.

—— "Hauriou, Suarez, and Chief Justice Marshall," *Thought*, VI, 1932.

—— "The Modern State and Catholic Principles," *Thought*, XII, 1937.

———— "The Influence of Roman Law on International Relations," *Thought*, VI, 1931-1932.

———— "Scholastic Philosophy and Modern Liberty," *America*, XX, 1918-1919.

———— "Burke and the Moral Basis of Liberty," *Thought*, XVI, 1941.

———— "The Two Traditions of Liberty," *America*, XX, 1918-1919.

———— "The American and French Revolutions," *Thought*, XIV, 1939.

———— "Bellarmine and the American Constitution," *Studies*, XIX, 1930.

Miltner, Charles C., C.S.C., "Social Unity and the Individual," *Thomist*, I, 1939.

Montagne, R. P. A., "Le contrat social," *Revue Thomiste*, VII, 1899.

Neibuhr, Reinhold, "Modern Utopians," *Scribner's Magazine*, C, 1936.

Obering, W. F., S.J., "Our Constitutional Origins," *Thought*, XII, 1937.

O'Keefe, Denis, "Democracy—An Analysis," *Studies*, XXVIII, 1939.

Parsons, Wilfred, S.J., "The Principle of Order in Politics," *The New Scholasticism*, XVI, 1942.

Petrie, Charles, "Equality of Opportunity Fact or Fiction," *Nineteenth Century*, CV, 1929.

Pollock, Sir Frederick, "Locke's Theory of the State," *British Academy*.

Radin, Max, "Roman Concept of Equality," *Political Science Quarterly*, XXXVIII, 1923.

Rahilly, Alfred, "The Sources of English and American Democracy," *Studies*, VIII, 1919.

———— "Sovereignty of the People," *Studies*, X, 1921.

———— "The Democracy of St. Thomas," *Studies*, IX, 1920.

———— "Significance of Suarez," *Studies*, VI, 1917.

———— "Suarez and Democracy," *Studies*, VII, 1918.

Russell, W. F., "Defense of Democracy," *Teachers College Record*, Dec. 1938.

———— Wm. F., "So Conceived and So Dedicated," *Atlantic Monthly*, CLV, 1935.

Ryan, J. A., "Fascism, Communism and Democracy," *Catholic Action*, XX, 1938.

Schlosinger, A. M., "The American Revolution Reconsidered," *Political Science Quarterly*, XXXIV, 1919.

Smith, T. V., "The Transcendental Derivation of Equality in America," *The International Journal of Ethics*, XXXV, 1924-1925.

"Socialism, Fascism, and Democracy," *The Annals of the American Academy of Political and Social Science*, CLXXX, 1935.

Stephen, Leslie, "Social Equality," *International Journal of Ethics*, I, 1890-1891.

"The Crisis of Democracy," *The Annals of the American Academy of Political and Social Science,* CLXIX, 1933.

Tobriner, Matthew O., "Equal Protection of the Law," *The New Republic,* LXIV, 1930.

Tucker, Wm. J., "The Goal of Equality," *Atlantic Monthly,* CXII, 1913.

Watt, S. J., "Suarez and Sovereignty of the People," *Studies,* V, 1916.

Welschen, R. R., "Le Concept de personne," *Revue Thomiste,* XXII, 1914.

Weyle, Walter E., "Equality," *The New Republic,* I, 1915.

Wright, Herbert, "St. Augustine and International Peace," *Thought,* VI, 1931-1932.

Zammit, P. K., O.P., "The Concept of Rights According to Aristotle and St. Thomas," *Angelicum,* XVI, 1939.

Zeiller, Jacques, "L'origine du pouvoir politique," *Revue Thomiste,* XVIII, 1910.

INDEX OF NAMES

CPSIA information can be obtained
at www.ICGtesting.com
Printed in the USA
BVHW052335090223
658265BV00032B/663